HOW HITLER HIJACKED WORLD SPORT

HOW HITLER HIJACKED WORLD SPORT

THE WORLD CUP, THE OLYMPICS, THE HEAVYWEIGHT CHAMPIONSHIP AND THE GRAND PRIX

CHRISTOPHER HILTON

The History Press

German sport has only one task: to strengthen the character of the German people, imbuing it with the fighting spirit and steadfast camaraderie necessary in the struggle for its existence.

Joseph Goebbels, Minister of Propaganda, 23 April 1933

First published 2012

The History Press
The Mill, Brimscombe Port
Stroud, Gloucestershire, GL5 2QG
www.thehistorypress.co.uk

British Library Cataloguing in Publication Data.
A catalogue record for this book is available from the British Library.

ISBN 978 0 7524 5925 7

Typesetting and origination by The History Press
Manufacturing Managed by Jellyfish Print Solutions Ltd
Printed in Malta by Gutenberg Press.

CONTENTS

INTRODUCTION

There is an inescapable reason why the Third Reich remains hypnotically fascinating even six and a half decades after it was buried. Nothing remotely like it had happened before, nothing like it has happened since and nothing like is remotely likely to happen again. The odds against the combination of circumstances which spawned it repeating themselves will always be heavily against, starting with a figure like Adolf Hitler.

In his twelve years of power he wreaked terrible havoc on many different fronts and that, by a great paradox, included the world of sport; a paradox because before he came to power he showed very little interest in it — apart from racing cars and what relevance it might have in military terms. Almost from the moment he had power all that changed.

He approached sport as he approached everything else, by being prepared to exploit it in the most shameless ways as long as it served his purpose. It brought an additional paradox because sport was built on exactly the opposite principles to those Hitler and the Nazis held, if indeed you can call what they believed principles.

To say that Hitler had no grasp of any sporting ethos would be an understatement of historic proportions. As one of his generals said, 'I searched constantly for signs of genius and found only the diabolical.'

His chilled, bloodied hand would reach deep into the Olympic movement *and* an Olympic Games, soccer's World Cup, Grand Prix motor racing, the World Heavyweight Boxing Championship, Wimbledon and the tennis circuit, and the Isle of Man TT motorbike races. To humanise this by making a random selection, that hand would reach for — sometimes fatally — a cyclist and several ice hockey players, a decathlete and a fencer, two sharecroppers' sons from Alabama, two tennis players (one an aristocratic homosexual, the other a Jew), an English public schoolboy and a patriotic German high jumper.

The treatment of the high jumper was most shameless of all because she held the national record but was Jewish and, rather than select her for the Olympic team, the Nazis picked a man because, being stronger, he would be sure to win. I will repeat that. *The Nazis picked a man to contest the women's high jump.* He did compete and, as if sport was exacting its own revenge for such a travesty, he finished fourth. You will see quite why he was able to be selected, and like so much of the Third Reich it does not make for happy reading.

Along the way, Hitler's policies created a furore across the United States, Britain, France and Sweden, who all agonised over boycotting his Olympics – those in 1936 in Berlin. Bitter words were spoken and bitter accusations were made in the United States, drawing in politicians, diplomats, the Jewish community, innocent young athletes and power hunters. A chorus of voices tried to define what a free country really was, and what it should do.

Racism would never be far away, either: not just anti-Semitism but the purest kind of white supremacy, which, in turn, denigrated black people. This was unfortunate because the denigration would involve two of the very greatest athletes, Jesse Owens and Joe Louis, the sharecroppers' sons.

Many individual stories have been told and it is senseless to pretend that they have not been. You can read whole books on the 1936 Olympics – including mine[1] – or what the mighty German racing cars did or the life and times of the homosexual tennis player, but this book is the first, I believe, to bring all the aspects together. In that sense, most of the rich cast of characters are meeting themselves for the first time, if I can put it like that. Here, for example, you will find one of the most politically charged soccer matches ever played, where an Austrian genius publicly taunted thousands of Nazis. Again, you will see.

A word about the structure. I have re-created German sport in great detail because it is the best way to appreciate what was being done to it, and an inevitable by-product of this is that the book also becomes a history of Germany's sports matches and competitions from 1933 to 1939. The first chapter traces Hitler's rise to power across the 1920s with, interwoven, the people and events who will form the backbone of the story. I have included the main political events to give it an authentic context, although I stress that this is a book about how politics manipulated sport rather than a straightforward political book. There is a big difference.

The next seven chapters trace in chronological order what happened to sport and sports people from the moment Hitler took power in 1933. Because the impact of the Nazis was so immediate and wide reaching, the text risked darting from this sport to that all across the profusion of the summers (and winters), so to make it easier to digest I have amalgamated some of the material, breaking the strict chronological order. The seven chapters take the narrative to the moment the war broke out in 1939. As it happened, four of his mighty racing cars would be thundering round the cobbled streets of Belgrade in a Grand Prix on that very day, bringing the era to a close with, aptly, a roaring noise.

Chapter nine has the same framework as the first chapter, but pitched forward to chart what happened to all the people who formed the backbone, while chapter ten speculates about what world sport would have looked like if Hitler had won the war. Some escaped the chilled, bloodied hand. Some didn't.

I offer sincere thanks to Tommy Wahlsten (vice chairman) and Linda Sandgren of the Swedish Olympic Committee; Michaël Guittard, Opérations et événements, Direction de la Communication et du Marketing, Fédération Française de Tennis; Irv Osterer and Patrick Houda of the Society for International Hockey Research; David Hayhoe for raiding his library for relevant books; Mail-Pressestelle team at info@dfb.de; Gabriella Strauss of BMW; Oliver Richtberg of the DTB press office; Thomas Grömer of the Austrian Tennis Federation; Dr Gunnar Streidt of the Rot-Weiss Tennis Club, Berlin; Scott Bowers, Group Director of Communications, The Jockey Club; Birgit Kubisch-Hillebrand; Eberhard Reuss, author of the definitive *Hitler's Motor Racing Battles* for permission to quote, for his thoughts and for sending photographs; Robert Cellini of *The Copenhagen Post*; Andy Shaw for directing me towards Eric Morse (a foreign and strategic affairs commentator at the Royal Canadian Military Institute in Toronto, who was responsible for international sports relations at Canada's foreign ministry – Department of External Affairs, as it then was – from 1973 to 1986); Jimmy Lindahl for researching Sweden's reaction to the 1938 World Cup when their first-round opponents, Austria, ceased to exist; Søren Elbech of danskfodbold.com and Andreas Werner for help with two amazing soccer matches; Jim Hendry, MBE, Honorary Archivist, British Cycling; David Oldrey, a member of The Jockey Club and eminent horse-racing historian; Arjen Zegers of the KNVB, the Dutch FA and Timo Bootsma, a historian who found and translated invaluable material on the 1938 Holland-Germany match which never happened; Kay Crooks of the Wimbledon Lawn Tennis Museum.

The chapter titled 'If …' is about the shape of world sport assuming Hitler had won the war and represents, by definition, speculation. I am indebted to John Woodcock, Ian Cole and Linda Carlson for reading it, offering opinions, and contributing. I also owe a particular debt to James and Nancy Pinion, the co-directors of the Jesse Owens Museum in Oakville, Alabama, for providing a superb selection of photographs (taken by their friend Charlie Siefried) and daughter Marcy who sent them in high resolution. The Pinions are retired and keep the museum going on 'donations, gift shop sales and annual grants from the State of Alabama'. They do it, unpaid, because they believe the Owens legacy should be kept alive. The museum can be accessed on www.jesseowensmuseum.org and reached at jesseowens@charter.net.

I have used many, many sources and each is acknowledged by chapter endnotes, but I must single out two books, *Hitler's Motor Racing Battles* by Eberhard Reuss and *A Terrible Splendor* by Marshall Jon Fisher (Crown), as treasure troves of basic information. The internet is now such a wealth of information that it would be churlish to pretend that I haven't been using it; I have. The websites are noted and their addresses given. Among them I salute The Golden Era of Grand Prix Racing (www.kolumbus.fi/leif.snellman/), which covers the 1930s in extraordinary detail. The Rec. Sport Soccer Statistics Foundation (http://www.rsssf.com/nersssf.html) is a mine of priceless information. The *Official Berlin Games Report* covers the 1936 Games in exhaustive detail.

BBC Four broadcast an important documentary in 2003, *Fascism and Football*, which contained a wealth of expert insights as well as provocative opinions and I have drawn from it. Again, in each case this is clearly accredited through chapter endnotes. *The Journal of Sport History*, vol. 16, no. 1 (spring, 1989) carried a beautifully researched and penetrating feature, 'A Tale of Two Diplomats: George S. Messersmith and Charles H. Sherrill on Proposed American Participation in the 1936 Olympics', by Stephen R. Wenn of the University of Western Ontario. I have drawn from this too, and it is also accredited through chapter endnotes. I am grateful for his generous permission to quote extensively from it. There is a full bibliography at the end which contains full citations to the texts referred to in the chapter endnotes.

Finally, a word for the (sometimes maligned) British Newspaper Library at Colindale, north London, which is a source of almost unlimited scope and importance. I have been using it for twenty-five years and have the deepest gratitude to it, and especially to the staff.

Notes

1 Hilton, *Hitler's Olympics*.

1

THE PLAYERS

Munich was a place of big, solid stone buildings, churches and museums inhabited by big, solid, beer-fed citizens. The politics among its population of 666,000 stood in direct contrast: volatile and, at its sharp edges, revolutionary.

On 1 April 1920, Adolf Hitler left the army to work full time for the National Socialist German Workers' Party, the *Nationalsozialistische Deutsche Arbeiterpartei*. The pronunciation of *Nationalsozialist* gave it the abbreviation the world would come to know so well and fear so much, *Nazi*. The party was based at a building called the Brown House in Munich and Hitler began to take it over. The local German Army Command was the 'ultimate arbiter of public order' and nothing officially to do with the Nazis, but Hitler had military friends and that allowed him to 'exercise with impunity his methods of incitement, violence and intimidation'.[1] He became party chairman a year later.

He looked like the army corporal he had been in the war and sounded like a raucous rabble-rouser with a wild look in his eyes. You would have predicted a sticky end, possibly very soon, as the volatility consumed him. Instead, across the next thirteen years, he manoeuvred towards power while in the most natural and usual way people who almost certainly had never heard of him were building their careers – mostly far removed from any kind of politics – in Germany, in Europe beyond Germany, in Britain and the United States. When he had power they would feel it.

Oakville can represent that. It was a very small place, lost in gently rolling farmland somewhere along the pencil-thin, pencil-straight roads of northern Alabama. Oakville was also poor and the bigotry of segregation cut wounds through it. Sharecroppers, tenants who worked the land for a percentage of the crop, picked cotton, but, because of the hilly terrain and woodland, corn was grown and molasses made. The black couple in the shanty dwelling – draughty, basic – had nine children and wished for no more but a tenth, a 'gift child', came. He was sickly, suffering from bronchial problems and pneumonia. They christened him James Cleveland Owens.

You would have predicted a back-breaking future picking the cotton, the segregation legally holding him forever from opportunity, as well as poverty and anonymity if he survived the bronchial problems and pneumonia. One day in 1922, while Hitler was beginning his journey to absolute power, Owens' mother said the family were going on a train. J.C. asked, 'but where we gonna go, Momma?' 'To a better life,' she replied. That was Cleveland, Ohio, and when he got there a school teacher asked him his name. He replied in a strong southern drawl, 'J.C. Owens'. The initials sounded just like the name the world would come to know so well and respect so much: Jesse.[2]

On a cloudy afternoon, with rain hanging in the air, the former corporal and the sharecropper's son would find themselves in the same place and what happened there between them – or rather, what did not happen between them – remains one of the most memorably evocative moments of the whole twentieth century.

You can argue that sport is an international activity, essentially about anybody on the planet exploiting their talent (which, as it happens, is one way of defining the Olympic Games). The competitor's background obviously has an impact in terms of opportunity[3] and by its nature it produces some wonderfully improbable encounters but rarely anything approaching the undercurrents which flowed into the stone-clad stadium that August afternoon when the corporal and the sharecropper's son faced each other.

In 1923 the Nazis staged a Beer Hall Putsch in Munich, starting at a political meeting at the biggest *keller*. Hitler climbed on to a chair and shouted, 'the national revolution has begun'. It hadn't. He fled, although by now the *Sturmabteilung* (SA), the storm troopers who formed the Nazi paramilitary force, numbered some 15,000 and the party itself 20,000.

At between six and seven o'clock on the morning of the *putsch* Adolf Hühnlein, an early party member and an unprepossessing man even though he had won the Iron Cross during the war, was dispatched with others to seize a police station. He failed and was arrested. He had no sense of humour, no mechanical knowledge and at the moment of his arrest seemed destined to be a figurine, not even an historical footnote.

Hitler would, in time, give him charge of all motor sport in Germany, so that he marched the European calendar of Grands Prix in his uniform and swastikas like an emperor. He embodied what Hitler had ordained: that racing would become an instrument of German power and a global demonstration of the superiority of our technology. The failed police station-seizer would have a stage – that stage – for his marching and, if appearances are anything to go by, he would adore it. You could tell by his body language. Hitler would also put Hühnlein in charge of all Germany's motorised transport, training it for war.

Hitler received a five-year prison sentence in April 1924 for the attempted *putsch*, but was eligible for parole in six months. He spent his hours writing a turgid and wild tome, *My Struggle*, the title of which the world would come to know so well in the original, *Mein Kampf*. Hitler was paroled in December. He had spent time in Vienna as a rejected artist and there he learned to hate the Jews.

Manfred von Brauchitsch, handsome but haughty, came from a strong military family and at 18 his father put him into an infantry regiment on Germany's north coast. He had a small inheritance and with it he bought a motorbike. He crashed, breaking his arm, his leg, four ribs and fracturing his skull. He left the army and recuperated in a cousin's forty-room castle. The cousin owned a powerful Mercedes and taught von Brauchitsch to drive. In time, he would win – and lose – some extraordinary Grands Prix, try to flee to Switzerland when the Second World War began and, after it, flee to communist East Germany. Before any of that, Hitler would make his uncle, Walther, commander-in-chief of the German army.

Max Schmeling, born just north of Berlin, grew up in Hamburg where his father worked for a shipping company. He had a strong, open, almost pug-like face and a thicket of hair cut across his forehead. At 16 he went to the cinema and the show included newsreel coverage of the World Heavyweight Championship between reigning champion Jack Dempsey and Frenchman Georges Carpentier at an outdoor arena in New Jersey. It produced boxing's first million-dollar gate and reached a large audience as one of the first radio broadcasts dedicated to a specific event. Dempsey stormed Carpentier and destroyed him in four rounds.

It also reached Schmeling. He bought second-hand gloves and, when he moved to the Rhineland, joined the local amateur club. He made such progress that by the time Hitler served his jail sentence he was contesting the German light-heavyweight title and fought for the first time as a professional that August, 1924.

In time, Hitler would use Schmeling as a model of Aryan supremacy against an American black sharecropper's son in far, far away Yankee Stadium in the Bronx – just a couple of weeks before the cloudy afternoon when Hitler and that other sharecropper's son found themselves staring at each other in Berlin. It was the same Schmeling who risked his life to save two Jewish children long after Hitler did get absolute power.

In 1925 the Nazis were holding mass meetings and the *Schutzstaffel* was formed to protect Hitler. The world would come to know it so well by its abbreviation: the SS. Heinrich Himmler, one of the most odious men in European history, commanded it.

Hans Stuck's father owned an estate at Freiburg, in the rolling hills and flatlands of south-eastern Germany not far from France and Switzerland (the Stucks were originally Swiss). Stuck served in the artillery in the First World War and when his commanding officer was killed he was sent to give the bad news to the family. The commanding officer's sister was called Ellen and, although five years older, they married. Stuck, tall and good looking, would always attract ladies – and marry twice again – but now he and Ellen 'set up home on a farm south of Munich'[4] and in the early mornings Stuck delivered milk from it to Munich.

He used to park his car at a garage and he became friendly with the man who parked next to him, Julius Schreck. Very soon Stuck would begin a career in motor racing and in time he and Schreck would shoot together on the farm. One day in 1925 Schreck arrived for a shoot and asked if his boss, who was in the car, might join them. Stuck said, 'Of course', and there was Hitler.

Stuck's racing career stalled and Schreck said he should meet Hitler. Stuck thought that mildly absurd when Hitler was working day and night to take over Germany, but Schreck arranged it, explaining that Hitler had not forgotten the day's shooting, and Stuck travelled to the Brown House. Stuck explained that the German companies had withdrawn and he didn't want to drive for a foreign company like Alfa Romeo or Bugatti. Hitler was evidently sympathetic but pointed out that the party couldn't finance a racing driver. He added, though, that 'You're an excellent driver, Herr Stuck. If you can avoid driving for a foreign firm I promise you that when I come to power the Reich will place a racing car at your disposal.'[5]

Stuck naturally assumed this was in the nature of a joke, 'the sort of thing only a fantasist says with a straight face. I mean – a Reich racing car!'[6] He would learn, as would the world, that Hitler didn't really make jokes. However fantastic his words were, he always meant them literally.

In 1926 Hitler fought off internal dissent and by summer 'felt strong enough to hold a mass rally in Weimar, in Thuringia, one of the few states in which he was still allowed to speak'.[7] Meanwhile, a club-footed, lecherous little man called Joseph Goebbels began to move up through the party hierarchy.

Lafayette is 'tucked away in the foothills of central East Alabama',[8] very close to Georgia. Bigotry overhung it. Sharecroppers bent their back here, just as they did in Oakville 160 miles away. Munroe Barrow married Lillie Reese, a daughter of former slaves, and they had eight children. They lived in a shack some 6 miles from Lafayette's wide streets, large trees and fine old houses. The seventh child was christened Joseph Louis Barrow, but the Joseph would be shortened and the Barrow dropped. He would be known as Joe.

In 1926, one report says the family was 'shaken' by an 'altercation' with the Ku Klux Klan. The word came down that Ford at Detroit did not mind hiring black people and, although Munroe had mental problems which put him into an institution, the family moved north. Joe and his brother worked for Ford. In time the idealised image of Aryan supremacy would be tested to destruction against the seventh child on, simultaneously, the largest stage in the world (the global audience devouring the World Heavyweight Championship) and the smallest (a boxing ring).

Rudolf Caracciola had a boyish face and an almost button nose. Despite his Italian name he had been born in Remagen on the Rhine to a family who ran a hotel. He didn't intend to make it his life and worked in a car factory at Aachen. That part of Germany was occupied by Belgium after the First World War and he got into a fight with some Belgians. He moved quickly to Dresden and worked as a sales representative, but he was crazy about motor racing and was soon racing a Mercedes. He would enter the German Grand Prix privately and win a very wet race. This was a genuine sensation. In time, he would advocate the Nazi cause in the spoken and printed word, lavishing praise on Hitler, both before and during the Second World War. He didn't after it.

That September, 1926, a distinguished-looking English teenager arrived at Rugby School (founded 1567). He had well-bred manners and well-bred features, dominated by a very prominent nose, almost a beak. Rugby, in the English Midlands, was an august establishment where, in 1823, William Webb Ellis first picked up a football and ran with it, creating the game of rugby. Thomas Arnold, a fabled headmaster, believed in a complete education to form adults. Baron Pierre de Coubertin, who would found the modern Olympic Games, visited the school several times and was deeply influenced by what he saw.

The teenager was called Richard Seaman and there was money in the family. They intended him to go into law and later, perhaps, stand for parliament. But he was only interested in racing cars and in time that would take him to the Mercedes team, although Hitler's permission had to be sought. He would fall in love and marry a beautiful young Bavarian, and his mother disapproved so much that she never spoke to him again because she knew war was coming. He would die at the wheel of the Mercedes and Hitler sent a large wreath to his funeral in London. What Seaman did and did not do remains controversial many decades later, as if escaping from Hitler remains almost impossible even for the purist sportsman and even from beyond the grave.

That September too, Matthias Sindelar, an 'awkward, edgy character',[9] made his debut for the Austrian soccer team. They beat Czechoslovakia 2–1 in Prague. Sindelar came from poor Czechoslovakian immigrant stock who had settled in a working-class district of Vienna. His father, a blacksmith, was killed in the First World War. Sindelar played soccer in the streets but, then and later, he looked so delicate he was known as the 'Man of Paper', even though he was a centre forward. He'd been play-ing for a team called Hertha Vienna but now joined FK Austria Vienna. In time he became one of the greatest of all players in one of his country's greatest teams. Then Hitler's Reich ingested Austria whole and Sindelar faced an immediate problem: he hated the Nazis and everything they represented.

During a match to 'celebrate' that – Austria v. Germany in Vienna – he taunted the Nazis, who in turn suspected him of Jewish connections. He refused to play for Germany and one January morning was found dead next to his former prostitute girlfriend. Carbon monoxide poisoning, said the officials. Few believed it then and few believe it now. By that time, more than the Austria ingestion, Czechoslovakia had been dismembered and part of it ingested by the Reich too.

A 13-year-old with a mop of hair curling down his forehead joined a sports club in his home town, Leipzig. He'd grow to 6ft, ideal for a long jumper. He was called Carl-Ludwig 'Luz' Long, and in time he would work as a lawyer in Hamburg. Eventually, he would also challenge the sharecropper's son from Oakville on the most public stage and, in doing so, become a trusted friend. With Hitler watching, it took rare courage. Long, with his warming smile and hair like breaking waves, had courage all right.

Across 1927 and 1928 the Nazis did not poll well but the party kept on growing. In the spring of 1928 soccer's international body, FIFA, met at the Amsterdam Olympic Games and the president, Jules Rimet, announced that a new, professional competi-tion was to be established. Up to then the Olympics represented the pinnacle. The new competition was to be open to all FIFA members. It would be first contested in Uruguay in 1930 and then in Italy in 1934. There, it grew so quickly that thirty-two teams went through a qualifying stage and sixteen contested the finals. Germany got through and, of the other fifteen, Hitler would absorb, occupy or declare war on ten. But neither Rimet nor anyone else could have imagined anything as fantastical as that while the Amsterdam Olympics was proceeding quite normally and FIFA had its momentous meeting.[10]

At Amsterdam, Helene Mayer – a blonde 18-year-old from Offenbach, a town on the river Main near Frankfurt – won the women's foil. Mayer was 'fresh, blooming, full of life, a wholesome portrait of German girlhood'.[11] Her mother happened to be Christian; her father Jewish. In time she'd find herself in California and in a tug-of-war between Hitler, who wanted her as his token Jewish Olympian, and her own sensibilities. At a certain critical moment she held the destiny of the Berlin Olympic Games in her slender, sensitive hands.

Here was another wonderfully improbable encounter whose undercurrents flowed from the strong-willed corporal in his capital city to the strong-willed woman in the Californian sun and back again. Truth would be a casualty of the tug-of-war – and very quickly.

Rudi Ball, a Berlin Jew, stood at 5ft 4in and weighed 140lb, which was no kind of a physique for an ice hockey player. His father bought him expensive Canadian skates when he was 15 and he proved fast and elegant; so fast and elegant that his career began at 17 in 1928. In time, he would help Germany to an Olympic bronze medal at Lake Placid but, as a Jew, be discarded for the Winter Games in the German heartland of Bavaria. Another leading player refused to take part if Ball was excluded, so Ball became the only Jewish man to compete in any German Olympic team in 1936.

Nor was that all. He remained in Berlin, playing to capacity audiences during the war, and afterwards immigrated to South Africa. The question remains, perhaps never to be answered: why did Hitler and the Nazis not kill him as they killed 6 million other Jews? There may have been valid reasons, as we shall see, although with the Nazis terms like 'valid reasons' can acquire their own dimensions.

A classically blonde, tall, elegant man – someone said that when he wore his red-and-white-striped blazer he looked more like a host at a garden party – he moved to Berlin. Gottfried von Cramm had been brought up on the family estate in another German heartland, Lower Saxony. Their summer residence, a castle that they'd had since the sixteenth century, had a tennis court. Von Cramm took to the sport and, when the family visited friends nearby, their estate offered two clay courts. Old, famous players were guests there too.

His parents wanted him to go into diplomacy but he had already decided to devote himself to tennis. He needed to get into the exclusive Rot-Weiss Club in Berlin, and did. As a player he was noted for his grace, difficult service and impeccable ground strokes, but it was not so much his shot-making skills as his elegant presence that captured the public fancy.

His elegance and grey-green eyes were immediately attractive to women but his desires lay elsewhere and 1920s Berlin, arguably the most sexually liberated city in the world, indulged in mass catering for that and just about anything else you wanted. Soon enough von Cramm would find the Eldorado Club and an Israeli actor called Manasse Herbst. In time von Cramm would be pressured to laud Hitler outside Germany and he would refuse; the Gestapo would watch him closely, and he would be tried and then jailed for homosexuality. That he was by then a world-famous figure, admired as much for his chivalry as his tennis skills, did not inhibit the Nazis from doing this in any way.

Along the way, as von Cramm was preparing to play in the quiet, leafy, middle-class London suburb of Wimbledon, he would receive a message from Hitler suggesting he did not lose. That is the mythology, anyway. The swastika flew among the other flags at Wimbledon and Hitler's sports minister sat in the Royal Box. As someone said, Hitler fully intended more than one swastika to fly over London one day.[12] If that had happened, what would have happened to Wimbledon? It's another question that can't be answered (but for my speculation on this and the possible fate of other sports, see chapter ten).

By 1929 the Nazi Party had 130,000 members.

In November the police in Lingen, a town on the Rhine near the Dutch border, reflected the exasperation of the residents by taking the driving licence of a young man called Bernd Rosemeyer. They had all had enough of him going through the village at 70kmph over cobbles, standing up on his motorbike, sometimes scattering pedestrians as he went. His father owned a garage and repair shop, and that was the way in to racing once he had received his licence back. He had intuitive balance and that would bring him many advantages in fast, dangerous cars on fast, dangerous circuits. After one of his victories Himmler made him a 'Storm Leader' in the SS. It was not something you could refuse and he did not.

With war beckoning he would show Germans power – the power Hitler ordained and nurtured, the power Hühnlein marshalled and refined – to an enormous, enthralled crowd in typical country house parkland set gently in the Midlands of England (not far, as it happened, from Rugby). The power was so extreme nobody there would ever forget it. This was heightened by the fact that the cars against them were little, pug-like, elderly British ones driven by good chaps with, for a little spice, a Maserati driven by a Thai prince among them.

Rosemeyer won and the leading non-German car – the Maserati – finished more than 5 miles behind him. The crowd had witnessed, whether they understood it or not, a precise preview of the beginning of the war.

Hermann Lang was born in 'humble surroundings' near Stuttgart, but his father died in 1923 and Lang's mother brought him and three brothers up 'under great difficulties'. He became an apprentice mechanic and raced motorbikes in 1929. By persistence and skill he reached Grand Prix racing, though von Brauchitsch was caustic about his lack of breeding. Because Lang, like the other drivers, had to belong to the Nazi motoring organisation, he was classified as a 'fellow traveller' after the war. He would be forced to defend himself hard.

In mid-summer 1929 thirteen cars finished the German Grand Prix at the majestic Nürburgring. A Bugatti beat a Bugatti, a Mercedes third, then two more Bugattis, another Mercedes, two Bugattis and a Maserati, a Bugatti and an Alfa Romeo. Hitler was interested in this. Within five years he would be part-financing the most powerful racing cars the world had ever seen and Grand Prix racing would belong to him.

Georg 'Schorsch' Meier, a Bavarian, worked his apprenticeship after he left school at 14. He heard the Bavarian State Police were starting a motorcycle section and he liked that. When he was 19, he applied and was accepted. In time he would take a BMW to the Isle of Man, that curious expression of Britishness set in the Irish Sea, with the war only weeks away. He would force the bike through the stone-clad villages and twisting lanes of the island and dominate it, watched by a lot of other German riders and officials. It felt just like an occupation.

Daniel Prenn was ranked eighth in the world by the great American tennis professional Bill Tilden. Prenn had fled the Russian Revolution and, like so many Jewish émigrés, settled in Berlin where a large Jewish community had been for centuries. The International Lawn Tennis Federation reinstated Germany after the First World War so they could enter the Davis Cup again. Now, at the Rot-Weiss Club, they beat mighty Britain 3-2 in one of the rounds, intoxicating the whole of Germany. In time, Prenn and von Cramm would become formidable Davis Cup exponents, but that was before Prenn understood where Hitler's anti-Semitic laws were really going and escaped to London. He took out British citizenship and played at Wimbledon, although never, as it happened, against a German. The luck of the draw, no less.

Laupheim, in southern Germany, was a small, ancient community, although Jews had only been allowed to live there from 1724. Since then they had settled, prospered and considered themselves quite normal members of the community. A long-legged, darkly attractive high jumper called Gretel Bergmann started to argue with her parents. She wanted to go to the University of Physical Education in Berlin but they felt that, at 16, she was too young. In time she would be ruthlessly exploited by the Nazis to prevent an American boycott of the 1936 Olympics, then discarded – and a male member of the Hitler Youth (the one mentioned in the introduction) was chosen to replace her on the theory that he would be bound to beat women and win the gold medal.

At the training camp she was forced to room with him because, under the anti-Semitic laws, the Nazis knew he would never dare risk a physical relationship with her. Nasty things happened to people who did.

Stan Cullis, who had had an unhappy childhood and wanted to be a journalist, played soccer in the streets of Ellesmere Port, Cheshire, and then for the local boy's team. He was so good that talent scouts hovered at the match, but his father, a passionate supporter of Wolverhampton Wanderers, said the boy would play for them, and he did. He was a centre-half. In time it brought him to the England team and a match in the Olympic Stadium, Berlin, where in the interests of diplomatic relations the British ambassador decreed the team must line up and give Nazi salutes. Cullis refused and was quietly dropped. The others did and would find themselves haunted for decades by photographs and film of them doing it. Escaping Hitler remained problematical for them too.

Some historians have even postulated that the match, and the salute, were a part of the British government's policy of appeasement, tacitly suggesting that it conveyed a sort of approval for Hitler to invade Czechoslovakia. That seems highly unlikely from whichever direction you approach it, but the fact that it can be made at all reflects the strange, ominous shadowland of the era.

In 1930, the German economy was floundering, the social democrats and communists were divided and Hitler exploited all that. He blamed the crisis on Jewish financiers and Bolshevicks, and in the September elections the Nazis became the second-biggest party in the Reichstag (the parliament).

As the crisis deepened into 1931, Germany was awarded the 1936 Olympics, something that would initially be treated with contempt by Hitler. This was until he understood that the Games could be mercilessly, unashamedly exploited and ultimately, after 1940 in Tokyo, held in Berlin forever.

On Saturday 11 April, a man called Augusto Turati – a fascist, a journalist, a leading Italian sports figure and a confidant of Mussolini[13] – stood on a long, broad avenue holding a flag. At exactly 1 p.m. he lowered it, setting in motion a cavalcade of ninety-nine cars. They started at intervals, accelerating down the avenue through vast crowds and out of Brescia, an otherwise anonymous town in northern Italy. The Mille Miglia, 1,000 miles and one of the most famous, fearsome motor races, had begun.

Sixteen hours and ten minutes later, on a brilliant Sunday morning, Caracciola – the man from Remagen – brought his open-top Mercedes back to Brescia and to victory. Caracciola was now globally famous because, all else aside, the Mille Miglia had been running for four years and he was the first non-Italian to win it.

Shortly afterwards Caracciola was summoned to the Mercedes factory at Stuttgart by Dr Wilhelm Kissel, the company chairman, who explained that Hitler had ordered an open-topped Mercedes for himself. However, he demanded modifications, not least a glove compartment which could accommodate a revolver. These modifications had taken time, the delivery date had come and gone and Hitler was displeased. Dr Kissel felt he might even cancel the order.

Caracciola's fame was to be deployed. Hitler could not have avoided knowing that he had not only won the Mille Miglia but had beaten a whole array of Italian drivers in their Alfa Romeos doing it. Caracciola, therefore, would travel to the Brown House at Munich and present the car to him. This would be followed by a demonstration run.

Caracciola drove the car to Munich and, while it was being washed, he and the Mercedes representative in Munich, Jakob Werlin, went to the Brown House, a typically heavy stone building decorated in what has been described as an 'anti-modern style'. Hitler had a portrait of Henry Ford beside his desk. They admired each other. It cannot have been a coincidence that both men were fiercely anti-Semitic.

Caracciola remembered:

At the entrance steps we were met by a tall, slim young man with wavy hair. It was Rudolf Hess.[14] He asked us to wait, and after a short time led us into a large room. In one corner of that room was a desk and behind it sat Herr Hitler. He got up and came toward us: a rather stocky man with a trimmed moustache and straight black hair that fell over his forehead. He congratulated me on my great success in Italy … His speech was clipped, tinged with Austrian-Bavarian accent. I thanked him for the congratulations and was searching for words to explain the purpose of my visit. But Hitler didn't even let me begin; Italy seemed to be a matter of burning interest to him. He wanted to know what living conditions were like there, whether the people were happy and how they felt about Mussolini.[15]

Caracciola, who knew almost nothing about any of this, repeatedly tried to turn the conversation back to the Mercedes and explain the delay. Hitler was having none of it and gave Caracciola a conducted tour of the Brown House, including the vast conference room and the safes with the cards of 500,000 party members. Evidently the 500,000th had joined that very day.

Caracciola thought it was a lot of people, but was not particularly interested because he had come about the car. 'Herr Hitler, the big Mercedes you ordered is now ready. I've come to demonstrate it for you. It turned out to be a very beautiful car and I'm sure you will like it. May I bring it here?'

Hitler thought for a moment and said he would prefer to see it in the garage. He would be there in half an hour – and was. The chauffeur, Schreck, who'd been a member of the party since 1921, explained to Caracciola that on no account should he drive at more than 30mph because any chance of an accident must be avoided.

Caracciola gave Hitler a tour of Munich and its outskirts at what he estimated was slower than walking speed. Hitler liked the car but had a favour to ask. Would Caracciola give Hitler's niece a short run in it? Hitler gave Caracciola an address and they drove there:

> Hitler went into the house and came back with a young, golden-haired girl. She was so pretty that it took my breath away … When we stopped in front of her house again she ran over to her uncle and exclaimed enthusiastically: 'Uncle, oh, Uncle, it's a magnificent car!' The uncle beamed. As we drove off she waved for a long time.[16]

Caracciola did not consider meeting Hitler important because 'I could not imagine that this man would have the requirements for taking over the government some day. He had made no impression on me as a personality.' Perhaps, Caracciola reflected, if Hitler had had 'the head of a Caesar, like Mussolini', he – Caracciola – might have said 'let me be number 500,001', but Hitler had not. The notion that one day soon Hitler would wield 'the power of life and death over a great nation' was so inconceivable it never crossed Caracciola's mind.

However, the historian William L. Shirer wrote:

> Hitler had now, by the start of 1931, gathered around him in the party the little band of fanatical, ruthless men who would help him in his final drive to power and who, with one exception, would be at his side to help him sustain that power during the years of the Third Reich, though another of them, who was closest of all to him and perhaps the ablest and most brutish of the lot, would not survive, even with his life, the second year of Nazi government.[17]

This was Ernst Röhm, the leader of the storm troopers, or SA. Röhm had been enticed back from abroad by Hitler and:

> immediately set to work to make the S.A. by far the most efficient of the Party armies ... The organization was closely modelled on that of the Army, with its own headquarters and General Staff quite separate from the organization of the Party, and its own training college for S.A. and S.S. leaders opened at Munich in June 1931. [One of] Röhm's auxiliaries was the N.S.K.K. – the Nazi Motor Corps, a flying squad under the command of Major Huhnlein. At the time Röhm took over, in January 1931, the S.A. numbered roughly a hundred thousand men; a year later Hitler could claim three hundred thousand.

The Nazi rise to power is straightforward at the factual level and infernally complicated at the human level. Perhaps Caracciola's experience reflects the latter with great accuracy. Perhaps nobody – or very few – could foresee what was coming in any way. That must surely include the people we have already met in this chapter, however varied their backgrounds and personalities, who were simply enjoying their careers in the wholesome, and arguably innocent, world of sport.

In 1932 the Nazis were fighting running street battles with the communists and became the largest party in a July poll.

Between 30 July and 14 August, the tenth Olympic Games of the modern era were held in Los Angeles. Re-created in 1896 at Athens, the Games had visited Paris, St Louis, Athens again, London, Stockholm, Antwerp, Paris again and Amsterdam. The governing body, the International Olympic Committee (IOC), moved their headquarters to the calm of neutral Switzerland in 1915, so they would be safe from predators while they made sure the Games grew from its European-centric base to embrace every corner of the world. Hitler would have his own ideas about that and the Games would be very vulnerable indeed.

A cyclist from Cologne called Albert Richter had hoped to compete at Los Angeles but his federation could not afford the fare. He would know great success across the decade, however, though he was quite open in his dislike of the Nazis. At the end of the decade he would be hauled off a train at the Swiss border by the Gestapo and dragged along the platform. His date of death is given as two days later.

In January 1933 the German Organising Committee for the Berlin Olympics met in the council chamber of Berlin Town Hall. The mayor, Heinrich Sahm, a lawyer and experienced politician who stood at 6ft 6in, gave them a warm greeting. He would become vice chairman of the committee. Dr Theodore Lewald, almost 70, bearing a certain dignity and intimately connected to the Olympic movement for decades, estimated some 4,000 athletes and 1,000 officials would attend the Summer Games. That compared with 1,408 who had gone to Los Angeles in 1932. He also explained that the existing stadium they proposed would not be big enough.

Lewald evidently nursed suspicions about what might happen if the Nazis took power because he formed the Organising Committee as a 'separate non-profit society' which was independent and, because of that, even if the Nazis stripped him and Carl Diem of the positions they held in German sport, they could not be dismissed from the committee. Registering such a committee would normally have taken around six weeks but Lewald, sensing imminent danger, used his contacts and had it done in an hour.

Six days after the Organising Committee met, Hitler became Chancellor of Germany. The circumstances of his getting the position, and the niceties of what it ought to have entailed, are academic. The consequences are not. Hitler exploited it so quickly that, by March, civil liberties had been suspended and whatever the Nazi Party did was above the law. In practical terms he had attained absolute power.

Many had reason to fear this and many more would come to fear it, but the world of sport can hardly have been among them. Hitler was a political creature who, as we have seen, showed no interest apart from fast cars (driven slowly), although some reports suggest he spoke favourably about shooting, boxing and wrestling which, in retrospect, becomes ominous. Certainly in *Mein Kampf* he wrote of boxing: 'There is no sport that cultivates a spirit of aggressiveness, that demands lightning-quick decisiveness, that develops the body to such steely smoothness.'[18] He saw sport as a way of training soldiers as well as enhancing racial purity. 'I want my youth strong and beautiful. I will train them in all of the athletic sciences. I want an athletic youth. That's the first and most important thing.'[19]

It seems clear that if a political creed united the three fascist dictators – Mussolini in power from 1922, Hitler from 1933 and Franco[20] from 1936 – a singular indifference to sport in general also united them. Hitler watched one soccer match – Germany lost and he left in disgust – and he never returned. Mussolini knew perfectly well the power of soccer and would manipulate it. Franco knew the depths of hatred between Real Madrid and Barcelona and he would use that like a blunt instrument.

What Hitler did show, to a degree quite separate from the other two dictators, was a pathological intent to exclude Jews from national life and, in time, exclude them from the life process itself. The domestic German sports were all suddenly within his absolute power, of course, and initially he would purge Jews from every sports club and association. That aside, there seemed to be no reason for him to interfere. Germany had played competitive soccer from 1894; for example, VfB Leipzig became the first national champions in 1903 and the game flourished. He had every incentive to leave it and the rest alone.

He would surely have a great many more pressing demands on every waking moment – from the ruined economy to the communists who wanted his power for themselves – than racing drivers, tennis players and small people playing ice hockey.

Wouldn't he?

The answer was coming, and very, very quickly.

Notes

1 Bullock, *Hitler*.
2 Baker, *Jesse Owens: An American Life*.
3 Opportunity can depend on historical legacy, of course: an all-American boy from, say, Alabama is very unlikely to become a cricketer in much the same way that a Jamaican who can sprint is likely to become a very good sprinter. But I have interviewed a Danish county cricketer (an opening bowler) which, alone, proves that all things in sport are available if you want them badly enough. Sport ought to be the ultimate meritocracy.
4 Nixon, *Silver Arrows*.
5 Ibid.
6 Reuss, *Hitler's Motor Racing Battles*.
7 Bullock, *Hitler*.
8 lafayetteal.com/default.aspx?MODE=AREA_HISTORY
9 *The Guardian*.
10 The sixteen countries were Germany, Italy, the USA, Spain, Brazil, Austria, France, Hungary, Egypt, Czechoslovakia, Roumania, Holland, Switzerland, Belgium, Sweden and Argentina. The five Hitler did not occupy or declare war on were neutral Sweden and Switzerland, Brazil and Argentina (too far away), and Spain, although of course German forces took part in the civil war there and Hitler made a concerted effort to persuade General Franco to join the invasion of the Soviet Union (he was unsuccessful and said he would rather have teeth pulled out than submit to another meeting with Franco).
11 Mogulof, *Foiled*.
12 Fisher, *A Terrible Splendor*.
13 Augusto Turati (1888–1955) was a dedicated fascist and held official positions in fascist organisations as well as occupying himself with several sports, including tennis, athletics and the Olympics.
14 Rudolf Hess (1894–1987) was Hitler's deputy but became increasingly marginalised as the war progressed and, in an episode still cloaked in mystery, piloted himself to Scotland to try to negotiate peace. Whether he was mad or sane – or lost forever somewhere between the two – is also cloaked in mystery. He was sentenced to life imprisonment at the Nuremberg Trials and died in Spandau Prison, Berlin.
15 Caracciola, *A Racing Driver's World*.
16 Ibid.
17 Shirer, *The Rise and Fall of the Third Reich*.
18 Quoted in Fisher.
19 Bachrach, *The Nazi Olympics*.
20 Franco's full name was Francisco Paulino Hermenegildo Teódulo Franco y Bahamonde Salgado Pardo de Andrade, which must have had interesting consequences when he had to fill in forms. I assume (without being flippant) that one of the advantages of supreme power is that you do not have to fill in forms any more. He ruled part of Spain from 1936 and the remainder from 1939.

2

THE INHERITANCE

A physical education magazine, *Forum*, asked several prominent sportspeople for their 1933 predictions. Several felt that if the Nazis took power they would naturally follow Italian fascism by giving sport a great deal of big government support. That would make it 'centralised and geared towards successful international competition to show not only pride and commitment to the Fatherland but also fitness and ability'.[1]

The predictions seemed entirely reasonable because they were made in a country that was still a rational place, whatever political and financial waves had buffeted it. Germany was a functioning multi-party democracy living under the rule of law with a capital, Berlin, famous for its science, its cocky irreverence, its culture and the sexual liberalism which attracted many and ensnared Gottfried von Cramm.

To recapture what the man in the street, never mind the sportsman on the pitch, might have predicted in those January days remains extremely difficult because it is a (using that word again) reasonable assumption that they did not foresee Germany becoming an irrational place. An irrational place with, within weeks, the multi-party democracy, the culture, the sexual liberalism and the rule of law absolutely destroyed.

Between Monday 30 January and the last day of March – two days short of nine weeks – Hitler curbed left-wing parties, expressed contempt for parliamentary democracy, authorised Nazi paramilitaries to become the police in Prussia, opened the first concentration camp (Dachau), began a merciless attack on Jews and, when the Reichstag burned down, ruled by decree. Hitler became the law, now able to make all his phobias and fantasies legally binding on every citizen.

The historian William L. Shirer[2] has set out in plain language Hitler's inheritance. He had:

> conquered Germany with the greatest of ease, but a number of problems remained to be faced as summer came in 1933. There were at least five major ones: preventing a second revolution; settling the uneasy relations between the *S.A.* and the Army; getting the country out of its economic morass and finding jobs for the six million

unemployed; achieving equality of armaments for Germany at the Disarmament Conference in Geneva and accelerating the Reich's secret rearming, which had begun during the last years of the Republic; and deciding who should succeed the ailing Hindenburg when he died.

In the midst of all this he found time to attend the Berlin Motor Show on 11 February and in a speech there announced state-sponsored 'national motorisation'. This would involve the manufacture of a small, affordable car (ultimately the Volkswagen, the 'people's car'), the 'abolition of vehicle tax, reduction of corporation tax and government support for road-building and motorsport'. This would involve 500,000 Reichsmarks to build racing cars. Cumulatively, they:

> were clear signals that, in Hitler's state, cars and car manufacturers would play a key role. From this, Nazi propaganda would successfully mythologise the Führer as the original 'creator of the autobahns', even though Munich highways engineer and Nazi Party member Fritz Todt had included in his job-creation programme the so-called *Ha-Fra-Ba* plans, which had existed since the 1920s.

Ha-Fra-Ba was short for an association from the Hanseatic area: the North and Baltic Seas, Frankfurt and Basel. The association envisaged a motorway from Hamburg, Bremen and Lübeck through Frankfurt in the centre to Basel in Switzerland, which – passing all the major Ruhr towns – would give Germany a mighty, mobile backbone.[3]

This Berlin Motor Show set an immediate mood and a tempo. Hitler intended to change Germany, fundamentally and quickly. Here already, in the tall, arched hall on the Kaiserdamm – a broad avenue beyond the city centre – he had begun. In the weeks to come, ranging over sport as well as everything else, the tempo would be maintained in an almost bewildering way.

We, however, are still at the Berlin Motor Show.

'What one dictator could see as a way of increasing international prestige could also become apparent to a rival,' a motoring author, David Owen, has written:

> And Benito Musolini's willingness to spend more and more money on sponsoring Alfa [Romeo]'s efforts to regain their domination of Grand Prix racing would see the company's production car efforts pushed more and more into the background. Yet it would be eclipsed in its primary target too – by the money and the backing poured into the reborn German racing efforts by Adolf Hitler, and by the power of the cars and the domination they succeeded in establishing, right up to the outbreak of another world war.
>
> During that long and inexorable decline, there would still be times when the brilliance of [designer Vittorio] Jano's P3 [car] would still shine forth as of old. But the sad fact was that Alfa could not keep up with the pace of innovation to be set by the new German teams. Try as they might, every advance in design or in performance would be too little, too late. With the absence of any kind of legal limit to even the balance between the teams, the race would increasingly go to the powerful.[4]

Dr Ferry Porsche had, with his father, opened a car design company in Stuttgart a couple of years before. Intrigued and excited by the idea of a people's car he telegrammed Hitler:

> As the creator of many notable designs in the sphere of German and Austrian motor transport and aviation and one who has shared your struggle for more than 30 years to achieve today's success, I congratulate Your Excellency on your profound speech at the opening of the German Automobile Exhibition. I hope it will be granted to me and my staff, in future and to an increased extent, to place our skill and determination at the disposal of the German people.[5]

Hans Stuck claimed in his memoirs that Hitler also found time to telephone him and recorded the conversation like this:

> Adolf Hitler here. You remember the time, Herr Stuck, when I told you the Reich would help you to build a racing car once I came to power? Well, I've finally got here. I've seen how you have remained loyal to Germany. You've had some fine successes for Germany in a German car, in Brazil and Argentina. Please draft the necessary proposals for me. When you are ready, come and see me![6]

Whether this conversation really happened, or happened in the way Stuck recalled, it cannot be verified but it has an authentic ring in two ways. Hitler, like so many people with strange powers, seems to have had a startling memory; what might have been a flippant remark – 'When I'm in power I will give you a car' – was not flippant because, as the world would discover, Hitler did not indulge in the flippant any more than he indulged in misleading jokes. The telephone call fitted the mood and tempo.

Porsche also nursed ambitions to design a racing car but soon after the Berlin show Werlin – the Mercedes representative at Munich, of course, and close friend of Hitler – was able to claim the 500,000 Reichsmarks for Mercedes. That excluded Porsche and it excluded everybody else too.

That February, the Berlin Chief of Police announced a 'comprehensive campaign' against the city's 'depraved nightlife' and as a first measure set the closing time for 'amusements with dancing of the homosexual kind' at 10 p.m. Soon after, Hermann Göring – in effect Hitler's deputy – began closing premises and the Eldorado, which von Cramm patronised and where he met his lover Manasse Herbst, was shut down. The Nazis reportedly used it as a local headquarters.

Herbst, a Jewish actor, understood where the merciless attack on Jews was already going. He and his parents obtained visas to immigrate to Portugal but a problem confronted them: how to get money – their life savings – out. Germany remained in straightened financial circumstances, the lean and desperate days of the great depression lingering, and exporting of currency was subject to very strict controls. You could only take the equivalent of 7 per cent of your property, for example. This was made worse because the strict controls were physically operated at the borders and

Jews were checked with particular zeal. The family intended to sail (presumably from Hamburg) but that would involve getting through the customs on the dockside.

Herbst thought he had a solution. He went to von Cramm's apartment in Berlin with 'a small satchel ... bulging with Reichsmarks'. Surely someone as famous as von Cramm could board a ship without a body search? Von Cramm agreed but when he arrived on the day Herbst was due to sail his pockets were empty. He had decided it was simply too dangerous, even for him. He explained the money was safe in a bank and he would try to get it to Portugal somehow.[7]

Hitler's Germany was already a dangerous place for Jews and would remorselessly become more and more dangerous. On 15 March, he proclaimed the Third Reich and the next day received Lewald and Sahm, the Olympic people:

[They] explained to him the significance of the Games and the plans for their presentation. The Chancellor declared in response to Dr. Lewald's remarks that he welcomed the allotting of the Games to Berlin and that he would do everything possible to ensure their successful presentation. The Games, he asserted, would contribute substantially towards furthering understanding among the nations of the world and would promote the development of sport among the German youth, this being in his opinion of vast importance to the welfare of the nation. He expressed his best wishes to the Organizing Committee for the success of its work and promised it his constant support.

An official statement printed in the German press informed the nation of the attitude of their Chancellor towards the Berlin Games. The preparatory work could thus proceed on a firm foundation and it was carried forward with all alacrity in order that a complete plan might be submitted to the International Olympic Committee during its annual meeting at Vienna in 1933. Three main problems were to be solved by then: the centres of competition, the accommodations for the athletes, and the date of the Games.[8]

Because this forms part of the official report it is couched in matter-of-fact phrasing and simultaneously diplomatic language. But even that cannot disguise the fact that clearly something very fundamental had happened between Hitler condemning the Games as the plaything of Jews and Freemasons (not to mention black people), insisting Germany would have nothing to do with them, and this talk of support. It may be that even Hitler discovered that saying things in opposition is easy and facing the real consequences of them in government is not at all the same; it may be that now Germany had the Games it was easier to take the path of least resistance. Germany might as well keep them. He had promised support but, as with any standard diplomatic communiqués, he hadn't actually promised anything. Support could be made to mean whatever he wanted.

At the meeting, Lewald spoke to Goebbels and asked for support from the Propaganda Ministry. Goebbels, a sharp political operator and a visionary in propaganda, saw – before, during or after this – the potential like a revelation. Here was a unique chance to portray the new Germany to the world, perhaps never to be repeated. Here was a chance to bring the world to Germany and let them experience it for themselves. Here, at the same time, was a chance to show the German people that the new government could organise the biggest sporting event and better than it had ever been done before – by Athens, Paris, St Louis, Athens (again), London, Stockholm, Antwerp, Paris (again), Amsterdam and Los Angeles.

Goebbels, susceptible to all manner of temptations (private and professional), did not resist this one. He would make sure Hitler did not either. The support from the Propaganda Ministry would be extensive and, ultimately, would be given in a way that had never been done before.

On 25 March the Organising Committee set the date for the Games, 1–16 August 1936.

Three days later Lewald (along with Carl Diem) met Goebbels again. Lewald secured the appointment, which was hardly surprising because he had 'influential friends in all ministries, as he had been responsible for the selection and training of most of the young lawyers in government service for a ten-year period …'[9]

Lewald and Diem submitted their publicity and transportation plans to Goebbels and secured his permission to set up a special commission to deal with this aspect of the Games' organisation.

As the anti-Semitism increased – 'it had become commonplace to see groups of storm troopers, armed with revolvers and pieces of piping, roaming the streets looking for Jews to beat up'[10] – Lewald and Diem faced a major problem. The International Olympic Committee was to meet in Vienna from 7 to 10 June and the question of the treatment of the Jews was bound to be raised. Any discrimination against them, in terms of the German team or any other team coming to Berlin, risked the IOC withdrawing the Games, which was absolutely within their power.

Moreover, the Winter Games were to be allocated at the Vienna meeting and, although they were confidently expected to go to the Bavarian resort of Garmisch-Partenkirchen, the IOC might show their displeasure by taking them elsewhere.

The first Winter Games had been in 1924 at Chamonix and the Summer Games in Paris that year, which might have established a custom of always holding them in the same host country, but, in 1928, they went to St Moritz and Amsterdam, returning to the same host in 1932 at Lake Placid, New York State and Los Angeles. In other words the custom was not established so strongly that Garmisch-Partenkirchen could be regarded as automatic. On top of that, the IOC would have plenty of time to find an alternative. It was a question of scale: Lake Placid attracted 306 competitors and Los Angeles 1,408. This meant that the Winter Games were still small enough to be manageable and it would be much easier to find a venue for them.

There was another dimension. The United States, easily the strongest Olympic country – to the point where a Games without their team would be diluted into meaninglessness – might well boycott Berlin in the face of all the anti-Semitism and, if they did, others could follow. The statistics are eloquent. At Los Angeles, the United States won 103 medals (41 gold, 32 silver, 30 bronze) with Italy next on 36 (12, 12, 12), Germany eighth on 21 (4, 12, 5). And if the United States wasn't going to go to Berlin it certainly wouldn't be going to Garmisch-Partenkirchen either.

The Nazis were trapped because their internal logic demanded they enact the persecution of the Jews, but that brought these external pressures they could not suppress. They would be forced to strike an uneasy compromise between the two, involving subterfuge, deception and outright lying – though that never troubled them in sport or in anything else. Yet by their actions nobody can doubt that the priority would be the Jews, not the Olympics, because the Nazis maintained the persecution – with no more than token public concessions – and only drew back when the Games were actually upon them, resuming immediately afterwards.

Domestically, the Nazis now had a free hand and Hitler Youth leader Baldur von Schirach moved quickly to seize control of some 400 other youth organisations. That happened in April and, by June, Hitler made Schirach *Jugendführer des Deutschen Reiches*, Youth Leader of Germany. The Hitler Youth became a quasi-military organisation promoting physical activity, including boxing, as well as, inevitably, war games.[11]

In the midst of it all the Nazis themselves faced a problem laced with irony, because Germany had a solid, organised, uninspired soccer team but Austria were known as the *Wunderteam*, a group of artistic players with flair and adventure. They had mauled Scotland 5-0, Germany 6-0 and 5-0, France 4-0 and Hungary 8-2. The team might possibly have peaked, however, because three months after Hitler took power they lost 2-1 to Czechoslovakia. Hitler would reach a novel solution to the problem of the Austrian team and tear Czechoslovakia apart.

So much interwove, here and everywhere else, and so much would bring unforeseen consequences.

Sepp Herberger, as assistant coach with the German team, joined the Nazi Party and would go on to prominence before and after the war. In the 1930s, however, 'he never had anything to do with ideologies but he was willingly used for the inhuman ideology'. Herberger would, too, co-operate with a Nazi propaganda film early in the war, *Das grosse Spiel* (*The Great Game*).[12]

One incident distils the Nazis' attitude to the Jews with perfect clarity, although the exact details are slightly obscure. On 12 April, so few weeks after Hitler came to power, Lewald resigned, under Nazi pressure, from his post as a German sports leader following publicity about his Jewish grandmother. Evidently there was also pressure to strip him of the presidency of the Organising Committee, with the aim of replacing him with Hans von Tschammer und Osten, soon to be *Reichssportführer* (the Reich's sports commissioner), something which, as we have seen, Lewald had taken precautions to prevent. Von Tschammer und Osten was an early Nazi (1922), a language teacher and a horseman who knew little – if anything – about sport. He had a withered arm from a First World War injury. Reportedly he regarded sport as a weapon to 'improve the morale and productivity of German workers', which was exactly the sort of approach to endear him to Hitler.

Whether Lewald, a deeply respected figure within the IOC, was – or could have been – actually dismissed is not clear but, either way, there was something of an outcry and he stayed in his post. Whatever some suggest, he was no more than a figurehead (or perhaps fig leaf so the Nazis could hide behind his respectability).

The fact that they needed his respectability saved him and forced them into another uneasy compromise. Hitler could control what happened in Germany but he could not yet orchestrate what happened beyond it – the internal, external problem – and with the Berlin Games now vulnerable he could not afford to alienate the country he needed, the United States, who were strongly represented on the IOC.

One of these April days, Max Schmeling was dining in a sports café in Berlin when a member of the SA[13] came up and said Hitler would like to entertain him to dinner in the Reich Chancellery, the stone-clad building on the wide, straight boulevard, housing some of the government ministries and foreign embassies. He waited in an ante room and then:

> I had barely walked over to the window when the door opened and Hitler appeared, surrounded by Goering, Goebbels and most of the other cabinet ministers. Without hesitating, Hitler came directly over to me and said, 'Good day, Herr Schmeling, how good of you to come. I wanted to invite you to join me for dinner.' He was shorter than I had imagined, but, more than anything else, there was none of the rigid, overdone intensity of his public appearances. When we had driven into the city … in the last few years, we would see his election posters in the villages and towns that we drove through, and [wife] Anny would always laugh at his resemblance to Charlie Chaplin. But in this moment there was nothing comical or absurd in his bearing; he moved about in a relaxed way, he was charming and seemed quietly confident in these surroundings. I answered, 'Herr Reichskanzler, thank you very much, but I have just eaten.' Hitler accepted that in a friendly manner and said only, 'Well, let's at least just chat a bit.'[14]

This lasted some 20 minutes and was, as Schmeling would remember, a jovial, informal gathering, which culminated in Hitler wishing him well in his fight against the American Max Baer, due in New York in June.

'As he was being driven home, Max concluded that the purpose of the meeting was to get him to spread the word, in interviews with the American press, that the doom merchants had got it all wrong and that everything in Germany was fine.'[15]

Baer had been raised as a Catholic, his mother's religion. Jewish law says that the matriarchy determines the religion. His father apparently was partially Jewish and Baer did identify himself as Jewish: he would wear a Star of David on his trunks against Schmeling. For once, the degree of Jewishness is not relevant because the group in the Reich Chancellery would have regarded Baer as a representative of a degenerate race (the Jews) who was at the same time a citizen of another degenerate race (the Americans) and would surely have emphasised that to Schmeling, with Goebbels keen to exploit the propaganda possibilities.

This was only the fourth month of Hitler in power, of course, and although the anti-Semitism was gathering pace it was not yet a sculpted, structured obsession to be paraded in detail in public at every opportunity. The Baer fight itself would demonstrate that and Schmeling reflected that 'most of his American friends were Jews, Joe Jacobs foremost among them'.[16]

In practice for the Monaco Grand Prix, Rudolf Caracciola was taking his Alfa Romeo down towards the quayside at, he estimated, 100kmph. He braked but the brakes gripped only one of the front wheels. The car skidded and he decided it was better to strike the stone wall there than plunge into the harbour. The impact was so brutal that he'd walk with a limp for the rest of his life and the injury added a curious dimension to the triumphant motor racing Hitler wanted so badly.

This needs context. Grand Prix racing began in France in 1906 and up to the First World War the French held five more races and the Americans held five. The French Grand Prix resumed in 1921 and the Italian began that year (in Brescia). A year later it moved to Monza before other countries came in: Spain (1923), Belgium at Spa (1925), Germany at the Avus and Britain at Brooklands (1926) – Germany moved to the Nürburgring in 1927 – Monaco (1929) and the Czechoslovakian at Brno (1930). The sport was not only well established and popular, but the seasonal calendar had a settled feel to it. Nobody could foresee that it was ripe for domination, least of all Caracciola, who was determined to drive again but could not be sure he ever would.

Three days after Monaco, an 'Aryans only' ruling was applied to German sport, including gymnastics. German sports clubs had to expel their Jewish athletes and were, from that moment on, not allowed to compete against them.

This was manifestly *not* an uneasy compromise to keep the Americans sweet but a basic expression of how the Nazis intended Germany to be, whatever anybody else thought. In that sense, it was their initial concrete response to the internal-external problem.

The ruling had a negative effect on 23-year-old Eric Seelig, the country's light-heavyweight and middleweight champion. He was Jewish and the Boxing Association expelled him. He would find frightening pressure brought on to him in a matter of weeks and it became so intolerable that he would flee Germany.

The 'Aryans only' then reached out and touched Daniel Prenn, the naturalised German, born in Poland of Jewish ancestry (some say Byelorussia, others say Russia or Lithuania). He was the leading German tennis player from 1928 to 1932 and during that time represented the country with notable success. Now the German Tennis Federation applied the rule. No Jew would be selected for Germany, including the Davis Cup. No Jewish or Marxist club could be affiliated to the Federation. No Jew could hold an official position in the Federation and 'the player Dr. Prenn (a Jew) will not be selected for the Davis Cup team in 1933'.

Fred Perry and Bunny Austin, leading British players, protested in a strong letter published in *The Times*, but the International Lawn Tennis Association did nothing. The letter said:

Sir, – We have read with considerable dismay the official statement which has appeared in the press that Dr. D.D. Prenn is not to represent Germany in the Davis Cup on the grounds that he is of Jewish origin.

We cannot but recall the scene when, less than 12 months ago, Dr. Prenn before a large crowd at Berlin won for Germany against Great Britain the semi-final round of the European Zone of the Davis Cup, and was carried from the arena amidst spontaneous and tremendous enthusiasm.

We view with great misgivings any action which may well undermine all that is most valuable in international competitions.

Yours faithfully,

H.W. Austin

Fred Perry

The small band of tennis professionals in the world who, by turning professional, had excluded themselves from the amateur game altogether did not protest and did not offer Prenn a place amongst themselves because 'Germany had become an important venue for the pro game. Responding to the times, the Meister of pro tennis in Germany, Roman Najuch, shortly resigned as coach of Poland's Davis Cup team because of "Poland's anti-German agitation."'[17] You can read a great deal into this, not least that as the Nazis began to push beyond the acceptable boundaries of human conduct they were already meeting such little resistance.

The tennis decree brought tragedy. Nelly Neppach, German champion in 1925 and a Jew, committed suicide by poison and gas. She was 34. The fact that she was now effectively excluded from tennis reportedly had a traumatic effect on her. In early May, the German Tennis Federation reported that the sport was now free of Jews. The official magazine *Tennis und Golf* covered the suicide in the most downbeat way, saying it was not shocking or tragic but, in a most chilling phrase, 'a problem has solved itself'.[18]

Whether the lack of resistance encouraged the Nazis is problematical because, by every utterance and every deed, they already regarded the rest of the world, especially the United States, with contempt and intended, as far as possible, to ignore it prior to conquering it. The letter from two tennis players about another, Jewish, tennis player must be seen in that context. It is a context which will become more and more familiar.

On 7 May 1933, Germany played a first-round Davis Cup tie against Egypt and won easily enough, 5-0. Between this May and July 1939, Germany would play a total of thirty ties against twenty-two countries. Of them, Hitler would absorb and/ or conquer thirteen, declare war on three, be allied to two and leave only four (more or less) alone: Switzerland, Sweden, Ireland and Argentina. There seems little reason to doubt that if he had won the war he'd have gone for each of these neutrals except Argentina (simply because it was too far away).

The Nazis did compromise a little in the anti-Semitic legislation. They would not bar 'non-German non-Aryans' from entering the major motor races at their two set-piece circuits, the Nürburgring in the Eifel Mountains near the Belgian border – which attracted truly enormous crowds – and the Avus circuit on the outskirts of Berlin, which satisfied the crowds from the capital who wanted to enliven their Sunday afternoons. The compromise was tolerated because the major races at these circuits would be fully reported in the foreign press. The non-German non-Aryan term meant, in plain speak, Jews. A French Jew, René Dreyfus, competed in the 1936 and 1938 German Grands Prix and even in 1939, driving a Delahaye, a French car.

Hitler evidently visited the Avus circuit on the outskirts of Berlin at the beginning of May to watch a special stage of the ADAC (Allgemeiner Deutscher Automobil Club) Reichsfahrt event although it seems he never attended a race there.[19]

Von Tschammer und Osten officially disbanded the *Deutscher Reichsausschuss für Leibesübungen* (German Commission for Physical Exercise – meaning sport) on 10 May. He was elevated to *Reichssportführer* two months later, placing the whole sphere of German sport within his authority.

The Nazis banned trade unions on, as it happened, the day the executive of the Organising Committee met with the task of taking 'into consideration the changes which had come about as a result of the National Socialist Revolution, to ensure the co-operation of the Reich Sport Leader, to introduce the principle of leadership and to take cognizance of the alterations emanating from the changes in the form of government'.[20]

It's hard to quantify this as anything but masterly understatement.

Baron Klaus von Oertzen, Chairman of Auto Union, had been urged by a fellow director to go to Hitler and lay before him a 'show-piece product' – a design for a racing car. Von Oertzen naturally consulted Ferry Porsche and, when the meeting with Hitler had been secured, took Porsche and Hans Stuck. Von Oertzen did not know Hitler at all, but knew that Stuck did.

Hitler had been expecting von Oertzen and nobody else, although there is some confusion over this. Certainly only Hitler and his secretary were present, and the meeting began so coldly it took some time to warm up. At some point Hitler shook hands with Porsche and said, 'We know each other.' This mystified Porsche but Hitler was right. They had met at the Solitude circuit near Stuttgart in 1926 when Porsche's Mercedes racing car was competing and Hitler attended with Werlin.

Von Oertzen would remember:

> In the course of the discussion Hitler turned down my request for capital backing for the Auto Union racing car and at the end of his explanation he said: 'Don't bother with it any more!' Then I took my courage in both hands and said to him: 'You know, Herr Reich Chancellor' – I never called him *mein Führer* – 'it's not so terribly long ago that you were collected in a Mercedes from your imprisonment in Landsberg. You said you wanted to start your Party work again but the press said to you: *Don't bother, Herr Hitler. We'll never listen to you again. It's all over for you …* Now you're saying the same thing to me, that I shouldn't bother with the racing car, I should give up, but I'm not going to do that. I *am* going to bother. It is the duty I owe to ten thousand workers.' Hitler did not like me talking like that. He looked at me twice very hard, then ignored my impertinence and turned to Dr Porsche.[21]

Ghislaine Kaes, Porsche's private secretary, must have been given full details of the meeting because he would remember[22] Hitler took Porsche to a window and they:

> talked for twenty minutes. I think the reason for this was that Porsche was an elderly man who had met many of the great men of the world and was not at all nervous in

Hitler's presence. Also, they were both from Austria and spoke the same language – I think Hitler took a liking to him. Porsche later told me that Hitler had asked him what he wanted. Porsche showed him drawings of the new engine he had designed … – a V-16. He reminded Hitler of his speech at the Berlin Motor Show a few weeks before, in which he had promised to boost the German car industry, and pointed out that the engine was designed for a racing car that would do great things for Germany in the new 750kg Formula races.[23]

Hitler explained that, two weeks before, he had agreed to fund the Mercedes racing programme for 500,000 Reichsmarks; as a consequence Auto Union and Porsche were too late. Porsche countered by saying it would be better to have two German teams competing against the might of the Italians. Hitler said Porsche didn't have a factory. Porsche countered by saying that Auto Union did. Hitler said that Auto Union had never built a racing car. Porsche countered by saying, 'No, but I have.'[24]

Von Oertzen remembered Hitler asking Porsche 'how he intended to build the racing car. There was a long discussion and Hitler was interested in all the technicalities. He had all sorts of knowledge that one would not have expected him to have. Then he brought the meeting to an end and said: "You'll be hearing from me."' Three days later permission came through.

Whether or not they discussed the people's car at the meeting, Hitler's wishes about that were clear. The car had to be able to carry two adults and three children, cruise at 100kmph (62mph), go 100km on 9 litres (l) of fuel, have an air-cooled engine and cost less than 1,000 Reichsmarks. It also had to be capable of carrying three soldiers and a machine gun. That evidently represented Hitler's idea of a family vehicle.

On 17 May Prenn won the Austrian tennis championships in Vienna, beating Harry Kinzl, an Austrian, 6-1, 5-7, 6-3, 6-1. As someone noted, Prenn, the hero of the year before, was now, in the German newspapers, a Jew and consequently not German at all. It did not matter that he was not a practising Jew nor, indeed, religious at all. It did not matter that he was married to a Christian.[25]

Within days Prenn and his wife fled to England, where he had a powerful benefactor in Simon Marks of the wealthy chain Marks & Spencer. Marks knew Prenn well from his vists to Wimbledon and now, as it seems, helped him become a British citizen. By 26 June, at Wimbledon, Prenn was representing Britain.

We are still in late May, however, and a motor race at the Nürburgring called the Eifelrennen. One German car, a Mercedes driven by the aforementioned haughty Manfred von Brauchitsch, faced an array of Alfa Romeos and Bugattis. He finished second to Tazio Nuvolari, a maestro regarded as one of the best drivers of all time, who danced his Alfa Romeo round the ring's 22km of twists and turns, ascents and descents.

Hermann Göring was there surrounded by an entourage of senior Nazi officials, quite a few of whom would be heard of again in the rearmament of Germany and the unleashing of the Second World War. There was the ambitious, industrious and intelligent Erhard Milch, who, thanks to his experience as a fighter pilot and his links with industry, was appointed Deputy Reich Commissioner for Aviation as soon as the Nazis came to power. Since May 1933 he had been permanent secretary in the ministry and a paid-up member of the NSDAP (Nazi Party). Göring was also accompanied by Colonel Walter von Reichenau, a senior official in the Army Ministry. In 1941, as a field marshal in Russia, he described the slaughter of the Jews of Kiev by the SS, as well as the bloody crimes of his own troops, as:

> the necessity of a harsh but just penalty paid by the subhuman Jews ... After the race Göring mounted the podium at the finishing line and addressed the spectators: 'You must have recognised how the new Germany is more intense and passionate about sport, and especially motorsport,' he boomed, while his words were being simultaneously transmitted on national radio. 'This event is valuable to the new Germany because we have been able to show that the things people are saying about us are not true. It can be seen that those Germans who slander us from beyond our borders have no right to speak in the name of Germany. Our guests will have become aware that ours is a Germany in which every individual looks again into a more peaceful future, that the country is experiencing an internal springtime. The people of Germany desire peaceful competition.'[26]

Göring[27] was not himself a sinister figure, neither physically nor in the primitive Nazi way. His presence at the race, and the entourage surrounding him, however, made clear the regime was watching motor sport closely and was already in the process of exploiting it. Hence the nationwide broadcast and the boasting. Within days of the Nürburgring – at a different racing circuit and then a tennis championships – these words would be given their true context.

Leo Steinweg from Münster was running a motorbike shop and competing successfully. He was a Jew. In May, he won the 175cc and 250cc classes at a race meeting near Wuppertal but reportedly refused to give the Nazi salute on the podium.

The German tennis authorities only entered von Cramm for the doubles in the French championships in Paris, even though Prenn, who would have made a strong partnership, was now in London. That von Cramm was denied a chance at the singles, with all the publicity and personal glory that might bring, could have been an ominous sign.

In the doubles, he and Kai Lund – regarded as a much the weaker player of the two – had a bye. In the second round the Czechoslovakian pair Roderich Menzel and Friedrich von Rohrer proved too strong, winning 6-4, 4-6, 2-6, 6-3, 6-3. Menzel – later to play for Germany – has been described as a 'huge, blustering player' and was an admirer of von Cramm's tennis; he attributed von Cramm's success to 'practicing like a professor of mathematics for 5 hours a day'. Menzel described von Cramm's tennis rise in military terms with a plan as 'well-judged' as 'the staff of an army would work out in the case of mobilisation'.[28]

This needs context. Tennis was much longer established than Grand Prix racing (Wimbledon from 1877, the US from 1881, the French from 1891 and the Australian 1905), although it was in no sense the global presence it has become. In 1933 the Wimbledon seeds were three Britons, two Americans, an Australian and a Japanese.

The entry carried an international flavour with entries from another fifteen countries – from as far afield as Egypt, Jamaica, Argentina and Uruguay – but only two of them survived the earlier rounds. France and Germany, however, habitually proved strong: their leading players were celebrities in their own countries and abroad. In other words, what had happened to Prenn and what was happening to von Cramm were not obscure events lost in a minor sport but ought to have become national topics. That they did not is very revealing and can only have strengthened the Nazi view that in practical terms they had a free hand.

In June, Hitler broadened his control of motoring. He ordered Adolf Hühnlein to separate the NSKK (*Nationalsozialistisches Kraftfahrkorps*, National Socialist Motor Corps) from the motor storm troopers (of the paramilitary SA) and make it independent. Hühnlein immediately Nazified all the German drivers' associations and automobile clubs, and a decree was issued: no further racing licences would be issued to 'Jews and other non-Aryans'.

That affected Leo Steinweg. He had already been forced to put a sign in the shop window saying 'GERMANS, DON'T BUY FROM JEWS!' Soon enough he would get a licence form to apply for a competition licence for 1934, but it included questions about Aryan ancestry. He knew at that moment his career had ended and much worse might be coming.

Hühnlein of course might reasonably have concluded that if the future looked dark for such as Steinweg, it looked very good indeed for him. He had been a professional soldier and joined the SA as early as 1925. He was no orator but a man to get things done (despite the police station debacle during the *putsch*), and that's what he would do.

Now Hitler broadened his control of all domestic sport, and this merely four months after taking power. On 2 June, the Nazi minister of education announced that Jews were to be excluded from youth and welfare organisations 'and that the facilities of such bodies were to be closed to them'. It was on that same day that Lewald was threatened with expulsion from the Olympic Organising Committee.

It was done with a breath-taking arrogance or absence of awareness because the crucial Vienna meeting was only five days away and there Americans would apply fierce pressure as they sought assurances that these measures would not be applied to Jews within the Olympic context.

The day before Vienna *The New York Times* reported:

> The Hitler government had already backed [trodden] water, after opposition by the Olympic Games Committee on a plan to depose Dr. Lewald on the ground his grandmother was Jewish and hand over the arrangements for the games [sic] to a government commissar. Germany does not wish to lose the games, which are expected to furnish Hitlerism with an excellent opportunity for propaganda.

The USA, Britain and France would try to move the Games from Berlin unless binding declarations were given that there would be no discrimination of any kind based on race or religion.

In Vienna, that American pressure came from three men, Colonel William May Garland, Commodore Ernest Lee Jahncke and Brigadier General Charles Hitchcock Sherrill, former sportsman and American minister to Argentina and Turkey. He had been an IOC representative since 1922.[29]

Before he left for the meeting, Sherrill spoke trenchant and uncompromising words about what he would be demanding. He invited the American public to 'rest assured that I shall stoutly maintain the American principle that all citizens are equal under all laws'. He expanded on that with a demand that there could be no question of barring German Jews from competing. *The New York Times* carried Sherrill's response to the proposition that what the German government did inside Germany was nobody else's business. Sherrill executed a slight feint.

'General Sherrill,' the newspaper printed, 'rejects the argument that the whole matter is an internal question. He maintains the Olympic Games and its rules cannot be violated by the entertaining nation.'

The New York Times reported that the German delegation arrived at the Festival Hall at the Academy of Sciences in Vienna with a 'promise from their government in their pockets'. The Americans 'demanded a specific assurance that Jews would not be excluded from the German Olympic team'. The German 'legation had to cable superiors in Berlin for instructions. Finally the Germans agreed to the broader guidelines.'[30]

According to research by Stephen R. Wenn,[31] Sherrill's 'public posture' altered as the 'participation debate intensified'. The Germans understood the absolute 'gravity of the situation' and made a 'strategic retreat'. On the opening day, Lewald said publicly that Germany would honour the IOC's rules. Wenn writes: 'It was also announced that Lewald had been reinstated to the Organizing Committee' – even with diminished authority.

Overall, the IOC had its assurances, although the Nazis 'baulked' at giving a specific pledge that German Jews would be on the German team and 'a number of last minute communiqués were required before Lewald could accede to such an IOC demand'. Subsequently in letters and speeches Sherrill would play the tough man who had played hard ball in Vienna and repeatedly describe this as his 'Vienna triumph', even in a letter to a New York rabbi.[32]

Was it? Had he?

The official IOC bulletin said:

THE GAMES OF THE XIth OLYMPIAD,
TO BE HELD IN BERLIN

August 1 – 16th 1936.

The president then dealt with the question of the Games of the XIth Olympiad at Berlin and gave an account to his colleagues of the negotiations, which had taken place since the change of government in Germany, with the delegates of the IOC in that country, in order to be:

quite sure that the guarantees given by the government in power in 1931, just as they had been given by the governments of countries where preceding Olympiads had been organised, could be considered as reliable, and that the application of the Olympic Rules dealing with the Committee of Organisation and the qualifications of participants would be scrupulously observed, even though certain limitations of our International Rules should seem to be inconsistent with recent orders laid down in Germany.

The president paid tribute to the Olympic spirit and to the loyalty of the German delegates, who, having done all they could to put the suitable ministers in possession of the facts of the situation, had succeeded in putting matters sufficiently in order in time to allow the statement to be published.

Sherrill would remember it as:

> a trying fight. We were six on the Executive Committee, and even my English colleagues thought we ought not to interfere in the internal arrangements of the German team. The Germans yielded slowly – very slowly. First they conceded that other nations could bring Jews. Then, after the fight was over, telephones [sic] came from Berlin that no publication [sic] should be given to their government's back-down on Jews, but only the vague statement that they agreed to follow our rules ... Then I went at them hard, insisting that as they had expressly excluded Jews, now they must expressly declare that Jews would not even be excluded from German teams. All sorts of influence was exerted to change my American stand. Finally they yielded because they found that I had lined up the necessary votes.[33]

Sherrill's position would harden so that – amazingly – the hard man would be playing hard ball in the opposite direction.

Lewald hailed what happened at Vienna as an assertion of sporting values over government power. Was it?

The problem which Sherrill, Lewald and everyone else faced was getting Hitler and the Nazis into proper focus. In 1933, despite the anti-Semitism, who could know the full depravity of what Hitler was going to do or how completely amoral he truly was? Who could know what the Nazis were really capable of? Sherrill and Lewald and the IOC would be hijacked but in their defence it is necessary to say that, even in 1939, there were those still trying to appease Hitler, still failing to get him into proper focus.

George S. Messersmith, head of the US Consulate in Berlin, appears to have got the focus right, however, although you can argue that as a professional politician he ought to have done. But how many professional politicians did not, including British Prime Minister Neville Chamberlain, until deep into 1939?

Messersmith began his correspondence about the Olympics to the State Department with what has been described as 'a far more cautionary tone' than the one the IOC adopted. Messersmith pointed out that although the Nazis were promoting sport and emphasising its importance they were banning Jews from taking part. Surveying the Nazis honeyed words he pointed out that that was not their 'real intention' and added he was not convinced American Jews would be safe during the Olympics, presumably including competitors as well as spectators.

The Winter Games went to Garmisch, to be held in February 1936, but the exact dates were not yet decided.

The American insistence was to become a great deal more complicated for America. It would involve strong personalities and sub-currents, and run like a sore for another three years. After that it would leave a legacy which tainted some of those strong personalities even decades later. That reached out and touched not only Sherrill, but also a man called Avery Brundage, one of the most controversial of all Olympic figures, as well as American diplomatic and consular officials in Berlin, including the ambassador and two consuls.

This, cumulatively, represented the first time Hitler's policies had a direct, destructive impact beyond Germany. It would not be the last.

While the IOC were meeting in Vienna, three professional tennis players – Bill Tilden, young German Hans Nüsslein and Brian Barnes – sailed for Europe on the *Bremen*. Tilden was a notorious homosexual and would become entwined with von Cramm for an associated reason.

In New York, the day after Vienna, Baer met Schmeling at the Bronx in a non-title heavyweight bout – the one for which Hitler had wished Schmeling good fortune. Baer did wear the Star of David on his shorts but, it seems, there were no political overtones to the fight. *The New York Times*, which carried extensive descriptions of the days before – up to the fact that 1,250 policemen would be on duty, including a contingent from the pickpocket division, and which ticket-holders should use which bridges – makes no mention of it being anything other than a boxing match. Even two days before, a writer called John Kiernan explored Baer's life, career and personality in a feature article 1,500 words long and made no mention of anything but boxing.

In the fight, Baer (described in traditional boxing terms as 'a larruping thumper from Livermore, Cal.') played the clown in the middle rounds after a strong start and, although Schmeling got in counter-punches, Baer defended well before the fight was stopped in the tenth round. Baer landed a heavy right to Schmeling's head, Schmeling's knees buckled and, helpless, Baer battered him mercilessly. Schmeling went down, got up and Baer battered him mercilessly again. The referee put an end to it.

Some days later, von Tschammer und Osten made a speech in Berlin during which he said: 'We shall see to it that both in our national life and in our relations and competitions with foreign nations only such Germans shall be allowed to represent the nation as those against whom no objection can be raised.'

In another speech, in Cologne, he said:

It is hardly fair to expect that state support be given to purely Jewish organisations, which, being composed almost exclusively of Zionists, are even today in sharp political conflict with the government. Just as Nationalist sports organizations during the past years continued to enlist and engage in activities without any material assistance by relying purely upon themselves, so, too, no other treatment can now justly be meted out to Jewish organizations. That certainly won't create any difficulty for them, because in their circles substantial private means are available.[34]

If these speeches sounded like a direct repudiation of what had been agreed at Vienna, which true Nazis gave a damn? Or did von Tschammer und Osten, and more particularly touchy-feely Goebbels, judge that such speeches would not have serious resonance beyond Germany and, as a consequence, reasoned they could get away with them without provoking the international community? Certainly, at moments in the future, when speeches like that might be very damaging, Goebbels would be vetting them.

Germany had four men in the Wimbledon men's singles, including von Cramm. He reached the third round where he was beaten 6-3, 6-4, 9-7 by American Clifford Sutter. However, von Cramm and Hilda Krahwinkel won the mixed doubles.

Prenn played as a Briton, of course. *The Times*, in its preview, said 'all the leading men in the world will be present and nearly 30 countries will be represented in the 64 matches in the first round of the Singles … No other game can attract its followers from so many corners of the earth. Among them will be one D. Prenn, the former German Davis Cup player, now for some kind of political reason discarded by his country, but playing as well as ever, as no doubt he will soon prove.' Interestingly, perhaps, the *Daily Express* – to select just one popular newspaper – carried an extensive preview but did not mention Prenn at all.

Prenn reached the fourth round but lost to American Ellsworth Vines 6-3, 6-2, 6-4.

The American professionals' tour reached the Blau-Weiss Club at Berlin (not to be confused with the Rot-Weiss) where a match was played using the Davis Cup format. Tilden and Barnes beat Nüsslein, Roman Najuch and Hermann Bartels four matches to one – Nüsslein took the sole German point, beating Barnes in four sets. The *Berliner Morgenpost* reported that Najuch should have won his match but received a wrong call. Goebbels and his wife Magda were in the crowd.[35]

No doubt they appeared as a charming, normal couple, applauding at all the right moments during a charming, normal tennis tournament. If Göring, at the Nürburgring or anywhere else, was not of himself a sinister figure, either physically or in the primitive Nazi way, that did not hold true for Goebbels. Göring appeared a wonderfully corpulent figure in the tradition of Henry VIII; Goebbels had a club foot and a face not dissimilar to a rodent. His presence at the tennis, deliberately or innocently, made clear he was watching and would know what was going on.

The Olympic Organising Committee had problems beyond the anti-Semitism. The stadium for the 1936 Games was supposed to be on a racecourse but who would pick up the bill? The official report said that the Reich 'could not be the under-lease of the Racing Association, and the government announced that either the City or the Reich itself should assume official responsibility for the completion of the new construction'.

At a meeting on 5 July this was agreed. It might seem a minor administrative matter, especially under the overall mood and tempo, but it carried enormous significance. It is still present today. Hitler could build the stadium he wanted without troubling himself about the Racing Association, and do it in the most normal way. He must have understood he was building a monument to himself.

Eric Seelig, the 23-year-old German light-heavyweight and middleweight champion, was preparing to defend his middleweight championship in Berlin on the morrow. Some Nazis came to see him and explained that it would not be a good idea for him to get into the ring because he would be killed if he did. That same night he fled to France to begin a new life.

Emmy and Leo Steinweg married in a civil ceremony because they had been warned that marriages between Aryans and non-Aryans would soon be illegal. Once married, they carried on running his motorbike shop although they cannot have known that, five years further on, the warning would assume a literal meaning when a sympathetic SS man would explain to Leo that it would be a good idea to get out of Germany very, very quickly.

The soccer authority DFB, which had a large membership inevitably reflecting all shades of political opinion (not that it mattered), held a short meeting in Berlin and 'submitted to new rulers and new *Gau*'.[36] The Nazi salute would be made compulsory; Jews and communists expelled.'A new organization, *Reichsbund für Leibesübungen*, was established and [Felix] Linnemann was appointed leader of its *Fachamt Fußball* which took over the operational affairs, whereas the DFB lost most of its duties until it was formally dissolved in 1941.'[37]

Hitler had seized German soccer.

The author Nils Havemann[38] gives some interesting reflections on that. The DFB was sceptical about the Nazis before 1933 but after 1933 it quickly became 'great enthusiasm'. The DFB had been damaged by the global economic crisis and was struggling with the introduction of professionalism. 'For the DFB this fight was life threatening because professionalism in their view would have led to a significant weakening of its position. Then after a few months it turned out that the Nazis would be against the professional sports.'

Havemann says that the DFB President, Felix Linnemann, moved swiftly to adopt the 'leader principle' – the Hitler principle, in fact, where the man at the top makes the decisions he wants – and senior DFB people regarded this as an advantage, not a burden. Havemann concludes that 'the enthusiasm for the regime in the first place was not ideological. Most at the DFB were careerists.'

Von Tschammer und Osten would head DRL and be intent on making it, and through it sport in general, a pure Nazi organisation to 'improve the morale and productivity of German workers' while, at the same time, becoming a source of national pride. From now on, sporting prowess became an entry to schools, universities and jobs. The DRL would stage enormous *Reichssportfest* events too.

Meanwhile, Hühnlein:

centres the nation's motorsport activities totally on the spectacular '2,000 Kilometres Through Germany' rally. This was a kind of German *Mille Miglia*, only on a larger and more extravagant scale, starting on 22 July in the – by German standards – highly sophisticated spa and casino resort of Baden-Baden. Within extremely tight time limits, the race was run at a breakneck pace along public roads across the length and breadth of the Reich.

Depending on the class of car or motorcycle, average speeds in the range of 80–100kmph (50–62mph) were required continuously over 20 to 34 hours ... It was a gruelling race that ended in disaster for many: only 103 out of 176 cars, 81 out of 212 motorcycles and just four out of 35 sidecar teams reached the finish under qualifying conditions. *Korpsführer* Hühnlein praised the spirit of the '2,000 Kilometres' racers: 'These men have achieved something superhuman. The true spirit of the Motor SA was alive, the spirit that fights selflessly for the sake of honour.'

He would add that Germany needed the fastest racing drivers but he did not add that in time Germany would need lots and lots of other drivers – and riders – because that is how an army moves. The NSKK would number some 500,000 of them by 1939.[39]

On 23 July importing banned books became punishable by death; three days later the Nazi government announced a programme of sterilising any Germans who were imperfect. By now some 27,000 people were in fifty improvised detention camps.

In August, amateur and professional tennis players met at the Rot-Weiss – a rare event, by definition, because the two were usually separate. A crowd of 5,000 watched Tilden beat von Cramm, who had just won the German championships in Hamburg. Von Cramm was now a very big name, and very vulnerable.

At the World Cycling Championship in Paris, Albert Richter (known as Teddy) from Cologne finished third in the men's sprint. He was one of three brothers born to a musical father; he had played the violin but at 16 discovered cycling and was soon competing. He was coached by a man called Ernst Berliner, a Jew, who also ran a furniture store which would be smashed up several times by the Nazis. Richter refused to wear the swastika when he raced and he did not like the Nazis. He would be on the podium of every championship he took part in from 1933 to 1939. He would remain vulnerable.

Bernd Rosemeyer was about to become a big name[40] and made sure he was not too vulnerable. There was a motorbike meeting at Hockenheim. 'During the entire Nazi period no German motorcycle racer was forced to wear a swastika armband during a race yet Bernd Rosemeyer, unlike his colleagues within the NSU factory team, did so at Hockenheim. Was his motive to further his racing ambitions, or did he wear this armband because he was a Nazi supporter?'[41]

In September, the Olympic Organising Committee began negotiations for:

the erection of a youth tent encampment near Rupenhorn[42] which would accommodate thirty young representatives of each nation at a great international youth rally. Another encampment organized on similar lines for the physical education students and instructors of the world was later constructed on the University Athletic Field near the Avus Race Track. Other centres were also planned ... The Hitler Youth also established an encampment in the midst of the Grunewald. A total of 11,148 youthful visitors were thus enabled to lead a simple camp life and attend the Games. The Prussian and Berlin Forestry Departments rendered valuable assistance in these preparations, and the tents for the international youth and physical educational student encampments were erected by the Second Company of the Fourth Pioneer Corps of the German Army. In the spacious army tents, each of which was adequate for a national group, a gay and festive atmosphere prevailed. The young representatives of the various nations thus became acquainted with one another and formed friendships. The Berlin populace enjoyed the presence of these young people in their colourful national costumes, and they in turn lent an air of freshness and enthusiasm to the Games through their participation.[43]

The International Amateur Athletic Federation decided the year before to examine organising a European athletics championship. The IAAF Council met in Berlin and appointed a European Committee. This in turn would lead to the first European Championships, in Turin, the following year.

Far in the background, the sixty-strong motor racing division at Auto Union had been working three shifts a day putting together the 1,622 components on their Grand Prix car. The first test runs were made on public roads around the factory.

On 5 October Hitler visited the Olympic construction site and it proved to be a decisive moment. The Official Report is as dry as ever:

Models of the new building and the remodelled Stadium as well as numerous plans were exhibited in the large gymnasium of the Sport Forum. After inspecting these, the group made a tour of the entire premises. In answer to the question of the German Chancellor as to why the necessary enlargement of the Stadium to a capacity of 80,000 spectators was to be achieved through increasing the depth of the Stadium rather than expanding it, Dr. Lewald explained that according to the lease contract with the Berlin Racing Association the Stadium might not extend over the race course or obstruct the view.

Hitler asked if the racecourse was essential and Lewald said it was not. Berlin already had two other courses and Grünwald had been running at a great loss. Hitler then made the sort of decision which dictators can make. The Grünwald course must go completely and if necessary be rebuilt somewhere else. That would allow the present site to become a giant sporting centre complete with a 'large open-air amphitheatre'. The architect, Werner March, murmured that the City of Berlin might object but Hitler brushed that aside:

The Stadium must be erected by the Reich; it will be the task of the nation. If Germany is to stand host to the entire world, her preparations must be complete and magnificent. The exterior of the Stadium must not be of concrete but of natural stone. When a nation has 4,000,000 unemployed, it must seek ways and means of creating work for them.

Five days later, at a pre-planned conference at the Reich Chancellery – with Hitler, Goebbels, Secretary of State Pfundtner, Commissioner of Woods and Forests von Keudell and the Olympic Committee – Hitler spread out his vision.

It was intended to take the world's breath away. Inadvertently it took Hitler's breath away too, and brought a crisis. Werner March drew up plans for the new stadium, 'a concrete structure with glass partition walls, reminiscent of a stadium recently built in Vienna'.[44]

The architect Speer, who was there, revealed that Hitler went into a rage and ordered Pfundtner to cancel the Games. He was head of state, the head of state had to open the Games and he 'refused to enter a glass-and-concrete monstrosity such as March had proposed'.[45]

Overnight, Speer 'made a sketch showing how the steel skeleton already built could be clad in natural stone and have more massive cornices added. The glass partitions were eliminated, and Hitler was content. He saw to the financing of the increased costs; Professor March agreed to the changes.'[46]

This Olympic Stadium would quickly became a stage for Hitler to walk in front of a global audience but also an iconic structure in itself, observing classical proportions and consequently timeless. The World Cup soccer final was played in it, quite naturally, in 2006 and the stadium required only minimal adjustments. How many, that July day seven decades later when Italy played France, saw him in their mind's eye still walking his stage?[47]

The American Consul General in Berlin, George S. Messersmith, began to devote 'an abundance of energy and time to investigation and documentation of developments in Germany regarding the plight of German-Jewish athletes'. He wrote a report to the Secretary of State, Cordell Hull, on 28 November 1933 (and another on 15 November 1935). 'Messersmith's personal papers reveal the intense interest and concern that he displayed in regard to the issue of participation. Messersmith wrote numerous dispatches to various officials at the State Department seeking governmental or departmental action.'

According to historian Stephen R. Wenn,[48] 'Messersmith's behind-the-scenes involvement in the participation controversy provides a fascinating contrast to the high-profile role played by a former diplomat, whose association with the IOC dictated a rather different stand.'

This was none other than Sherrill, who had engaged in the 'trying fight' in Vienna. Wenn writes that Sherrill's:

> attitude towards the discrimination paralleled the position adopted by Brundage. Sherrill pressured the Germans into promising to abide by all Olympic statutes, and also to guarantee the equal rights of German-Jewish athletes. However, once

this promise was obtained, Sherrill publicly ignored all indication that the Germans were failing to honour their pledges. While Messersmith toiled in Germany (and later following his transfer to Vienna in 1934 in Austria) gathering critical information and providing reports to the State Department concerning the Jewish situation, Sherrill vociferously campaigned for the support of an American Olympic entry.[49]

The pace remained relentless.

Hitler had made Germany walk out of the Geneva Disarmanent Conference in October and now 95 per cent of the population approved that.

A few days later Auto Union took their new racing car to the Nürburgring and unloaded it from the trailer in great and laboured secrecy. Storm troopers patrolled the circuit, and the area around it, and chased any spectators away. Hans Stuck took the car out on to the short circuit. Another driver, Alfred Rosenberger, would claim he drove it as well and was only two seconds slower than Stuck. Hühnlein's 'Aryan clause' precluded Rosenberger, a Jew who had financed Porsche, from ever driving it in competition.[50]

Five days after this, Mercedes tested their new racing car round the perimeter of their factory. The most famous rivalry in all motor sport history had begun.

Three days following, the American Amateur Athletic Union, meeting in Pittsburgh for their annual convention, passed a resolution which requested the IOC to tell Germany that if Jewish athletes were not allowed to prepare for and participate in the Olympics the Americans would boycott it. The president of the AAA was a strong man too. He was called Judge Jeremiah Mahoney.

Official preparations were continuing smoothly. By December:

> the day and hour of every event in all of the 19 forms of sport had been definitely fixed, and few changes were made after this date. This was of vast importance from the point of view of organization because the dates and hours of commencement of the various events had to be decided upon before the printing of tickets could begin, and since in order to avoid attempts at counterfeiting these were to be printed on special security paper, a considerable amount of time had to be allowed.[51]

And that was the first year.

In a certain way, 1934 would be more interesting still because Mussolini had positioned himself to demonstrate how a major sporting event like the World Cup could be exploited and manipulated. Hitler, watching Italy so closely, would draw all the appropriate conclusions.

Mussolini knew about exploitation and manipulation.

'For propaganda purposes' Mussolini 'was allowed to pose for press photographers sitting in Nuvolari's victorious Alfa Romeo.' Being Italian, the fascists placed a lot of importance on *bella figura*, always anxious to make a grandiose impression. But in this, as in everything else, they would fail in just as spectacular a fashion as their later, far more brutal, counterparts in Hitler's Reich. Yet it was precisely these grossly exaggerated gestures of power that made Italian fascism the model for the aesthetically far more amateurish Nazis:

> The *NSDAP* chieftains also honoured battle and victory, paid tribute to futuristic technology, and yet at heart were sworn enemies of the modern – which, ironically, they attempted to suppress with the methods of contemporary culture, that is to say, with highly sophisticated techniques of mass-manipulation. It was a strange brew, whose intoxicating effect clouded any sober assessment of the actual circumstances. By worshipping and taking ownership of German racing heroes and German engineering skills, motorsport offered the Nazis the ideal platform from which to present themselves, at moments of glory, as successful and progressive shapers of the new Germany and, alongside the triumphant German drivers and their unbeatable racing cars, to parade as victors on the stage of history.[52]

As 1933 drew to a close, President Roosevelt was being urged by a senior Jewish advisor, Judge Samuel Rosenman, not to go near the Olympic problem. It chimed with isolationism. Roosevelt even told William Dodd, when he was appointed ambassador to Germany, that America would not interfere in domestic German affairs until it involved American citizens directly. This policy would have a significant bearing on the official American reaction up to the 1936 Olympic Games.

Here, already, was a potential source of inter-American friction.

In Berlin, Messersmith was motivated to impart basic information about what was really happening in Germany. He wanted the American Olympic Committee and the American Athletic Union to have that information so that they could make properly informed decisions about going to the Olympics. In these final, fading days of 1933 it was not at all certain that they would go.[53]

Notes

1 Kruger, Murray, *The Nazi Olympics*.
2 Shirer, *The Rise and Fall of the Third Reich*.
3 Reuss, *Hitler's Motor Racing Battles*.
4 Owen, *Alfa Romeo*.
5 Reuss, op. cit.
6 Ibid.
7 Fisher, *A Terrible Splendor*.
8 Official German Olympic report.
9 Kruger, Murray, op. cit.
10 *Chronicle of the Twentieth Century*.
11 www.historyplace.com/worldwar2/hitleryouth/hj-prelude.htm.
12 Havemann, *Fussball unterm Hakenkreuz* (*Soccer Under the Swastika*).

13 SA, *Sturmabteilung* – storm troopers, a paramilitary organisation instrumental in helping Hitler to power.

14 Quoted in Myler, *Ring Of Hate.*

15 Ibid.

16 Ibid.

17 www.tennisserver.com/lines/lines_02_10_05.html.

18 www.tebe.de/artikel2234.html.

19 www.kolumbus.fi/leif.snellman/gp3306.htm.

20 Official German report.

21 Reuss, op. cit.

22 Nixon, *Silver Arrows.*

23 750kg Formula meant that between 1934 and 1937 a car's maximum weight was 750kg (1,653lb). In 1938 the regulations changed restricting the engine capacity.

24 Nixon, op. cit.

25 Fisher, op. cit.

26 Reuss, op. cit.

27 The Nuremberg Trials, in which the leading Nazis were tried for crimes against humanity, produced (and there is a consensus among eyewitnesses) a truly amazing spectacle. The supposed mighty, fearsome figures, who held the power of life and death over a continent, turned out to be mediocrities, provoking incredulity: how could these people have done it? Göring was the exception and emerged with a kind of stature and an intellectual ability.

28 Quoted in Fisher.

29 Wenn, Stephen R., 'A Tale of Two Diplomats: George S. Messersmith and Charles H. Sherrill on Proposed American Participation in the 1936 Olympics' in *Journal of Sport History*, vol. 16, no. 1 (spring 1989).

30 Schaap, Jeremy, *Triumph: The Untold Story of Jesse Owens and Hitler's Olympics* (ESPN).

31 Wenn, op. cit.

32 Ibid.

33 Quoted in Mandell, *The Nazi Olympics.*

34 Schaap, op. cit.

35 www.tennisserver.com/lines/lines_02_10_05.html.

36 *Gau*, an ancient term for a German region, revived by the Nazis.

37 en.academic.ru/dic.nsf/enwiki/363321.

38 Havemann, op. cit. The Havemann quotations are taken from his interview with *Speigel Online Sports*, 2005.

39 Reuss, op. cit.

40 German children used to shout 'Who do you think you are, Bernd Rosemeyer?' to anything travelling fast, much as British kids did about Stirling Moss and later Nigel Mansell.

41 Reuss, op. cit.

42 Rupenhorn, just outside Berlin.

43 Official German Olympic report.

44 Hart–Davis, *Hitler's Games*.

45 Ibid.

46 Speer, *Inside the Third Reich*.

47 In fact Hitler opened the 1936 Olympics on Saturday 1 August and the 2009 World Cup final was played on 9 July, so it was in fact twenty-six days short of exactly seven decades.

48 Wenn, op. cit.

49 Ibid.

50 Reuss, op. cit.

51 Official German Olympic report.

52 Reuss, op. cit.

53 Wenn, op. cit.

3

SECRETS OF POWER

On 1 January 1934 the law for sterilising 'inferior' German citizens came into effect. Of everything which had happened since 30 January 1933 this was the first time the Nazis were prepared to violate human bodies for reasons other than the political. They felt ethically – although Nazis and ethics are difficult to reconcile – that the imperfect had no right to live and, if they were alive, they had no right to procreate.

Hitler was, of course, quite prepared to violate human bodies for political reasons. Moving into 1934 only two groups of people could threaten him: the 2.5 million storm troopers and the army. Hitler decided to placate the army, which naturally disliked and distrusted the storm troopers, with a savage purge. Hundreds died in what would become known as the Night of the Long Knives.

The army was delighted. However, in:

> making common cause with the lawlessness, indeed the gangsterism, of Hitler ... the generals were putting themselves in a position in which they could never oppose future acts of Nazi terrorism not only at home but even when they were aimed across frontiers, even when they were committed against their own members.[1]

That was mid-summer and by then Hitler would have all the power he could ever need. He intended to use it, and to keep the tempo relentless.

The vision of this – which, with the benefit of hindsight, becomes more and more terrifying – and the world of sport proceeding, or trying to proceed, quite normally governed by completely different ethics, is yet another irony of the 1930s.

On 4 January Hitler attended meetings in the Brown House at Munich. Cannily, Mercedes shipped their racing car there and Goebbels noted in his diary: 'Went out for coffee with Hitler. He is touchingly nice to me. Inspected the new racing car at Mercedes. A fantastic job. First class!'

Moving into 1934 sport did proceed quite normally, showing its different faces.

As we saw, the International Amateur Athletic Federation had set up a special committee to examine holding, for the first time, a European championships. A permanent committee followed and it met in Budapest on 7 January. The championships, it decided, would be held that September in Turin. There were no world championships (until 1983) because the Olympic Games were regarded as supreme, but Turin would provide an authentic form line for the 1936 Games, not least for the German team.

The hijack of Grand Prix racing began on 12 January. Auto Union took their racing car to the Avus, Hans Stuck at the wheel, and the press found a name for it: 'The fuselage on wheels.' Soon, Ferry Porsche would be sending a letter to Hitler, again putting forward a people's car.

The Olympic preparations continued. The Propaganda Ministry:

> took charge of the more general forms of publicity and transportation arrangements. The initial meeting of this body was held on January 15th, 1934 under the chairmanship of Reich Minister Goebbels, on which occasion the Olympic Publicity Commission under the chairmanship of Ministerial Councillor Haegert and sub-committees for transportation, press, radio, film, art and budgetary questions were formed.[2]

A week later the executive committee was 'in a position to make new plans as regards the centres of competition on the basis of the considerably changed state of affairs' – Hitler having committed the government to full backing.

> The first problem was that of selecting halls for the indoor events such as wrestling, boxing and possibly also gymnastics, and we decided for the time being on one of the large halls at the Exhibition Grounds, the Municipal Authorities having generously offered to remove it from their own exhibition plans and place it at our disposal. It was not until 1935 that the erection of the Deutschland Hall was decided upon and we could relinquish our original plans.[3]

Both motor racing teams went to the Italian circuit of Monza, near Milan, to test. The weather was clearly one attraction (although northern Italy can be snow-clad) and the track itself, essentially a test of speed, another. Mercedes fielded von Brauchitsch but he would crash so heavily – perhaps a tyre failure – that the car could not be repaired at the circuit. Auto Union fielded Stuck, Willy Walb (actually team manager) and a prince, Hermann zu Leiningen.

Pressure was coming from the Minister of Transport in Berlin for the teams to nominate their drivers for the season because, after all, Berlin was paying. Dr Kissel of Mercedes deflected this by saying a decision had not yet been made, did not mention that von Brauchitsch had crashed at Monza, and signed his letter 'yours faithfully' rather than the ubiquitous and prudent 'Heil Hitler'.

At the beginning of February the Austrian Socialist Party rose, although they were eventually crushed. This is the first time in our story that the volatility of Austria has revealed itself and in time the country's politics would prove a fertile breeding ground for Hitler and the Nazis, creating – among all else – mystery, death and destruction in Austrian soccer.

This would be centred around politics, of course, and be spiced by the inescapable fact that as a team Austria were better. This needs context. The season before, Germany lost 3-1 to Italy in Bologna, drew 3-3 with France in Berlin, beat Belgium 8-1 in Duisburg, drew 2-2 with Norway in Magdeburg, beat Switzerland 2-0 in Zurick and Poland 1-0 in Berlin.

By contrast, Austria beat France 4-0 in Paris, lost to Czechoslovakia 2-1 in Vienna but drew 1-1 with Hungary, beat Belgium 4-1 in Vienna, drew 3-3 with Czechoslovakia in Prague, 2-2 with Hungary in Vienna, 2-2 with Scotland in Glasgow and beat Holland 1-0 in Amsterdam.

This set several undercurrents flowing for the World Cup in Italy in May.

Then, on 14 January 1934, Germany beat Hungary 3-1 in Frankfurt.

Into February, Goebbels invited the Olympic Organising Committee to consider the 'working plans drawn up by the chairmen of the different sub-committees'. During it the possibility of a Torch Run was raised. It would be a propaganda coup on a Goebbels scale, although the suggestion did not come from him. The plan was for it to begin in Olympia, Greece, and thread through the countries between there and Berlin, with local runners bearing the torch for a kilometre before handing it on to the next runner. The torch would arrive on the day of the opening ceremony at the stadium in Berlin where it would light the Olympic flame at the stadium. This would be prepared with military efficiency and thoroughness with recce parties, special torches which would be difficult to put out (and with back-up torches in case one did), a carefully chosen course and plenty of publicity so that the local populations could watch the extraordinary spectacle go by. Its passage would inevitably convey a sense of mounting excitement, moving hour by hour towards Berlin, and climaxing with the flame entering the stadium and lighting a specially constructed bowl which would burn throughout the Games. As the last runner entered the stadium Hitler would have arrived and be standing on his own balcony surveying *his* Games:

> It was also decided at this meeting to emphasize and develop the artistic aspect in decorating the Capital City for the Games, to enlist the talents of German artists for the designing of posters, diplomas and medals, and to combine the Olympic Art Exhibition with a large national display which would bear the title, 'Germany'.[4]

Austria began their run towards the World Cup with a friendly against Italy on the afternoon of 11 February in the Benito Mussolini Stadium, Turin, in front of 54,000 people. Matthias Sindelar did not play for Austria, while Italy's backbone came from Juventus who provided seven players. Austria won 4-2 with three goals by Karl Zischek, a prolific scorer throughout his career.

The internal and external contradiction reached out to the Unites States. Into March, the disquiet over Germany, the Olympics and Jews produced a mock trial at

Madison Square Gardens, New York, attended by 20,000 people. Some twenty-two witnesses testified against Hitler and one, a former governor of New York, said Hitler had introduced the 'law of the caveman'. This meeting, full of ferocious statements, increased the pressure over whether America would send a team to Berlin or not to such a pitch that Avery Brundage, who had become president of the US Olympic Committee, decided he must go and see for himself.

In Berlin, Hans Stuck drove the Auto Union at the Avus and broke three world records: the highest average speed over a timed hour (217.1kmph/134.9mph), 217.0 kmph/134.8mph over a measured 200km and 216.8kmph/134.7mph over a measured 100 miles. On the straight Stuck reached 265kmph (165mph).

The relentless pace was assuming a different dimension because Auto Union were leading – in headlines, anyway – over Mercedes, who had to be concerned about whether Caracciola would be able to drive ever again (his Monaco crash as bad as that), and about whether their stated policy of employing only German drivers could be sustained. It could not. The Mercedes team manager, Alfred Neubauer, reached for an Italian, Luigi Fagioli, then 36:

> Built like a middleweight boxer with brawny arms, wide, wide shoulders and no neck to speak of, Fagioli had an aggressive stance which matched his personality. True, he liked a joke and had a winning smile, but he had a fiery temper allied to a colossal belief in his own ability and he regarded racing as a very serious business.[5]

How would this mesh with Teutonic efficiency and Hitler's ambition to show the Grand Prix world what Germany could do? Undercurrents might be flowing towards the soccer World Cup but stormy waters were moving towards Mercedes.

Dr Kissel sent a message saying their second racing car was not ready for inspection and added that the next financial instalment of 50,000 Reichsmarks now fell due – but he did not add that that Ernst Henne, a celebrated bike rider, had crashed a Mercedes in testing at the Nürburgring. Henne was thrown clear but landed, face down, in a stream and was saved from drowning by a farmer's wife who happened to be passing. The Ministry of Transport continued their pressure on the teams but in fact Grand Prix cars from both were behind schedule and, for propaganda reasons, Hühnlein decided they could not make their debut outside Germany. That meant missing the Monaco Grand Prix in April. Guy Moll, born into a wealthy Jewish family and French, would win that race in an Alfa Romeo from Louis Chiron, a Monaco grandee, who would become infamous for accusing a woman of collaborating with the Gestapo during the war.

The Grand Prix teams needed to work out their calendar for the season. They would meet Hühnlein in Berlin and agree to compete in the Grands Prix in France, Germany, Switzerland, Italy, Spain, Czechoslovakia and one at Rome (which would be cancelled). They would also go to the *Coppa Acerbo* in Italy, a road race named after Tito Acerbo, brother of prominent fascist Giacomo Acerbo, and take on three mountain climbs. The tempting date for the debut was the Grand Prix on the Avus at Berlin on 27 May, not to be confused with the German Grand Prix in mid-season.

The cars of both teams would be known as the Silver Arrows, although the origin is controversial and disputed.

'So it was that Auto Union and Mercedes-Benz were quite often on the road across Europe simultaneously, each with three different convoys of trucks, in order to get their silver racing machines to the track on time, or else to get them back to the factory for necessary refits,' Reuss writes:[6]

> This exemplary perfectionism was still only emerging during the Silver Arrows' first season, but later was largely the result of sheer force of numbers: in their best years both stables could each call on at least 12 race-ready cars, an immense supply, which was to push foreign competitors ever further back in the running.
>
> However, for the 1934 season the two German rivals would have the use of only three or four driveable Silver Arrows each, at best. This sometimes resulted in technical and organisational bottlenecks ... The first thing was to catch up on the foreign manufacturers. In Hühnlein's ringing words at a press conference before the Avus race: 'Come one, come all! May fortune smile on us or not! What does it matter? German drivers are once more joining battle in German machines!' But ... Henne knew the truth: 'We'll have to drive for our lives if we want to outstrip the foreigners.'

Because thirty-two countries had entered the soccer World Cup, qualifying matches were needed to reduce the number to sixteen for the competition proper. As a consequence, Germany met Luxembourg in Luxembourg on 11 March and won 9-1. This was enough to take them to Italy.

Austria met Switzerland in a friendly in Geneva and won 3-2. They'd have one more friendly, against Hungary in Vienna on 15 April, before their World Cup qualifying match, again in Vienna, against Bulgaria. They beat Hungary 5-2 and dealt with Bulgaria 6-1. The Austrians, known as a *Wunderteam*, were perhaps slightly past their best although their coach, the 'authoritan anglophile' Hugo Meisl, was one of the 'dominant figures in European soccer between the wars'.[7] Someone else[8] has written that Meisl was 'the Pitt, Disraeli, Bismark and Napoleon of Austrian soccer rolled into one'.[9] More than that, the 4-2 crushing of Italy in Turin in February seemed to represent a preview for the whole competition.

The internal and external problem touched a film with Max Baer in it. On 16 March *The Prizefighter and the Lady* opened at the Capitol Theatre in Berlin, although Dr Goebbels had not wanted it to. He had already banned an English film, *Catherine the Great*, whose leading role was played by an Austrian Jew and émigré. The official reason for the ban was her émigré status (itself stretching credulity), but clearly the fact that she was a Jewess lay behind it. Stretching credulity even further, Goebbels evidently took no exception to the rest of the film.

Messersmith, the US Consul General, took a keen interest in what was happening to *The Prizefighter and the Lady*. He said that if Goebbels banned it, serious consequences would follow and for Goebbels the decision was by no means an easy one. Reportedly he 'had not forgotten what Baer had said after he knocked out Schmeling: that every punch that he threw that night was aimed at Adolf Hitler'.

Permission was sought from the Propaganda Ministry, of course, to show the film, which had been dubbed into German. That took it to Goebbels' desk and his inclination was to ban it. 'One of his lieutenants was quoted by the American press as saying that he had "scruples against the film as not being in harmony with the purpose of the new Germany because the chief character is a Jewish Boxer."'

Perhaps under the weight of Messersmith's words, the German foreign minister, a man called Konstantin von Neurath – who had not joined the Nazi Party so far – petitioned Goebbels who 'reluctantly' cleared it to be shown.[10]

In the background, preparations for the Olympic Games continued. In the six months after Hitler decreed a new stadium be built, a special Reich Stadium Construction Department had been created and work began immediately. The Olympic Organising Committee would be able, this spring, to announce that 'all the plans had progressed to the point where they could be submitted to the international sporting authorities for approval from a technical point of view, and a second memorandum was issued, the first edition of the *Blue Guide Book*. It represented a decided advancement over the memorandum of the previous year. It would be submitted to the IOC's Executive Committee in May in Brussels.'[11]

On 20 April, Göring denied that Germany was secretly rearming.

In direct contrast, Gottfried von Cramm went to the French Open tennis on the slow, peaceful, reddened clay of Roland-Garros as a seeded player (as did Roderick Menzel, a naturalised German born in Czechoslovakia, and Prenn, whose name would have a Union Jack against it, of course).

Prenn was knocked out in the third round by a Slovakian Jew, Ladislav Hecht, 2–6, 6–1, 2–6, 7–5, 6–3. In the quarter finals von Cramm met Menzel and his 'training discipline paid off',[12] because the weather was fiercely hot; he took the first two sets 6–2, 6–3, but lost the next two, both 6–3. Von Cramm still looked fresh and overwhelmed Menzel 6–3 in the fifth set.

That brought him to Giorgio de Stefani, a left-hander and Italy's leading player who had been runner-up in the Amateur French Championships at Roland-Garros the year before. The match was uncannily like a variation on the theme of the quarter final. De Stefani took the first set 6–3, von Cramm seemed to have closed the match down by taking the next two sets 6–4, 6–1, but de Stefani struck back to level the match in the fourth set, 6–3. Von Cramm's training discipline proved decisive again because now he overwhelmed the Italian 6–2.

That brought him to the asthmatic Australian Jack Crawford in the final. Crawford, who had been the leading player in the world, liked to take a slug of whisky at moments of great tension in a match. He would need a slug or two before von Cramm was done with him.

Von Cramm won the first set 6–4 but Crawford struck back at him, 9–7, 6–3. Von Cramm drew on his fitness and took the fourth 7–5 then overwhelmed Crawford 6–3.

'When others were wilting in the heat and humidity, Cramm would look more refreshed than ever.'[13]

The victory confirmed his status as a leading German sportsman.

The character of the Nazi regime was becoming clear externally, or rather to those who visited from the external world, and this within eighteen months of Hitler taking power. That May, the British soccer club Derby County made a four-match tour:

When they eventually reached the German border it was to find a country swathed in swastika emblems ... Dave Holford was a 19-year-old outside-left from Scarborough, excited to be included in the tour party, despite his lack of experience: 'Everywhere we went, the swastika was flying. If you said "Good morning," they'd reply with "Heil Hitler." If you went into a cafe and said "Good evening," they would respond with "Heil Hitler." Even then, you could see this was a country preparing for war.'

On the pitch, Derby lost three times and drew once. Twice they conceded five goals in a match and were surprised by the standard of their hosts' game. All agreed, however, that if the football had been hard work, overall the tour had been an enjoyable one with good hotels and plenty of time to relax and enjoy the scenery.

There was, however, one overriding blot on the collective memory ... these Derby players were ordered to give the Nazi salute before each game.

Full-back George Collin, who captained the side when Tommy Cooper left for England duty, remembered their dilemma: 'We told the manager, George Jobey, that we didn't want to do it. He spoke with the directors, but they said that the British ambassador insisted we must. He said that the Foreign Office were afraid of causing an international incident if we refused. It would be a snub to Hitler at a time when international relations were so delicate. So we did as we were told. All except our goalkeeper, Jack Kirby, that is. Jack was adamant that he wouldn't give the salute.

When the time came, he just kept his arm down and almost turned his back on the dignitaries. If anyone noticed, they didn't say anything.'[14]

The politics of the Olympics continued just as the preparations did.

An 'active publicity campaign' began for the design of the official Olympic poster, which was not as trivial as it might sound. The poster would fulfil three distinct functions: to encapsulate the mood and place where the Games were being held, to attract the public to buy tickets and, historically, to take its place with the posters from other Games as a living historical tableau, each Games immediately identifiable by its poster even many decades later. The conditions for designing the poster would be announced that summer and the Publicity Committee established an office at the Organising Committee's headquarters.

At the political level, the regime still feared that their anti-Semitic policies would prevent the Americans coming. During an IOC meeting in Brussels, the German Organising Committee was able to present a progress report, though the Jewish question had not abated.

General Sherrill, the self-appointed scourge of the Nazis at Vienna when Lewald was fighting to save the Games for Berlin, was sure the IOC would look favourably on the German preparations. He would explain (in a letter to Brundage) about how the IOC:

> feels about Germany's compliance with the agreement I secured from them last June in Vienna. A very detailed statement was given our Exec. Com. by Lewald and Diem. To make assurance doubly sure, I had up from the Paris office of the 'N.Y. Times' (property of Mr. Ochs, a Jew) their Herb Matthews, and, after the close of the Ex. Com.'s afternoon session, I put him with Lewald and Diem into another room and let him question them to his heart's content. What he reports ought to satisfy American Jewry.

Lewald gave the interview to Matthews – the most direct way to reach American politicians, officials and public, on his own behalf and that of Sherrill – in an open attempt to explain, clarify and placate by setting out the 'true' position.

It appeared with a 'Brussels 8 May' dateline under the heading:

> Reich Keeping Faith on Olympics, Says Official, Denying Bar to Jews

> Germany will not only abide but her promise not to discriminate against German Jews at the 1936 Olympic Games in Berlin, but she will also give every facility for training and competition to Jewish athletes, Dr. Theordore Lewald, German representative on the German Olympic Committee, told this correspondent today.

Lewald reiterated the assurances which had been given in Vienna and accepted that Americans still nursed misgivings over the question of whether Jews would in reality be selected for the German team.

This turned on the phrase that Jews would not be excluded 'in principle', with its obvious ambiguity. Some critics, he said, were accusing Germany of preparing to renege on their commitment by wielding the ambiguity. Lewald assured Matthews that Germany would honour the Vienna promise and there 'will be no qualifications or restrictions of any kind upon the admission of Jewish athletes to the German Olympic team'.

Stephen Wenn has written:[15]

> As with all German promises in this regard, Lewald's words represented a bold-faced lie. Jews were excluded from all clubs eligible for national championship meets, and some were forced to practice in cow pastures because of restrictions placed on the use of training facilities … Sherrill's action indicates that he was devoutly committed to American participation. The concern over the 'hideous' treatment of the Jewish athlete had been surpassed by the perceived importance of the Olympic movement.

In the interview, Lewald produced some revealing statistics – revealing because in any ordinary circumstance it would not have occurred to anybody to research, never mind reveal, them. Subconsciously, it betrayed the way people were having to think. Lewald pointed out that he had been researching how many Jews took part in previous Olympiads and he had discovered in the British team at Los Angeles, of the seventy-four competitors, only one was a Jew. The American team there, 400-strong, had only five Jews. The four Games that Germany contested before Hitler came to power – Amsterdam, St Moritz, Lake Placid and Los Angeles – involved 412 competitors and only three were what was called 'non-Aryans', a euphemism for Jews, of course.

The page of *The New York Times* in which the interview appeared was itself revealing. Above the interview was a deep photograph four columns wide of Hitler at Tempelhof Airport, Berlin, proclaiming in front of rank after rank of soldiers how peaceful the Reich was – a speech heard by 2 million radio listeners. The column next to the interview had a story: 'ANTI-NAZI CLERGY PUSH WAR ON FOES'. This was about the efforts of the leaders of opposition to Nazify the German Protestant Church.

Messersmith subsequently sent a message to the State Department stating bluntly:

I had the chance to talk with General Sherrill at Ambassador Morris' house in Brussels some months ago. It was quite clear then that General Sherrill was so much interested in having us participate that he would be willing to accept what he knew to be hollow statements and promises.

This was the crux. Brundage and Sherrill agreed that American participation was essential to the survival of the Olympic movement and that the German-Jewish question would not be allowed to override that. It was a momentous decision.

If the Brundage-Sherrill posture had a strangeness about it – in terms of grandees who ought to have been coveting the Olympic ideal but were in the process of violating it, and would continue to do so – a different strangeness gathered at the Avus circuit on the outskirts of Berlin.

Neither Auto Union nor Mercedes had been ready to go to Monaco and they did not travel to lucrative Tripoli, Libya, a month later, although whether this was under Hühnlein's decree that the great debut must be in Germany or whether they were still not ready is unclear. They were certainly, they thought, ready for the Avus – Mercedes would soon find they were wrong – although both drew 'a veil of silence over their cars'.[16] One Berlin motoring publication wrote that 'during the practice sessions, why were Auto Union and Mercedes-Benz constantly roped off and surrounded by a cordon of SA soldiers? Doesn't this encourage rumour-mongering? All the other companies told us the capacity of their engines; only the Germans kept it secret.'

According to Reuss, 'even the Nazi-dominated press could scarcely elicit any information from them' and 'until the end of the Third Reich' both teams 'continued to cultivate an obsessive secrecy about their racing cars'.

Practice began on Thursday 24 May, a beautiful, mild day and:

at a stroke, the noise and speed of the new silver racing cars altered the public's perception. From then on, the Nazi strategy of sheer overwhelming power found its motor-racing counterpart in the appearance of the new national racing cars: the futuristic-looking Auto Union, whose VL6 power unit had such an immensely deep, hollow roar because the supercharger was fitted between the carburettors and the engine; and the front-engined Mercedes-Benz, which was different not only visually but acoustically too, its eight cylinders producing a shrill and distinctive shriek because the Roots supercharger pumped air directly into the carburettor and thence into the engine. The result was a concentrated assault on all the senses, comprising a roaring din, breakneck speed, gleaming metal and an acrid smell reminiscent of burnt almonds, which came from the rhizinus oil added to the fuel. These silver projectiles electrified not just the spectators lining the track, but also the volubly droning radio commentators.[17]

Mercedes had hired limping Caracciola; he had never driven anything as fast and his hip still gave him great pain. At the end of practice, Mercedes withdrew because they were having fuel-pump problems. That did not prevent an immense crowd making their way to the circuit even in the rain. Stuck launched the Auto Union into the lead but his clutch failed, opening the race to Guy Moll[18] in a Ferrari. August Momberger, an enthusiast rather than leading driver, came third and set the fastest lap.

This was the first, faltering step towards domination. From here the two German teams – or at least one of them – would contest a further eight Grands Prix in 1934, fourteen in 1935, twelve in 1936, sixteen in 1937, nine in 1938 and eight in 1939. To dominate this would be, in the context of the 1930s, the most expensive and extensive concerted effort sport had ever seen: sixty-eight races, each requiring an immense effort in logistics, organisation and personnel.

That same day the World Cup began in Italy. What followed was a demonstration of a straightforward hijack by Mussolini who 'colonised the game as a means of shoring up support for his fascist regime' because by this time 'football was emerging as an international sport around which international identities could be moulded'.[19]

The 'Duce himself would appear, heavy-chinned and smirking under a yachting cap …'[20] He prepared to finance, if necessary, the whole competition and take ownership of it too:

> At times, Italy appeared to have more sway than the official organiser, FIFA. Mussolini dictated which referees would oversee each match, and once on the field their behaviour immediately led to talk of corruption. The referees of two Italy matches were suspended by their home countries because of the poor standard of their officiating.[21]

Mussolini drew on the 'athletic imagery of the Roman Empire' as a reassertion of Italian power and even presented a trophy hugely bigger than the one used in the first World Cup, in 1930. He had to upstage even that.

On the opening day, Italy launched the competition by beating the United States, although there were seven other first-round matches. Austria beat France 3-2 after extra time in Turin, Germany beat Belgium 5-2 in Florence and in Trieste Czechoslovakia beat Roumania 2-1. The match was refereed by the Belgian John Langenus, who had handled four matches in the 1930 World Cup, including the potentially explosive final between Uruguay and Argentina.

Langenus would be confined to the Trieste match and said of the competition:

> In the majority of [other] countries the World Championship was called a sporting fiasco, because beside the [Italians'] desire to win, all other sporting considerations were non existent and because, moreover, a certain spirit brooded over the whole Championship. Italy wanted to win, it was natural, but they allowed it to be seen too clearly.[22]

The structure was knock out.

Italy beat Spain 1-0 after a replay in Florence, although the Swiss referee, Rene Marcet, would subsequently be suspended by the Swiss FA for the way he handled the game. Austria beat Hungary 2-1 in Bologna, Czechoslovakia beat Switzerland 3-2 in Turin and Germany beat Sweden 2-1 in Milan. That made the semi-finals Italy *v.* Austria in Milan and Czechoslovakia *v.* Germany in Rome.

The Italian match was refereed by a Swede, Ivan Eklind, and his performance remains controversial. One allegation is that Mussolini selected him and had dinner with him the night before the game so they could discuss the 'tactics'. Another is that the referee actually headed the ball to an Italian player. The Austrian inside-forward Josef Bican would say 'when I passed the ball out to the right wing one of our players, Cizek, ran for it and the referee headed it back to the Italians. It was terrible! Unbelievable!'

The match was played on a sodden pitch with standing water like mini lakes, which slowed and hampered the delicate Austrian ball players spearheaded by Sindelar. Italy won 1-0.

Czechoslovakia beat Germany 3-1.

That day at the Nürburgring, Mercedes contested a Grand Prix, called the Eifel – named for the mountains surrounding the circuit – with two cars, one for Manfred von Brauchitsch and the other Fagioli. Caracciola was not yet considered fit enough to participate, particularly because the race stretched to fifteen laps of the 22km circuit making 342km (212 miles).

The start had to be delayed for a long time because fog shrouded the circuit and rain drenched it. On the opening lap an Austrian crashed and was killed. Fagioli led from von Brauchitsch, Stuck in the Auto Union third. On the second lap Fagioli was ordered by the Mercedes team manager to let von Brauchitsch through – von Brauchitsch was a German, of course. Fagioli did but during his refuelling vented his rage on the team manager and then 'with one lap to go, simply abandoned his Mercedes on the track in disgust'.[23]

Von Brauchitsch beat Stuck by more than a minute but there was a more potent time gap. Louis Chiron, third in a Ferrari-prepared Alfa Romeo, finished 5 minutes and 43 seconds behind von Brauchitsch. The power which Hitler wanted to demonstrate had just been demonstrated. It would continue, remorselessly, and for simplicity it can be most easily expressed in a progressive scorecard, race by race, of the 157 Grands Prix they would contest from now to the Second World War. Leaving the Nürburgring, the Germans had won one and lost one (the Avus debut).

On 7 June Germany beat a dejected Austria 3–2 in the third place final at the World Cup. Italy met Czechoslovakia in the final in Rome at the stadium of the National Fascist Party. Mussolini would preside over it like a Roman emperor and there are dark tales that he behaved like one too, suggesting that the Italians players might meet the fate of those who lost in the Coliseum. In the stadium he saluted the crowd, milking every moment, and they roared their approval of him.

Referee Eklind's performance in that final remains even more controversial. He was invited to meet Mussolini alone, before the match.

A Czechoslovakian author, Miloslav Jensik, has said:

If anybody was going to be invited it would have been normal to invite the captains of the two teams, possibly with the referee as well, but when our players learnt that he had only invited the referee they were horrified. It was a conformation of their darkest fears because they knew what had taken place in the semi-final between Italy and Austria.

The Czechoslovakian goalkeeper, Frantisek Planicka, would say, 'we have been cheated out of victory. The atmosphere in the Stadium was tense. Eklind was in Mussolini's box. We didn't know what was discussed there, but we had an inkling. The man stopped clean passes, blowing his whistle, and overlooked bad fouls.'

Italy won 2–1 after extra time. 'The Italians' win in Rome did more than anything to cement the popularity of Il Duce. For the Italian people to celebrate victory, it was also to celebrate Fascism.'[24]

Mussolini had given a complete demonstration of exploitation. With the Olympic Games in Berlin only two years and two months away, the lessons and possibilities cannot have been lost on Hitler. In one important sense he had been much shrewder than Mussolini because he would not try to fix officials or events. In another, and at the public level, it was an even more blatant attempt to portray a political ideal through imagery based on *the* major sporting championship, an Olympic Games. Some even claim he made the manipulation of sport into an art form.

Germany would play two more soccer matches in 1934 – both friendlies – beating Poland 5–2 in Warsaw and Denmark 5–2 in Copenhagen. However, the side was simply not good enough to allow Hitler to exploit it in the way Mussolini could. As someone said, to project the power of a nation through soccer you have to have a good team and even the Nazis could not alter that.

In a bold and disturbing political move Hitler would take Germany out of the League of Nations,[25] a move which would inevitably alienate the German government from the international community. By contrast, soccer would provide a normality to reassure nervous European neighbours and simultaneously act as a cover for what Hitler really intended – especially when he eyed the nervous neighbours. In summary, what Hitler could do was exploit the team by showing what true, innocent sportsmen they were, especially in defeat. That would be done twice, in London and Berlin, but not yet.

The Olympic movement met in Athens between 16 and 19 June:

> to celebrate the fortieth anniversary of the revival of the Olympic Games. The plans of the Organizing Committee were approved and the Olympic programme was extended to include canoeing and four different classes in the yachting regatta … Our plans for the Festival Play and the re-institution of the custom of awarding victors wreaths of oak leaves, as well as the designs for an official chain of office for the members of the International Olympic Committee, were also accepted. The idea of organising a torch relay run from Olympia to Berlin was greeted as an ingenious thought and found the hearty approval of the entire Committee.
>
> … The Athens decisions provided us with a firm basis upon which to build and we could begin work on the thousands of details. It must be admitted that perfect organisation demands a prophetic gift, which we did not at all times possess in an adequate degree. It was extremely difficult, for example, to predict the number of athletes and spectators who would come to Berlin, or how many telephone connections would be necessary in order to ensure perfect communication during the various events.[26]

Wimbledon began on Tuesday 26 June; von Cramm was seeded but behind Jack Crawford and Britain's Fred Perry.

On Saturday 30 June practice was going on for the French Grand Prix at the Montlhéry circuit near Paris.

That day Hitler launched a purge of the storm troopers, known historically as the 'Night of the Long Knives'. Hühnlein had reportedly been a good friend of Ernst Röhm, the SA leader. The purge was swift, unexpected and brutal as the SA was physically decapitated. Hühnlein's office and house were searched but, of course, he was at Montlhéry. This, it seemed, saved his life.

At Wimbledon, Henkel beat Kleinschroth in the first round but lost to Crawford in the second, where Hans Denker lost to Austin and Menzel lost to Harry Hopman, later a celebrated Australian coach. It left von Cramm, who had a first round bye, facing Anker Jacobsen of Sweden. He dispatched him 6-2, 6-3, 9-7, and now faced Buster Andrews of New Zealand. He dispatched him 6-1, 6-4, 6-4, and now faced Vernon Kirby, a leading South African. He was 'quite unable to produce the form that won him the French Championship against Kirby. A malignant germ is this "Wimbledon throat" and it reflects great credit on von Cramm that he not only played but captured a set when for the most part he looked ready to collapse.'[27] Kirby, knowing that von Cramm liked to play at full speed, slowed and his ground strokes were so well placed that von Cramm went down 2-6, 6-2, 4-6, 2-6.

On the Sunday at Montlhéry, Caracciola returned to Grand Prix racing, the limp noticeable. By now, approaching only the third Grand Prix of the 157, the power of the German cars was manifest for all to see (and hear). In testing a fortnight before, Fagioli had taken the Mercedes round in 5 minutes and 11.8 seconds, destroying the old record by more than 7 seconds. In practice von Brauchitsch took 5 seconds from that.

Louis Chiron (Alfa Romeo) made a tremendous start before the German cars moved on him, but one after another they encountered mechanical problems and melted from Chiron who won it. That made the scoreboard: won one, lost two.

The German Grand Prix at the Nürburgring became the centrepiece of the whole season for Mercedes and Auto Union. Since this was the first German Grand Prix there under Hitler – the Eifelrennen, on the same circuit but only over fifteen laps (347km/215 miles) was not the same thing – the nature and scope of the race needs context. The circuit comprised eighty-eight left-hand and eighty-four right-hand corners, so many that even experienced drivers could not remember them all. Many corners were completely blind.

It followed the contours of the land, undulating through tree-clad foothills so that much of it might be in deceptive shadows. It was a lethal place and across the years it would exact a terrible toll.

The Nürburgring suited many of the Nazi concepts perfectly, however. It was an overtly macho place, perfect to demonstrate how superior the German cars were and, because it drew immense crowds, the demonstration would be very public. The German Grand Prix became a martial occasion, with swastikas and men in uniform wherever you looked, led by strutting Hühnlein, who was clearly in his element.

In practice the circuit exacted an immediate toll. Von Brauchitsch crashed so violently that he broke an arm, a shoulder blade, his collarbone and five ribs. The consolation for Mercedes was that Caracciola began to drive like a champion again.

Stuck led from the start of the race, Caracciola after him and that formed a pattern. They traded fastest laps and neither could break the other until Caracciola's engine failed. Stuck brought the Auto Union safely home. That made the scoreboard: won two, lost two.

The *Coppa Acerbo* was a road race run at Pescara on the Italian Adriatic coast, named after one of Mussolini's Cabinet ministers, Giacomo Acerbo, in memory of a brother killed in the First World War. In practice on the long seafront straight a Mercedes newcomer, Ernst Henne, reached 300kmph.

The race, run after rain, suited Caracciola, who was known as a master in the wet, but he crashed towards half distance and although the Italians in their Italian cars tried to swarm Fagioli he brought his Mercedes home a clear winner. That made the scoreboard: won three, lost two. During the race Moll crashed and was killed.

Avery Brundage prepared to go to Germany for six days on what, in journalese, would be a fact-finding mission. Brundage, from Detroit, competed in the 1912

Games in Stockholm (in the decathlon) and became something of an Olympic fanatic. He made a fortune with his own construction company and that allowed him to follow his fanaticism. It also made him vulnerable to deception: the man himself was, and is in retrospect, a disconcerting combination of the worldly and innocent. When he reached Berlin, he would need the worldliness, as the innocence would render him terribly vulnerable.

Whatever Brundage's motives, he confronted the conundrum that also confronted politicians and diplomats trying to deal with Nazi Germany: where do you find yourself when a major European power, globally acclaimed for its philosophers, artists, writers and scientists, is run by people who have no regard for the truth? Whatever they promise is worthless, and what in practical terms can anyone make of that? The question remains whether Brundage even tried.

Before his visit the Germans said that twenty-one of their Jewish athletes would take part in Olympic training. Whether this was to placate Brundage is not clear. What is clear is that Brundage did speak to some Jews, although, significantly, always in the presence of what have been described as 'Nazi chaperones'. The seduction of Brundage was complete. He described the Olympics as 'an international event [which] must be kept free from outside interference or entanglements, racial, religious or political. Certain Jews must understand that they cannot use these Games as a weapon in their boycott against the Nazis.'

Messersmith, the US Consul General in Berlin, emphatically disagreed. He messaged the State Department:

> Should the Games not be held in Berlin it would be one of the most serious blows which National Socialist prestige could suffer within an awakening Germany and one of the most effective ways which the world outside has of showing to the youth of Germany its opinion of National Socialist doctrine ... [it is] inconceivable that the American Olympic committee should continue its stand that sport in Germany is non-political, that there is no discrimination. Other nations are looking to the United States before they act, hoping for leadership; the Germans are holding back on increased economic oppression against the Jews until the Games are over. America should prevent its athletes from being used by another government as a political instrument.

In a sense, Brundage and Messersmith represented two different and very distinct battle lines, and now battle had been joined.

Already, in only the year after he had taken power, Hitler was forcing people within the Olympic movement to make uncomfortable choices, and forcing diplomats like Messersmith to try to intervene.

This was only an aspect, of course. The speed with which the Nazis had implemented their policies was reflected in how – in only this year from 1933 to 1934 – the country appeared to have been Nazified. A racing driver, Thomas Cholmondeley-Tapper, born in New Zealand, resident in Britain, caught that. On 19 August, the

German hill climb was run at Freiburg in the Black Forest. Cholmondeley-Tapper competed and would remember that, apart from the hill climb:

> there were two other motoring events at the Freiburg meeting, a trial and a rally, and since German enthusiasm for motor-sport runs very high, the town was packed with spectators – some who had come simply to enjoy the fun and the perfect weather, and also many representative groups from Nazi organizations who were camping in the woods on hills outside the town. I remember that the typical German fervour of the various youth organizations was a source of some irritation, since they appeared to spend entire nights marching round the town to the accompaniment of militant choruses.[28]

Cholmondeley-Tapper, though he would be offered a drive with Mercedes a couple of years later, was no more than a valuable witness. Hitler's chilled hand was about to reach out and take hold of another driver, Richard (Dick) Seaman.

The Swiss Grand Prix, at Bremgarten near Bern, was a major race at another very dangerous place, the circuit slicing through woodland, the drivers unprotected. It hosted motorbike races from 1931 and now welcomed the cars. Auto Union and Mercedes sent full teams. Remarkably, von Brauchitsch had recovered enough to be able to drive although he 'had to be helped in and out of the car in considerable pain and had a pillow to support his back when driving'.

Before the Grand Prix, Seaman won a minor race and then no doubt watched fascinated as Stuck forced his Auto Union into the lead, hunted by Tazio Nuvolari in a Maserati. The nature of the circuit allowed Nuvolari to display his skills but the car eventually broke down. Stuck won it from Momberger in another Auto Union and that made the scoreboard: won four, lost two.

So far, in the broad picture of Nazi sport, motor racing was a dramatic diversion from the main event, which would be the Olympics.

The Amateur Athletic Federation held their twelfth congress in Stockholm on 28 and 29 August. There the Swedish Gymnastic Federation's leaders said they would like to show their own form of gymnastics in Berlin, using 1,000 performers. The national form was active or passive joint movements and stretches designed to increase flexibility, reduce pain and maintain health. The German organisers were 'heartily in favour' because, beyond the accepted Olympic sports, the Games are 'in their most exalted sense a means of education and should for this reason be instructive in their nature'. They wanted the Games to act as an 'Educative Festival':

> Supported as always by the generous hospitality and co-operation of the German Army, we were able to offer the Swedish gymnasts the extremely low price of 2.50 Reichsmarks per day for lodgings and meals at the military barracks at Döberitz … We had naturally planned a gymnastic demonstration by a German team and had included this in the programme of the Marathon Day.

When the inclusion of the German and Swedish gymnastic demonstrations in the Olympic programme was announced we received other inquiries and were finally able to welcome seven national teams who presented their performances at the conclusion of the athletic competition on the various days. The spectators also evidenced great interest in these demonstrations, usually remaining in the Stadium until they were finished even though at times the long, exciting athletic competitions necessitated their being postponed until twilight.[29]

What would happen in Turin, where the first European Athletics Championships were being held (men only), might have provided a preview to the Olympics but in reality did not. Thirteen countries won medals and the Germans led with seven gold, two silver and three bronze, but Britain and the USSR did not send teams.

Adolf Metzner, German champion at 400m since 1931, had a medical background and a political background he would subsequently seek to conceal. At 23 he joined the SS and later the Nazi Party (during the war he served in the Waffen-SS). In Turin he duly took the 400m but in Berlin for the Olympics there would be the Americans – if they came.

Erich Borchmeyer took silver in the 100m, beaten by Chris Berger of Holland, but in Berlin there would be Jesse Owens – if the Americans came. Hans Scheele won the 400m hurdles but would face the Americans and Canadians in Berlin – *if* the Americans came. Wilhelm Leichum won the long jump but the man who finished third, Luz Long, would challenge Jesse Owens, help him, lose to him and befriend him. Gustav Wegner won the pole vault but he would not compete in Berlin. Hans-Heinrich Sievert won the decathlon, adding to the three world records he had set in the past year, and was physically regarded as a typical superior Aryan. But in Berlin he was injured and did not compete (except in the shot putt).

The championships showed that, if the Berlin Games were to be the authentic pinnacle, the Americans had to be there. That in turn led Germany back to the uneasy compromise of being faithful to their creed – the Jews were the source of all evil and must be removed from daily life – whilst proclaiming their devotion to the Olympic ideal, which meant not removing Jews from daily life. That they were able to sustain this absolute contradiction must say a great deal about other people, and particularly about Avery Brundage: the American Olympic Committee would decide to participate in the Olympics.

The Italian Grand Prix at Monza on 9 September carried undertones. Here were the mighty German teams in the heart of Italian motor sport, with a great many Italian cars and drivers pitted against them. The Pescara circuit down on the coast for the *Coppa Acerbo* was not the same thing. Monza, a town in its own right but with the industrial and suburban sprawl of Milan reaching out towards it like tentacles, offered a purpose-built track in use, as we have seen, since the early 1920s. Because motor sport was an Italian passion – great drivers, great cars – the Grands Prix drew vast, fanatical crowds. If Hitler was to win a race – and into it must be factored the inevitable dictatorship rivalry with Mussolini over prestige – this was the one to win.

Against the Germans would be ranged four Alfa Romeos and four Maseratis (as well as two Bugattis, of Italian pedigree but very French).

'Before the start of the race the cars and drivers paraded past the grandstands raising their arms in a fascist salute.'[30]

Stuck led from Fagioli but Caracciola came up into second place and the race became a re-run of the German Grand Prix, Auto Union holding off Mercedes. Stuck pitted eventually – the radiator had burnt his feet – and the heavy, constant braking the circuit required proved too much for Caracciola. He pitted, almost passed out and had to be lifted from the car. Fagioli took over and won it. That made the scoreboard: won five, lost two. A distinct shape was already forming.

The Grand Prix teams went to the Spanish race at Lasarte on 23 September and, although Stuck led, he had mechanical problems and Fagioli won it in his Mercedes from Caracciola in another Mercedes, Nuvolari (Bugatti) third: won six, lost two. The distinct shape was becoming clearer and clearer.

They would complete the season in the Czechoslovakian Grand Prix at Brno. There, Nuvolari tested an Auto Union and Stuck – amazingly – tested a Mercedes. A crowd of 350,000 saw a hard race on a hard circuit, which involved intense duelling between Fagioli's Mercedes and Stuck's Auto Union. Stuck won it, Nuvolari again third in the Maserati: won seven, lost two.

One of the Italians, Piero Taruff, reflected that the:

> Germans had come back into racing ... and life was not easy for us Bugatti drivers. It was a time of great technical progress ... I do not believe that manufacturers in those days understood much about a car's behaviour on corners; they did not yet know about 'slip angles' and the 'cornering power' of tyres and so were ignorant of the effects of 'oversteer' and 'understeer' on a car's behaviour, and of how these could be diminished or increased to produce the desired characteristic. This was largely because design was usually entrusted to excellent draughtsmen, brought up on practice rather than theoretical engineering. This began to appear very clearly under the new Formula setting a limit to maximum weight; the successful firms were those rich in technical resources, like Mercedes-Benz and Auto Union, who left everyone else behind.[31]

It was the first example of the Nazi state showing its raw power in a sporting arena. It would not be the last.

In October, while the Organising Committee were deciding to include polo and basketball, Hitler and Reich Minister of the Interior, Dr Frick, visited the Olympic site to monitor progress. Hitler:

> expressed several wishes for slight changes and announced the plans that had been made for the artistic adornment of the buildings. It was just a short time thereafter that he assumed the full patronage over the Games, replacing the late Reich President von Hindenburg. The favourable weather conditions of the late autumn and early winter of that year enabled rapid progress to be made at the Reich Sport Field.[32]

A group, the Honorary Youth Service (185 boys and 70 girls), was founded. They were selected from Berlin sporting clubs on linguistic ability and 'external appearance'. They would be trained for two years and, during the Games, render:

> valuable assistance in their white costumes. Several were assigned to each national team, performing errands and similar tasks at the Olympic Village and other centres of activity, and acting as messengers during the competitions. The girls were given the attractive task of accompanying the victors at the time honours were awarded and of placing the wreath of oak leaves upon their heads.[33]

That October, entrance prices were announced and the ticket office was due to be fully equipped by 1 November.

After the American Olympic Committee's decision, attention shifted to the American Athletic Union's meeting in December. This was important for all the obvious reasons, not least that the AAU 'supplied significant moral and financial support to the Olympic entry'. There was another important factor, however. Each athlete's eligibility form had to bear a signature from both bodies.

The New York Times encapsulated this by writing that 'American participation in Germany without the AAU would be akin to trying to run a horse race without a horse. The jockey might go the distance but not very well.' Brundage felt that, because the AOC had taken the decision it had, the AAU was 'morally' obliged follow. The AAU did not agree and postponed a decision.

The battle lines were still being drawn even though the battle really had begun.

Notes

1   Shirer, *The Rise and Fall of the Third Reich*.
2   Official German Olympic report.
3   *Deutschland Halle*, used for boxing, weightlifting and wrestling in the Olympics – it was reportedly so big that aviator Hanna Reitsch flew a helicopter there – the first time it had been done indoors.
4   Official German Olympic report.
5   Nixon, *Silver Arrows*.
6   Reuss, *Hitler's Motor Racing Battles*.
7   Glanville, *The Story of the World Cup*.
8   Jeffrey, *European International Football*.
9   William Pitt the Younger (1759–1806) was Britain's youngest prime minister at 24. His father had also been prime minister, hence the term 'the Younger'. Benjamin Disraeli (1804–81) was a leading politician for three decades and Britain's only Jewish prime minister.

10 Schaap, Jeremy, *Cinderella Man*.

11 Official German Olympic report.

12 Fisher, *A Terrible Splendor*.

13 Ibid.

14 youandyesterday.com/.../Derby_County:_Players_saw_Nazi_war_preparations.

15 Wenn, *Journal of Sport History*, vol. 16, no. 1 (spring 1989) and *A Tale of Two Diplomats: George S. Messersmith and Charles H. Sherrill on Proposed American Participation in the 1936 Olympics*.

16 Reuss, *Hitler's Motor Racing Battles*.

17 Ibid.

18 Guy Moll, leading French racing driver with family funds.

19 news.bbc.co.uk/2/hi/uk_news/magazine/3128202.stm.

20 Glanville, op. cit.

21 news.bbc.co.uk/2/hi/uk_news/magazine/3128202.stm.

22 Quoted in Glanville.

23 Snellman, *Golden Era of Grand Prix Racing* and www.kolumbus.fi/leif.snellman/

24 news.bbc.co.uk/2/hi/uk_news/magazine/3128202.stm.

25 League of Nations, formed after the First World War to prevent war. At its peak it had fifty-eight members.

26 Official German Olympic report.

27 *The Times*, London.

28 Cholmondeley-Tapper, *Amateur Racing Driver*.

29 Official German Olympic report.

30 Snellman, op. cit.

31 Taruffi, *Works Driver*.

32 Official German Olympic report.

33 Ibid.

4

JUST ONE JEW

If there is a certain irony in the fact that Hitler could not exploit the national soccer team, internally and externally, what happened internally reflected with great accuracy what the politics of the Reich meant.

By now the reorganisation of the domestic game was almost two years old. The huge scattering of little regional leagues embracing some 600 clubs had been brought into a *Gauliga* (sixteen *Gaus*) and the number pruned to 170. This brought strength to the *Deutscher Fussball-Bund* (German Football League, DFB) because stronger teams were playing stronger teams.

The German Cup began in 1935, called the *Tschammerpokal* after von Tschammer und Osten, and was won by FC Nuremberg. It continued until 1943 (and resumed in 1953, no longer called the *Tschammerpokal*).

If anyone wanted to join a DFB club they had to be recommended by two non-Marxists and, of course, Jews were barred. Reportedly some clubs, Alemannia Aachen and Bayern Munich among them, tried to mitigate this. As we have seen, the DFB was slowly but remorselessly absorbed into, and subjugated by, the Reichssportführer, the same von Tschammer und Osten.

France occupied the coal-rich German Saarland after the First World War and some teams played in the French Second Division. One, FV Saarbruecken, won the league but was denied promotion.

FC Schalke 04, from the industrial area of Gelsenkirchen, dominated domestic soccer:

> Over a dozen seasons from 1933 to 1945 Schalke accumulated an astounding record, winning 162 of 189 *Gauliga* matches, drawing 21 and losing only 6. On the way they scored 924 goals and gave up just 145. From 1935 to 1939 they did not lose a single league match. The club's dominance throughout this period led them to be held up for propaganda purposes by the Nazi regime as an example of the 'new Germany'. This was despite the fact that many players were descended from Polish immigrants, most notably the two stars of the team, Fritz Szepan and Ernst Kuzorra.[1]

In 1935 Germany played eighteen international matches and won fourteen, although some of the victories were against smaller countries like Luxembourg, Ireland, Finland, Estonia, Latvia and Bulgaria.

By now von Tschammer und Osten presided over the German National Olympic Committee as well as the Sports Ministry; Lewald remained as the figurehead. The Official Report said:

> The progress made in the work of preparation was announced to the National Olympic Committees in January, 1935 through our first circular letter, which also contained information concerning the costs and planning of expeditions as well as a time-table, the regulations for sojourn in the Olympic Village and the conditions governing the sale of admission tickets. Up to this time we had carried on a 'direct correspondence' with the various countries, but the idea of a circular letter proved to be practical, and we sent out a total of eight in all.
>
> … Our attention was directed in an increasing degree to the extension of our technical organization, and we began with the problem of providing the necessary sporting facilities. The courses for the road races, the Marathon event, the 50 kilometre walking race and the 100 kilometre cycling competition were laid out. The German technical departments for the various sports approved the plans of Dr. Diem, the authorities promised to take the necessary steps for closing off the stretches and the German Railway agreed to stop transportation on the Potsdam-Nauen route, which would be crossed during the long-distance cycling race. The *Reichsamt für Landesaufnahme* (Reich Department of Topography) measured the courses and designed a topographical map which was distributed in July, 1935. The long-distance runners and cyclists of the various nations were thus able to begin final training, taking into consideration the degrees of incline and decline they would meet with in Berlin.

The advance sale of Olympic tickets began on 1 January. The tickets – 4.5 million – had been printed:

> falling into 660 different classes and categories. The international travel offices as well as the National Olympic Committees were entrusted with the sale of tickets, and the ticket office fulfilled written orders directly. The first tickets to be offered for sale were the Olympic Stadium passes, which entitled the owner to admission to every event in the Olympic Stadium, sporting as well as artistic. The German quota in this category was sold out in four months.[2]

By now the political grip was tightening on sport generally. Guido von Mengden, journalist and ardent Nazi, became the public relations officer of the Sports Ministry and would advise von Tschammer und Osten. He would also edit *NS-Sport*, the ministry's mouthpiece. The ministry would also produce a sports magazine and propaganda tomes, *Sport und Staat* (*Sports and State*), chronicling organised sport.

Hans Stuck married Paula von Reznicek, a leading tennis player and journalist who had a Jewish grandparent. This brought danger and the Gestapo took a keen interest: anti-Stuck banners decorated one German motoring competition, a hill climb. The story after that is tortuous, but Stuck would find himself needing a friend in high places and that friend, Hitler, played hard to get.[3]

This, however, remained in the background, as did the potential American boycott. Though once Sherrill had his promise about equal treatment for Jews he 'publicly ignored all indication that the Germans were failing to honour their pledges'. He also staunchly campaigned in favour of and for support of an American Olympic entry.

Meanwhile, Messersmith, who continued to work in Germany gathering information about the Jewish plight, had been appointed Minister to Uruguay but a resignation took him to Vienna:

> The Austrian position was one that demanded an individual intimately familiar with the European situation and its unsettled political climate. Charles C. Burlingham, a New York lawyer and Presidential advisor on federal judicial appointments, told Roosevelt one week before Messersmith was appointed to Vienna that America needed a 'strong man' in Austria.

However:

> the revelation that Messersmith was to receive the Austrian position met with a different reception in Germany. The [New York] Times reported that the cancellation of Messersmith's transfer … 'has greatly interested German official circles, in which it is not too much to say it has aroused conflicting sentiments.' Although the Germans were gratified that a man such as Messersmith, who was conversant with German viewpoints, would be serving in Vienna, they were aware of his hard-nosed and uncompromising work ethic. He had proved to be a difficult man to deal with, and the Germans were aware of his hostility towards National Socialist policy.[4]

The Olympic Organising Committee started publishing the regulations booklets in five languages once it had approval at the IOC meeting in Oslo in February. The internal and external problem remained fundamentally insolvable.

Jim Wango, a professional black African wrestler, had become something of a celebrity in Nuremberg, beating white wrestlers easily one after another. In early March he was wrestling when Julius Streicher, a notorious Nazi Jew-baiter and Nuremberg resident, appeared. Streicher stopped the wrestling and an official newspaper, the Frankische Tageszeitung, quoted him as saying:

> We are in favour of sporting contests, including wrestling, in the compass of sports involving strength. What we oppose is the linking of sport with dirty business

interests and sales gimmicks. It is a sales gimmick, an appeal to inferior people, to subhumans, to put a negro on view and let him compete with white people. It is not in the spirit of the inhabitants of Nuremberg to let white men be subdued by a black man. Anyone who applauds when a black man throws a white man of our blood to the ground is no Nuremberger. No woman married to a negro can expect anything from Nuremberg.

The problem was not reconciling a creature like Streicher to any Olympic ideal, but concealing the Streichers from the rest of the world until the Olympics had been safely delivered. No doubt Messersmith did not fail to notice this incident. Vienna was not *that* far away.[5]

In a Gallup poll, 43 per cent of Americans said they were in favour of a boycott. Although Messersmith:

> approached the issue of participation in terms of its political and diplomatic impact, he shared the concerns of private citizens, politicians, various newspaper columnists and public interest groups that campaigned for an American boycott. These concerns included a fear for the safety of competing American athletes, the political exploitation of the Olympic movement by the Nazi hierarchy, the reprehensible treatment of the German-Jewish sport and general populations, and the apparent indifference to the discrimination displayed by sport leaders such as Sherrill and Brundage.[6]

It was not so easy because the modern world, a web of inter-connecting interests, rarely is. There were sporting bodies like the National Collegiate Athletic Association which understandably felt great sympathy for young athletes who had been training for Berlin since Los Angeles in 1932 – if not all of their lives – and would lose their chance of competing. The four-year Olympic cycle can be unforgiving: it was possible to have been just too young for Los Angeles and just too old for the 1940 Games.

There were also feelings (which would find powerful echoes in 1980 and 1984) about a boycott setting a precedent, which could inflict serious damage on the Olympic body, and that the sportsmen of one sovereign country had no business occupying themselves with the internal politics of another sovereign country. It was what Sherrill was saying.

Did Hitler read these nuances, these currents, these shifting sands the width of the Atlantic away? Instinctive politicians have a wide radar, but the question has no answer. During the spring of 1935, the tempo was maintained.

Max Schmeling had been beaten by an American, Steve Hamas, in Philadelphia in early 1934 and was now offered a chance to rectify that in a return in Hamburg.[7] Schmeling brought his manager, Joe Jacobs, over to Berlin a few days before. Jacobs was booked into the Hotel Bristol but when he arrived he found his reservation had been cancelled. The Jew was not welcome. Schmeling took care of that and, reportedly, although Jacobs was prevented from being in Schmeling's corner, he could have a ringside seat.

When Schmeling had won he was garlanded by a wreath with a swastika on it and, like the rest of the crowd, gave the Nazi salute. Evidently Jacobs did this, but with his cigar still in his hand, and winked at Schmeling.

It provoked controversy in the German newspapers about Jews, Jewish boxing managers and sport.

Neil Allen, a long-time sports journalist with a keen interest in boxing, has written:

> The record from the 1930s clearly shows that Adolf Hitler, through his propaganda minister Joseph Goebbels, put great pressure on Schmeling to get rid of Joe Jacobs. The Nazis were furious at a film showing the end of a Schmeling victory in 1935 in Germany depicting Jacobs giving the Nazi salute with a cigar in his hand and winking at his boxer. On his return to New York the shameless Jacobs told outraged friends 'The "Heil" didn't count because the fingers of my other hand were crossed behind my back.[8]

The aftermath of the fight resulted in Schmeling enduring a prickly, innuendo-laden meeting with von Tschammer und Osten, who suggested he ought to concentrate his career on Germany rather than America and Americans. Subsequently Schmeling met Hitler, taking his wife with him. Hitler exercised his charm on Mrs Schmeling, while Schmeling tried to explain that he intended to remain with Jacobs. Hitler, he felt, was not really listening.

Amazingly, Jacobs kept managing Schmeling until his death in 1941, although, as Neil Allen points out, Schmeling:

> had far less success when Dr Goebbels complained to him about his friendship with a German sculptor named Josef Thorak because Thorak's wife was a Jewess. Eventually Frau Thorak fled to asylum in England while Schmeling was harangued again by the powerful Goebbels for having met up with Jewish friends in Holland.[9]

The Grand Prix season began at Monaco, although only Mercedes was ready, the race therefore at their mercy. Caracciola, Fagioli and von Brauchitsch filled the front row. Fagioli led with Caracciola chasing and as the race developed a Frenchman, Philippe Etancelin – born wealthy – brought his Maserati up towards Caracciola. On the run to the Gasometer corner (today *Rascasse*) Etancelin forced through on the inside but Caracciola responded, re-taking him on the run up to Casino Square. Both cars broke down, leaving Fagioli in splendid isolation. That was: won eight, lost two.

The race in Tunisia was then major, although the Mercedes and Auto Union teams would not be going. Achille Varzi[10] had secured a drive for Auto Union, who sent a modified 1934 car for him. Varzi demanded to be paid in Lire because getting Reichsmarks out of Germany had become so difficult. Auto Union said he would be a private entry and could keep any start and prize money. Then they changed their minds. It was a good investment. Varzi dominated the race and won by almost 4 minutes – won nine, lost two.

The Tripoli race dovetailed into Tunisia perfectly, a week between them. Libya, of course, was part of Italy's empire and the race felt Italian. The circuit, Mellaha, was then the fastest road course in the world. This time Auto Union fielded Varzi and Stuck against the Mercedes of Fagioli, von Brauchitsch and Caracciola. The race would be a story of extreme heat, tyre wear, punctures, pit stops and, in Stuck's case, a terrifying fire from which he emerged shaken. Varzi led and looked the likely winner despite banging wheels with Nuvolari's Alfa Romeo, but near the end his tyres shredded, giving the race to Caracciola.

Two weeks later they were at the Avus. The Grand Prix was run over two heats of five laps and a ten-lap final with the top four from each heat qualifying. Stuck led from Varzi, the Mercedes of Fagioli, Caracciola and von Brauchitsch after them. Fagioli surged past Varzi and closed on Stuck who had a tyre burst at 290kmph. Like Mellaha, tyres were being shredded but Fagioli looked after his and won. That was: won eleven, lost two.

Work continued on the Olympic Torch Run. Permissions were sought and secured from the countries it would pass through and:

> we could begin final preparations such as conducting numerous experiments and trials in order to obtain a torch which would burn for the required length of time and under all conditions. It soon became obvious that torch holders would be needed, and to our gratification the Friedrich Krupp Firm in Essen offered to produce these in stainless steel. The directions and regulations pertaining to the relay run were printed in the languages of the five countries through which it was to pass and circulated.[11]

The entire route was to be inspected in September.

Season tickets for various sports went on sale in June and within a month had raised the first million Reichsmarks.

The Grand Prix cars went to the Eifel race at the Nürburgring where von Brauchitsch, returning for the first time since his crash, was stunningly fast in practice. The race was started in the modern way, using lights (red going to yellow, then 15 seconds later green). The weather cloaked the circuit in rain and, in other places, coated it in sunlight. Von Brauchitsch led but suffered plug problems so Caracciola and Rosemeyer duelled. Rosemeyer impudently overtook in front of the grandstands with three laps to go but, on the last lap, Caracciola out-accelerated the Auto Union and won by 1.9 seconds.

Hitler's investment had brought its dividend. Of the first six cars, only one – the Alfa Romeo of Louis Chiron – was not German, and of the fourteen races the Germans had contested since they came into Grand Prix racing as, essentially, Hitler's teams, they had won twelve and lost two.

A week later, at Montlhéry for the French Grand Prix, the German power was having direct consequences:

> The French organizers were trying to hinder a German walkover by adding three chicanes to the track. The chicanes lowered the speed considerably and also put great strain to the brakes ... The Bugatti entry was full of controversy ... The car used in the race appeared at midnight and was moved with the organizers' collusion without scrutineering into the Bugatti pit.[12]

The race provided further evidence of the power. Deep into it the Mercedes were running in formation at the front under team orders when Fagioli burst past Caracciola. They raced, much to the fury of team manager Alfred Neubauer. Fagioli's car developed a problem and he fell away. Von Brauchitsch followed Caracciola obediently home; won thirteen, lost two.

Auto Union did not go to the Penya Rhin race at Montjuich, Barcelona, because their new engine had developed problems and the priority was to have them solved by the German race. Mercedes fielded two cars and they finished first and second (Fagioli from Carraciola). Only Nuvolari in an Alfa Romeo could stay anywhere near them, and that made it won fourteen, lost two.

That was the end of June.

While the cars accelerated round Europe and North Africa, leaving their immense echoes, Gottfried von Cramm adorned the tennis courts but was no less celebrated for that. German tennis appeared strong and in depth: in Paris, Roderick Menzel reached the quarter finals while von Cramm proceeded almost majestically to the final and faced Fred Perry, von Cramm the master on clay and Perry decidedly not the master on it. The year before, Perry could have completed the Grand Slam but at the French he was beaten in four sets by Giorgio di Stefani. Now, however, Perry was at the peak of his abilities, unbelievably fast and with a 'murderous wristy forehand'.[13]

Perry was a canny player. He 'did not need obvious signals to home in on an opponent's weakness − his antennae picked up the smallest sign ... He attacked Gottfried von Cramm when the normally inscrutable German baron gave off the subtlest of distress signals − a slight draining of blood from his cheeks revealing pale pink spots. Also, he worked on von Cramm's obsession with tidiness by leaving the lining of one of his trouser pockets hanging out during a match, knowing how much it would irritate his opponent.'[14]

Perry took the first set 6–3, von Cramm the second 6–3, then Perry's speed and strength became decisive as he took the third 6–1 and the fourth 6–3.

It does not seem to have been a memorable final. Von Cramm kept serving the 'unhappiest of double faults' and Perry was not at his best because that was difficult against 'the many signs of nervousness that are betrayed by von Cramm'. *The Times* correspondent wrote about 'anxious hitting' although von Cramm saved five match points in the fourth set.

In the women's event, however, Hilde Sperling beat Simone Mathieu of France 6–2, 6–1.

On the day Perry was beating von Cramm, Prenn was winning the Middlesex Championships at Chiswick.

At Wimbledon, Donald Budge, a Californian destined to be one of the great players, met and defeated Bunny Austin. Thereby hangs a tale which stands in the most revealing (and damning) contrast to what the Nazis were doing. Budge was anxious to meet von Cramm socially. During Budge's match against Austin, Budge had displayed what he considered perfect sportsmanship. A linesman gave Austin a line call which was obviously wrong because the ball struck the chalk and, as was the custom in those days, Budge deliberately served a double fault to give the point back to Austin (people did not challenge decisions publicly because that was bad form).

Von Cramm, known as the custodian and arbiter of etiquette on court, congratulated Budge on his victory but, to Budge's consternation, discreetly accused him of poor sportsmanship. Budge wondered quite what he had done wrong and von Cramm explained that, by serving the double fault, he had humiliated the linesman in front of 15,000 people. Budge never did it again.

Von Cramm himself had come through the fourth round against American Gene Mako, born in Budapest but emigrated aged 7 via Italy and Argentina. He was tall, strong and a pin-up, but von Cramm hammered him 6-0, 6-1, 3-6, 6-1. Von Cramm came through his quarter final, beating Australian Vivian McGrath 6-4, 6-2, 4-6, 6-1. He and Budge met in the semi-finals and von Cramm won comfortably, 6-1, 8-6, 6-4. He met Perry in the final and had recovered from Paris so completely that he forced Perry to play the best match of his career so far. 'And the first appearance of von Cramm in the final round, the finest German player to have lived so far, was a triumph in itself and rightly earns him the position of second player in the world.'[15]

The Davis Cup was a major event and Germany moved through the Interzonal round with a bye, then beat Italy 4-1, Australia 4-1 and Czechoslovakia 4-1 to face the United States at Wimbledon. Germany had not won the Davis Cup and it offered enormous prestige for Hitler as well as Germany. Von Cramm was about to demonstrate that his ethics and sense of fair play overrode that.

On the first day, he beat Wilmer Allison 7-5, 11-9, 6-8, 6-1, but Henkel lost to Budge. Next day in the doubles von Cramm and Kai Lund met Allison and John Van Ryn, a celebrated partnership. The match moved into a fifth set and the Germans missed five match points. At this moment von Cramm and Lund both went to return a shot down the middle of the court and, as it seemed, Lund not only got to it but hit a winner – and a sixth match point.

Von Cramm, however, pointed out to the umpire that the ball had nicked his racket before Lund hit it and therefore the point had to go to the Americans. The German team captain, Heinrich Kleinschroth, did not see it that way.

Von Cramm has been reported as saying to Kleinschroth:

> When I chose tennis as a young man, I chose it because it was a gentleman's game, and that's the way I've played it ever since I picked up my first racket. Do you think that I would sleep tonight knowing that the ball had touched my racket without

my saying so? Never, because I would be violating every principle I think this game stands for. On the contrary, I don't think I'm letting the German people down. As a matter of fact, I think I'm doing them credit.

Von Cramm played a 'dead rubber' match against Budge, the tie already lost, and after a lively start fell away, his heart not in the match.

Fisher speculates that 'maybe he was thinking ahead to his imminent return to Berlin, the omnipresent Gestapo, and the problems of Manasse's money'.[16] Nor was that the only way of considering von Cramm's situation. He was in no sense a prod- uct of Hitler or the Third Reich and consequently vulnerable for that alone. He was a homosexual and vulnerable for that. He placed his ethics above those being pressed on him by the Third Reich and was vulnerable for that. He had publicly befriended Prenn, the Jew who fled, and was vulnerable for that. He played tennis, which was associated with grass-like lawns and no physical danger whatsoever, which was hardly likely to endear him to a man who fully intended to tear the Soviet Union to pieces once he had crushed Western Europe.

Also Göring had repeatedly urged him to join the Nazi Party, a move that would have immediately lessened the vulnerability. He refused and clearly did have a lot to contemplate as he journeyed back to Berlin.

The pressure continued to grow in the United States over the Olympics. Brundage and Sherrill faced opposition from several politicians, including New York Representative Emanuel Celler. Moreover, the Amateur Athletic Union's president, Jeremiah T. Mahoney – a former Olympian himself – came out with a resolute call for a boycott. It was not a position he would renegotiate.

Nor was Brundage in any mood to renegotiate either. 'The fact that no Jews have been named so far to compete for Germany does not necessarily mean that they have been discriminated against on that score,' he said. The meaning: they might not be good enough. Brundage would add that amateur sport 'cannot, with good grace or propriety, interfere in the internal political, religious or racial affairs of any country or group'. It was the same argument as before, and very convenient if you were trying to persuade people to go to Berlin.

Seven weeks after this, Hitler announced in Nuremberg what would become known as the Nuremberg Laws. Jews lost their German citizenship, lost the protec- tion of the law and were forbidden from marrying Aryans.

The New York Times reported that 'fear of losing the Games' through the boycott campaign and what was described as 'political Catholicism' had forced Goebbels to order foreign correspondents in Berlin to be obstructed and some expelled. This was an attempt to intimidate them into not reporting what was happening to the Jews.

Auto Union were still not happy with their engines and did not go to the Belgian Grand Prix at Spa but Mercedes did and Caracciola won. It was not straightforward. After pit stops Fagioli caught Caracciola and attacked, shaking his fist at Caracciola. Neubauer called him in, Fagioli erupted and von Brauchitsch took over the car, bringing it home second. That made it: won fifteen, lost two.

The German Grand Prix would be the only one in 1935 which a German car did not win. Nuvolari chased down von Brauchitsch in an Alfa Romeo, whose tyres were shredding, but could not afford a pit stop. Nuvolari danced the Alfa Romeo round the Nürburgring, drew his intuitive mastery over the full 22km and, when von Brauchitsch's tyre finally exploded, swept by to win. The winner's garland engulfed and dwarfed him. The organisers had been so sure a big German would win it they had ordered it to be made that size. Nor was the Italian national anthem available for the victory ceremony because, again, the organisers had been so sure a German would win it. Nuvolari had it on a record he always carried in his briefcase.

The aftermath produced a specific image, Hühnlein giving the Nazi salute while next to him Nuvolari raises his arm like a flipper in an uncomfortable compromise.

He was not the last man who would have to make this compromise, and Adolf Hühnlein, who reported directly to Hitler after the races, would have to explain that an Italian in an Italian car had beaten all the Germans. Nor was it the last time he would have to file a report which the Führer might not like to read. Anyway, that was: won fifteen, lost three.

Auto Union went to Pescara for the *Coppa Acerbo* in August but neither Mercedes nor Maserati did. Then Stuck's car cracked a cylinder head and could not be repaired. In the race Varzi led but Rosemeyer, starting from the back of the grid, reached second, but locked his brakes and flew over a ditch then between a telegraph pole and a bridge – the gap only 5cm wider than the car. Varzi won it and that was won sixteen, lost three.[17]

The New York Times dutifully reported the sense of gathering crisis over Jews and the Olympics, pointing out in one issue, 7 August, that high jumper Gretel Bergmann had been excluded from the German championships; a small Jewish newspaper in London was claiming Goebbels had sent out a memo to the Jewish sports association instructing them not to permit their athletes to train for the Olympics and, further, instructing them not to reveal that the memos had been sent (*The Times* said this story had yet to be verified); Baillet-Latour, in Vienna, said it was still possible to take the Games from Germany but 'I cannot imagine the German sports authorities not fulfilling their obligations'; Diem, in Paris, renewed Hitler's pledge that promises would be kept; in Boston, Massachusetts, 1,500 people representing 200 Jewish organisations demanded the American athletes not go to Berlin.

At this point, General Sherrill went to Germany with the object of getting a fencer, Helene Mayer, or Bergmann included in the German Olympic team. Mayer had won gold at the Amsterdam Games in 1928 but her father was Jewish and now, expelled by her home Offenbach Fencing Club, she had decamped to the United States. Clearly if Sherrill could get assurances that she would be picked his stance would be vindicated and a boycott much harder to enforce. Bergmann, an outstanding high jumper, had decamped to Britain where she took part in the British national championships. Avery Brundage believed the inclusion of one Jew would be decisive in swaying the American public.

So Sherrill, buoyed by the belief that he had single-handedly forced the Nazi government into concessions at Vienna, would go to Germany. Mayer, meanwhile, said she would try to get into the German team and had been promised that the Vienna assurance was true.

Sherrill subsequently said that von Tschammer und Osten had, in Berlin, given him a luncheon on Hitler's instructions and Sherrill assumed this was code for the fact that Germany intended to fulfil the Vienna assurance. He was, it seems, very wrong in reading a meaning into the luncheon, especially the meaning he did.

Sherrill met Hitler on 24 August in Munich, because the Nuremberg Rally was due just up the road (and, not that it was relevant, as practice for the Swiss Grand Prix was going on). Sherrill said later, 'It was dreadful nerve for me to tackle him in his own Munich home, but I am only a private citizen, and he can't eat me.' Not literally, anyway.

In Munich, Sherrill tried to persuade Hitler that one Jew would change everything and reminded him of the Vienna assurance. Hitler said he was unaware of this and Jewish participation was impossible. It must have been a bad moment for Sherrill, who then hinted that Germany might lose the Games. Hitler responded by saying the Games would be 'purely German'.

The Swiss Grand Prix was run in heavy rain. Caracciola, the 'Rain Master', avoided crashes and comfortably held off a late thrust by Fagioli. That was: won seventeen, lost three.

On 26 August, the two leading German heavyweight boxers, Schmeling and Walter Neusel, met in Hamburg in front of 95,000 spectators. The promoter was Walther Rothenburg, Schmeling's manager was Joe Jacobs, Neusel's was Paul Damski. All three were Jewish – and Damski, who had fled to Paris, did not risk returning for the fight. Why did the Nazis permit the fight? Author Partick Myler[18] feels it was because they were 'no doubt fearful that intervention could create a public backlash', although in due course both boxers came under 'strong pressure' to leave their managers. The pressure on Schmeling we have already seen.

Schmeling stopped Neusel, and after the Baer defeat that opened up possibilities in America again. It would create two of the most charged events in all sporting history, and Hitler's chill hand would be felt in both.

On 30 August, Sherrill sent a letter to the IOC president, Henri Baillet-Latour:

> I urge you to talk personally with the Führer, and show him the *Ministerium des Innern* June, 1933 letter you received in Vienna from Berlin about the exclusion of the German Jews from the German 1936 team. You are in for the greatest shock of your entire life. It will be a trying test even for your remarkable tact and savoir faire; and the sooner you meet the situation, the better the hope for your success, instead of a destructive explosion.

There are contradictions here because Hitler invited Sherrill to the Nuremberg Rally and he spent four days there. During this time Sherrill had another meeting with von Tschammer und Osten, and subsequently a Jew would be permitted, meaning Mayer.

Messersmith, monitoring closely, would charge that Sherrill was 'knowingly presenting a false picture of the German-Jewish situation'.[19]

Sherrill, in correspondence, subconsciously revealed how fascinated he was with Hitler, even down to how little personal protection he needed, and described the furnishings of the Brown House. If Hitler hypnotised him, he would not be the first or last.

The pressure continued to mount, and Lewald went to the United States on what has been described as a 'publicity campaign'. He said that 'the Olympics without America simply would not be the Olympics. It is unthinkable.'[20]

Dr Lewald revealed that he intended to send a personal invitation to Helene Mayer for the Olympic trials due in February 1936. This would be:

> with all expenses paid … We do not have any way of knowing if she has retained her skill after four years, but we hope she will come over. Believe me, we wish more than anybody in America that we had some Jewish athletes of Olympic calibre. But we have none, and I believe no one in America would want us to put a second rate athlete on our team just because he is Jewish. That certainly isn't the Olympic spirit.[21]

This was a falsehood and Lewald must have known it because Bergmann, in London or anywhere else, was one of Germany's leading highjumpers, if not the leading high jumper.

The pressure grew again because Mayer did not receive the Lewald letter.

On 27 September *The New York Times* said that von Tschammer und Osten had written to Sherrill enclosing his official invitations to Mayer and Bergmann. There was another assurance, that they would 'receive the same treatment as other candidates, although they are Jewesses'.[22]

Had he? Bergmann did not receive this letter, either. The most obvious explanation is that Mayer, Bergmann and Lewald were being shamelessly used, certainly to forestall trouble at the Amateur Athletic Union convention in December. No doubt the Nazis reasoned if they could safely negotiate a path through that, however they did it, the Games would suddenly be too close for any boycott. With every passing day, as expectations rose, a boycott would be harder and harder to secure.

Far away from these machinations, Monza had a new layout with five chicanes, four of them made by straw bales, for the Italian Grand Prix. The chicanes put much pressure on the cars and only five out of seventeen starters survived. Stuck won it from Nuvolari (Ferrari), making it won eighteen, lost three.

The Spanish Grand Prix was run at Lasarte and attracted a small entry: sixteen, including the customary four Auto Unions and four Mercedes. Stuck led, as he so often did, but stones on the track played havoc. Varzi pitted with a bloody face after his windscreen was smashed, and the same thing happened to Rosemeyer and Fagioli. Stuck had gear problems and Caracciola won it.

The Czechoslovakian Grand Prix at Brno completed the season and it attracted only fourteen entires – the four Auto Unions but only three Mercedes against three Alfa Romeos being run by Ferrari. Mechanical failures decimated the field, leaving Rosemeyer to win it, beating Nuvolari (Ferrari) by 6.5 minutes: won twenty, lost three.

Piero Taruffi, the Italian driver, captured the mood within racing. Through Stuck, he was offered a chance to drive the Auto Union in testing at Monza:

It was the first rear-engined model that I had driven, and was immensely powerful; but the driver's seat was too near the front, which was a drawback because it made it harder to sense rear-wheel slides. This was demonstrated in a spell of acceleration when, after a few laps I had, as I thought, become used to the car. A chicane made of straw bales had been placed at the end of the Lesmo straight.

Presumably one from the Grand Prix – forming a quick left-right-left. Taruffi came to grief there and was annoyed it might ruin the good impression he'd been creating:

Naturally the other candidate for fourth place on the team, von Delius, seemed pleased at my discomfiture, and I remember him laughing and making sweeping motions with a broom … I lost a marvellous opportunity and von Delius joined the team as number four. A few months later he was killed at the Nürburgring on the long left-hand bend after the straight. I was very sorry, but once again I came to the conclusion that it's no good fighting against fate.[23]

In late 1934 von Tschammer und Osten sought to 'bind' Germany's athletes to the Nazis with camps for political education and national training regimes. Those already chosen for the Olympics took part in a 'special public ceremony' which was broadcast. These athletes promised to obey the Reich Sports Office guidelines and 'swore that they would be worthy representatives of Germany, the Fatherland and the Games'.[24]

In October, Judge Mahoney made himself busy. In a speech in New York he spoke of 'some who went to Germany with the intention of keeping their eyes closed' – a clear reference to the Brundage and Sherrill trips. When asked if that is what he meant, Mahoney grinned and said he had not named any names. He did, however, speak of 'my dear friend Sherrill' who 'spent four days with Hitler and patted him on the back and said "old sport Hitler"'.

He responded to Lewald:

You state that Germany has no Jewish material of Olympic calibre. Is it not because the outstanding German Jewish athletes are either dead, exiled or barred from training and from competition with Aryans, and that they are enveloped by a hatred so intense that it is impossible for them to develop and display their prowess?

It is not important whether or not Miss Helene Mayer is part of the German team. It is important that Miss Mayer has not been invited to participate in the German Olympic tryouts because of her non-Aryan extraction until this month. It is important that it was four times announced that such an invitation had been extended to her, but as late as September 30, she had not received it.[25]

The mystery deepened because Lewald claimed Mayer had been invited and she had accepted. He produced a telegram allegedly from her saying 'sickness' had prevented her answering before.

The pressure on Mayer was unremitting because, living in the United States, she saw that if she refused the invitation – or did not go along with whatever subterfuges the Nazis were indulging in – she alone might be responsible for an American boycott and the wrecking of the Games. If she refused and there was a boycott, she had to consider what impact that might have on her family, still in Germany. If she accepted, she had to consider that she was giving legitimacy to the Nazis and, at a stretch, actually condoning them. She then had to contemplate what might happen to her when she went back to Germany, a place now so transformed that Lewald felt impelled to give assurances about the physical safety of Jewish visitors to the Games. More of this in a moment.

The cold hand of Hitler had reached out and taken hold of Helene Mayer very roughly indeed.

The subterfuges are encapsulated in a dispatch early in November from the British ambassador to Berlin, Sir Eric Phipps, to London. Hitler was:

> taking an enormous interest in the Olympic Games. In fact he is beginning to regard political questions very much from the angle of their effect on the Games ... The German government are simply terrified lest Jewish pressure may induce the United States government to withdraw their team and so wreck the festival, the material and propagandist value of which, they think, can scarcely be exaggerated.

And now they had got their one Jew.

It is, of course, a rich and wonderful irony that Hitler, self-appointed candidate for the position of ruler of the world, found himself in the late autumn and winter of 1935 hiding behind the skirts of a 25-year-old Jew in sun-kissed California.

Baillet-Latour went to Berlin and met Hitler, who promised anti-Semitic propaganda would be taken down for the Olympics, including Garmisch-Partenkirchen, and also in cities where foreign visitors might be going. Although Baillet-Latour reported this publicly, the German press did not mention it at all and the Propaganda Ministry refused to comment. Baillet-Latour seemed satisfied, as well he might have been with the future of the Games in doubt, but all he really had was that most dubious of twentieth-century artefacts: Hitler's word.

In early December, Germany was due to send a soccer team to play England at White Hart Lane, a match with obvious and explosive political potential. All else aside, London had long been a centre of Jewish life in Britain. There would be anti-fascist demonstrations but overall the whole visit allowed the Germans to demonstrate their humane, sensitive face. They were well dressed and very well behaved.

The match came to represent a military operation, although as we shall see it was not intended to look like one.

The Germans flew into Croydon on the Monday – the match was on Wednesday. They were assigned three German-speaking Scotland Yard detectives to protect them from demonstrations. The party was met by the German ambassador, Leopold von Hoesch, and they brought with them a silver cup, inscribed in German, which they would present to the Football Association as a token of their appreciation for England's friendship and sportsmanship.[26]

As the Germans arrived a delegation from the Trades Union Council was at the Home Office presenting a protest to the Home Secretary, Sir John Simon. The soccer team's trainer, Otto Nerz, countered by saying: 'We have had no message from Herr Hitler, and our visit to England to play your team has nothing to do with the government. It is purely a private fixture between the German and English Football Associations.'

However, Sir Walter Citrine of the TUC warned Simon that there might be anti-Nazi demonstrations and that the German government was using the match for political purposes. He would subsequently add that the Nazis were subsidising the huge influx of supporters that was due.[27]

The day before, while the players went to the ground for light training with police protection outside, plans were drawn up to receive 10,000 German spectators. Seven boats were due at Dover and Folkestone between 3 a.m. and 6.30 a.m. the next morning and sixteen special trains would transport the 8,000 anticipated to London. Some 1,600 were expected on a liner at Southampton where the soccer club would welcome them on the quayside and then three trains transport them to Waterloo Station. The *Daily Mirror* led their front page with '12,000 GERMANS HERE', and predicted that moving the German supporters around would be 'the greatest achievement in the history of tourist traffic'. One paragraph in the report said: 'Two reasons lie behind this elaborate scheme. One is to make the visitors as comfortable as possible; the other to demonstrate how a tremendous piece of organisation can be carried out without any militaristic display.'

That afternoon the German team went on a sight-seeing tour of London and in the evening attended a music hall with the English teams.

The next day *The Times* reported: 'Here and there traffic was dislocated, and at one time Leicester Square might almost have been mistaken for a Berlin *Platz*, but of demonstrations and counter-demonstrations feared by imaginative people there was none.' The Germans wore no political emblems – swastikas – and had only small flags to wave during the match.

A police van outside Victoria Station monitored possible problems as the Germans arrived – the first train at 5.30 a.m. – and they were given information in German. 'Everything had been carefully planned. Drivers in coaches in which the Germans were taken sight-seeing were given sealed orders including the routes they were to take and the stopping places.'[28]

Some of the Germans brought a laurel wreath so large it needed three men to carry it. It was taken to the Cenotaph and bore an inscription: 'IN MEMORY OF THE BRITISH DEAD [of the First World War] FROM 1,500 GERMAN FOOTBALL SUPPORTERS WHO HAVE TRAVELLED TO ATTEND THE ENGLISH-GERMANY GAME.'

Leicester Square did resemble a platz. It was closed to traffic so coaches could use it as a depot and was full of Germans. It even had German newspaper placards. 'Mounted and foot police escorted parties to the restaurants where luncheon was served in relays.'[29] A loudspeaker mounted on a police car in Piccadilly offered in German help for any visitors who had gotten lost.

White Hart Lane had a heavy police presence from 2 hours before the match and so did Park Lane, where the coaches would come along: a policeman every 10 yards. However, *The Times* observed that the only anti-Nazi 'feeling was the attempted distribution of literature, a few scuffles as police took possession of the pamphlets, and one or two protests – "Stop the Nazi match" – scrawled on walls'.

The two teams were cheered as they came on to the pitch together and some felt the Germans were given a warmer reception than the English. Before the start, as the teams lined up to face each other in the traditional way, the Germans gave the Nazi salute. One historian, Ulrich Linder, in his book *Strikers for Hitler,* explains that the match was intended 'to communicate, to show the British public that German people are no monsters, Germans are civilised, Germans can behave. Before 1936 they tried to hide their real intentions and football helped exactly to achieve that.'

It worked. England won 3-0 and the British press applauded the conduct of German players and supporters alike. The Nazi government's view: 'The political soldiers of the Führer had won.'

That evening, the president of the Football Association, Sir Charles Clegg, spoke at a dinner given for the German party and players. They were, for the first time on the visit, all dressed in brown.

Clegg attacked the TUC, who had been so critical of the match, for interfering with sport:

> We, as English sportsmen, desire to express our regret at the annoyance to which our visitors have been subjected. I may say that it is annoyance over which we, as the ruling body of English football, had no control. The Trades Union Council have thought fit to interfere in a matter which was absolutely outside their business. I have no hesitation in saying that they have no justification whatsoever for interfering. This is the first time the TUC has interfered with football. I hope it will be the last time.

Dr W. Erbach, leading the German party, assured the Football Association that they were not annoyed. The king was toasted and, as Clegg proposed it, all the Germans rose and stood to attention. Everybody sang the National Anthem. A second toast followed, 'To the leader, Adolf Hitler'. The Germans gave the Nazi salute.

After dinner everybody sang *Auld Lang Syne* and then Fritz Szepan, the German captain, used a cigar as a baton and conducted the rest, who had formed themselves into a choir, in singing several German songs.

The Times carried a leading article the following day admonishing those who had foreseen in the German spectators something they were not. It admonished those identifying 'a football team and its supporters with the authors of the dictatorship and the agents of brutality which have disfigured the Nazi regime'.

This drew a 'Letter to the Editor' from a J.N. Duckworth of Hawks Club, Cambridge, pointing out several recent instances 'of how Englishmen in Germany have received the greatest welcome and the greatest encouragements'. Specifically, he recounted how the Cambridge University rowing crew had been overwhelmed with hospitality: 'In Frankfort [sic], short of declaiming Hitler in the streets, we were free, if we so wished, to commit any excess of breach of courtesy, and nothing but a wise nod of the head and probably an expressive "Mad Englishmen" would be forthcoming.'

Both the leader and the letter capture the dilemma so many others faced when they were confronted with innate ordinary German correctness and warmth at one level and, at the level above, a political system which was almost impossible to reconcile with that correctness and warmth.

The pressure continued to grow on Lewald, who may have been a figurehead but who was proving an extremely useful one. The boycott did naturally dominate the Amateur Athletic Union's convention in December at the Hotel Commodore, New York. There were 5 hours of speeches and the argument lurched to and fro. Perhaps Fred L. Steers of Chicago, a vice president, caught the mood:

> There is no case yet against Germany in anything where the IOC has authority. Germany hasn't yet selected her team any more than we have. What you are trying here is not a case of sporting discrimination but a moral judgement on Germany as a whole, which we have no right to impose on our athletes.

At the end Mahoney, as president of the union, accepted that the move to boycott the Games had been defeated. The vote – sixty-one against fifty-five – had, Mahoney added, made it impossible for him to stand for re-election. Brundage was unanimously elected as his successor, putting him in an immensely strong position and virtually guaranteeing the Americans would go to Berlin. Mahoney, however, said he now felt free to continue the struggle of preserving 'the honour of American athletes', in scarcely veiled code for continuing the fight.

Evidently the convention 'greatly distressed' Lewald, who approached Messersmith and gave him an assurance that foreign Jews would not be in physical danger during the Games – Messersmith might have been tempted to retort: why should they be in any danger? And why do you feel impelled to say so? Messersmith pointed out that it was nothing to do with that. It centred on the fact that Jews could not qualify for the German team, which destroyed one of the central tenets of the whole Olympic spirit.

Lewald reportedly fell silent.

Messersmith pointed out to Washington that any further assurance from Lewald was worthless because he 'possessed no independent authority'.[30] Senator Augustine Longeran of Connecticut had been approached by a constituent who asked him to support the boycott. Sensibly, Longeran asked Secretary of State Cordell Hull for his view.

Hull replied:

The question of participation, of course, does not fall within the competence of any agency of this government but it is a matter exclusively for determination by the private organizations directly concerned. I am sure you will realize therefore that it would not be appropriate for me to make a statement which might be construed as in any way interfering with the freedom of decision of these organizations.[31]

The diplomats were going to remain extremely diplomatic.

Mahoney would continue to have an ally too, in Messersmith whose 'persistence deserves admiration. Although continually frustrated by a lack of response on the issue from Washington, his reports became even more numerous. The fact that he maintained intimate contact with the situation following his transfer to Vienna indicates that he truly felt that participation had serious ramifications.'

The British author Duff Hart-Davis has raised the intriguing question of the consequences if the boycott had succeeded and the Games moved to a more acceptable country. 'Nazi prestige would have suffered a serious blow, and the rest of the world made to think much harder about what was happening in Germany. Whether that would have achieved any practical result is another matter.' He suggested that by the end of 1936 German re-armament had reached a point where any chance of 'halting Hitler physically had gone for the time being'.

It can also be postulated that a boycott would have insulted and enraged Hitler to the point where he would have moved faster to do what he was going to do anyway.

It leaves two questions. What would the backlash to a boycott have been like for Jews in Germany, and by extension those who fell into Nazi hands when the conquests began? And what would the backlash have been like for Jews in the United States if they were perceived to have engineered the boycott and prevented American athletes from competing in an Olympic Games?

The man hiding behind Helene Mayer's skirts seemed to corrupt everything he could, and it did not matter which continent.

Notes

1   en.wikipedia.org/wiki/FC_Schalke_04.
2   Official German Olympic report.
3   forix.autosport.com/8w/stuck.html.
4   Wenn, 'A Tale of Two Diplomats' in *Journal of Sport History*.
5   Quoted in Hart-Davis, *Hitler's Games*.
6   Wenn, op. cit.
7   Summarised from Myler, *Ring of Hate*.
8   www.boxing-monthly.co.uk/content/0503/two.htm.

9   Ibid.
10 Varzi was, in his time, regarded as a great driver who became a drug addict (see chapter nine).
11 Official German Olympic report.
12 Snellman, *Golden Era of Grand Prix Racing.*
13 Fisher, *A Terrible Splendor.*
14 Henderson, *The Life of Fred Perry.*
15 *The Times,* London.
16 Fisher, op. cit.
17 Snellman, op. cit.
18 Myler, op. cit.
19 Wenn, op. cit.
20 Mogulof, *Foiled.*
21 In Mogulof, quoting *The New York Times,* 26 September 1935.
22 Quoted in Mogulof.
23 Taruffi, *Works Driver.*
24 Bachrach, *The Nazi Olympics.*
25 Quoted in Mogulof.
26 From www.london.diplo.de/.../Interwar__Years__Seite.html:

Of the Weimar period there is only a pathetic little memorial, the tombstone which Ambassador Leopold von Hoesch put up in the front garden of 9 Carlton House Terrace on the spot where he buried his beloved dog, an Alsatian. *Giro, ein treuer Begleiter! London, im Februar 1934, Hoesch,* the inscription reads. Two years later the ambassador died from a stroke in his Carlton House Terrace residence. He was only 55, but continuous worries about his new masters who had taken over in Berlin in 1933 and the strain which they put on Anglo-German relations were too much for him.

The British government bid him an impressive farewell. His coffin was taken on a gun-carriage from Carlton House Terrace to Victoria Station. The funeral cortège was led by two companies of the Grenadier Guards while a 19-gun salute was fired in St. James' Park.

27 *Daily Mirror,* London.
28 *The Times,* London.
29 Ibid.
30 Wenn, op. cit.
31 The Olympic movement has not been able to escape politics, of course, although there is a rich seam of irony in this talk of an American boycott because, in 1980, President Jimmy Carter forbade the American team from attending the Moscow Games – the Soviet Union had invaded Afghanistan (compounding the irony, as I write these words, the United States is in the ninth year of its Afghan invasion). Margaret Thatcher, who wanted the British team to follow the American move, discovered that the British IOC was independent. They chose to attend but at

the opening ceremony carried the Olympic flag rather than the Union Jack. The American 1980 boycott provoked the Soviet Union and most of the Eastern Bloc to boycott the 1984 Los Angeles Games.

5

OLYMPIC HEIGHTS

The 1936 Olympic Games in Berlin will always belong to two men, the Austrian corporal and the sharecropper's son. Seeing it this way has become virtually a historical truism, and rightly so, but it's a shame because the year contained far more than the Summer Games, and the Summer Games contained far more than the two men.

By year's end, Hitler would have impressed the world, gotten away with anti-Jewish sanctions, combined a successful Winter Olympics with the Summer, have an invincible grip on Grand Prix racing, be celebrating a blue-blooded German who won the French Open and reached the Wimbledon final, and glorifying a model Aryan (photographically, anyway) who went to the United States and whipped a black man for the World Heavyweight Championship.

Even those Germans with the most profound misgivings about the whole Nazi experience must have been impressed, and those who supported the Nazis were now far into deification. The triumphal progress – from early February when the Winter Games began to mid-October when the German soccer team charmed Glasgow and Dublin – confirmed, accelerated and deepened it all.

Hitler began the New Year with legislation banning Jews from employing anyone under 35 and, a day later, told the League of Nations that his treatment of Jews was none of their business. He felt the league was interfering with German sovereignty, and therefore restricting him which, by 1936 and the deification, was intolerable.

There is a story, however, that when Baillet-Latour, as president of the IOC, went to Garmisch-Partenkirchen before the Winter Games[1] and saw all the anti-Semitic posters and placards he told Hitler they would have to come down or the Games would be called into question. If this is true, Baillet-Latour must have been the last man to tell Hitler what to do. The veracity of the story is suspect because Goebbels at least understood the damage rampant, public anti-Semitism could do before and during the two Olympic Games. As a result the posters and placards came down, in Garmisch-Partenkirchen and Berlin, and the rabid publication *Der Stürmer* was withdrawn.

Rudi Ball, the leading German ice hockey player and devastating goal scorer, became a central figure because, as a Jew, he was living in voluntary exile in France. He had symbolic value. His teammate, Gustav Jaenecke, made the extraordinary (and dangerous) decision to refuse to play unless Ball was picked. Ball himself made a condition of returning that his family could leave Germany. The Nazis realised they were not cornered because, by picking Ball, they gave themselves cover against charges of anti-Semitism, allayed the Americans calling for a Berlin boycott and increased Germany's chances of an ice hockey medal.

The Winter Games faced an immediate problem: a lack of snow. Hitler could not govern the weather and chaos threatened. Some competitors decamped to St Moritz for training while contingency plans were actioned:

A giant Olympic ski-jump, with a tower 142ft high, had been completed in the winter of 1934. Around its base, where the jumpers would land after travelling up to 300ft through the air, was a stadium with space for 150,000 people. The Riessersee bob-run had been remodelled and rebuilt, with curves sharper and more steeply banked. To check the angles and the gradients, a car had been driven down the run during the summer months, and now, in the winter, it had been lined with blocks of ice cut from the Riesser lake. On the valley floor a new ice stadium, with an artificially cooled rink 100ft by 200ft, had been built: the wooden stands surrounding it could accommodate 12,000 spectators, and they included a post office and press headquarters, with 10 soundproof booths for broadcasting – facilities which seemed ultramodern in the context of winter sports. The whole complex had been tested, and found satisfactory, during the German championships of 1935.[2]

The Nazis were nervous. Here was the first chance to spread before the world the Germany which they wanted everyone to see, and the unprecedented preparations for a Winter Games mirrored that.

Sir Eric Phipps, British ambassador in Berlin, messaged Anthony Eden, the Foreign Secretary, just before the Games were due to begin: 'The German government attach enormous importance to the Olympic Games from the from the point of view of propaganda, and hope to be able to take the opportunity of impressing foreign countries with the capacity and solidity of the Nazi regime.'[3]

Snow did fall …

The seriousness of the Nazi approach was also mirrored by the fact that although Hitler (as head of state) opened the Games, he took with him many of the leading Nazis, including Goebbels and Göring.

Apart from the absence of the anti-Semitic posters and placards, the Nazis were 'extremely nervous' that some unforeseen incident would disturb the image they had created and were still creating. The American team arrived and a special envoy from the Ministry of Foreign Affairs was sent from Berlin to 'cosset the United States contingent' while 'special care' was taken to protect the Spanish team from any form of racism because their swarthy features made them distinctly non-Nordic.[4]

The Games attracted competitors from twenty-eight countries (675 men, 80 women) and seventeen events. These included Alpine skiing events for the first time, although the Austrian and Swiss racers boycotted the Games because ski instructors were considered professional (and thus ineligible).

Sonja Henie, a Norwegian figure skater who had competed at the Chamonix Games in 1924 then won at St Moritz in 1928 and Lake Placid in 1932, now added Garmisch with all seven judges placing her first. She was so popular that 'police had to be called out to control the crowds around her in places as far apart as New York City and Prague'.[5]

In the ice hockey Germany, even with Ball, faltered and finished fifth while Great Britain (with a stiffening of Canadians) took the gold medal. One incident did threaten. The Germany-Canada match became so physical that officials – and Göring and Goebbels – implored the crowd to remain calm and exhorted the players to chase the puck rather than each other.

Overall, the image was enhanced, not least by the efficiency of the transport from Munich, which allowed a total of 500,000 spectators to watch the Games. William Shirer, American broadcaster and journalist, wrote:

GARMISCH-PARTENKIRCHEN, February

This has been a more pleasant interlude than I expected. Much hard work for Tess and myself from dawn to midnight, covering the Winter Olympics, too many S.S. troops and military about, but the scenery of the Bavarian Alps, particularly at sunrise and sunset, superb, the mountain air exhilarating, the rosy-cheeked girls in their ski-ing outfits generally attractive, the games exciting, especially the bone-breaking ski-jump-ing, the bob-races (also bone-breaking and sometimes actually 'death-defying'), the hockey matches, and Sonja Henie. And on the whole the Nazis have done a wonder-ful propaganda job. They've greatly impressed most of the visiting foreigners with the lavish but smooth way in which they've run the games and with their kind manners, which to us who came from Berlin of course seemed staged. I was so alarmed at this that I gave a luncheon for some of our businessmen and invited Douglas Miller, our commercial attaché in Berlin, and the best-informed man on Germany we have in our Embassy, to enlighten them a little. But they told *him* what things were like, and Doug scarcely got a word in. Most of the correspondents a little peeved at a piece in the *Völkische Beobachter* quoting Birchall of the New York *Times* to the effect that there has been nothing military about these games and that correspondents who so reported were inaccurate. Westbrook Pegler especially resented this. To-night he seemed a little concerned that the Gestapo might pick him up for what he has writ-ten, but I don't think so. The 'Olympic spirit' will prevail for a fortnight or so more ...[6]

In late February, the German soccer team made a brief Iberian tour, beating Spain 2-1 in Barcelona and Portugal 3-1 in Lisbon. However, in March they lost 3-2 to Hungary in Budapest.

By then the Germans had entered the Rhineland, the area of Germany which had been de-militarised under the Treaty of Versailles after the First World War. Germany retained political control but were forbidden to have troops in it. Hitler gambled that the French would not use force if he sent the German army in, and they did not.

The Grand Prix season began at Monaco in April where Louis Chiron, who had signed for Mercedes, put the car on pole from Nuvolari in the Alfa Romeo. Rain drowned the race and on the opening lap one of the cars left oil at the harbour side chicane. On the next lap cars spun and crashed in all directions but eventually from it Caracciola emerged in the lead and on a strategy of not stopping for fuel or tyres. The race now turned on whether he could run safely to the end – another driver had dropped petrol when he hit a wall and ruptured his fuel tank. He did run safely to the end and beat Varzi (Auto Union) by 1 minute and 48 seconds. That made the big scoreboard won twenty-one, lost three.

The Monaco Grand Prix was entirely normal and innocent but the next race, at Tripoli, certainly was not. Libya was an Italian colony and Mussolini was in the process of proclaiming a fascist *imperium* – power – which made Italy great again. In fact the *Gran Consiglio del Fascismo*, the highest body in the country, made the proclamation on the day before the Tripoli race. The events in Rome 'made the sporting event an important political demonstration' for Mussolini.[7]

Clearly the Germans knew of this in advance because although Hühnlein could not attend the race (he was needed elsewhere) Hitler's Head of Chancellery – Philipp Bouhler, a very powerful man – flew from Berlin in special plane, calling at Rome. Dr Karl Feuereissen, the Auto Union team manager, was told to take charge of the arrangements for Bouhler and his party when they landed. Was Feuereissen also told of the political significance?

Stuck, the Austrian, led in his Auto Union but was given a 'SLOW' signal from the pit and obeyed it, allowing the Italian Varzi to come up in his Auto Union. The race reports are unclear, and understandably so, but Varzi eventually won it by 4.4 seconds (a very tight margin in the era) and both drivers reacted with fury when they realised what had been going on – Varzi because he felt humiliated, Stuck because he felt cheated. Whatever, that made it won twenty-two, lost three.

A week later they raced at Carthage but there was (and is) no suggestion of political meddling. Quite the contrary. Varzi led but on the long, fast straight a gust of wind seems to have destabilised the car and it spun, somersaulted repeatedly and thrashed itself to pieces. Varzi was unhurt. Caracciola won it by two laps from an Alfa Romeo and that made it won twenty-three, lost three.

Fred Perry was in the wrong mood and the wrong physical fitness for the French Open, although he reached the final against von Cramm. He had been injured the year before and not perhaps fully recovered, and although he was contemplating turning professional he did not feel Britain was making much of an effort to keep him amateur.

In Paris, von Cramm took him into a fifth set, the stage at which Perry's speed and strength crushed opponents. Von Cramm's service had murder in it, he was playing long, straight drives and Perry's backhand broke down. Von Cramm took this fifth set 6–0 and regained the title.

Moving into June, Varzi indulged his temperament in Spain when the cars contested the Penya Rhin Grand Prix at Montjuich, Barcelona. Auto Union had two kinds of car and Varzi could not have the one he wanted (it went to Rosemeyer) so he refused to race. Nuvolari (Alfa Romeo) returned after injury and won it from Caracciola in the Mercedes by 3.4 seconds. That made it won twenty-three, lost four.

The Eifelrennen at the Nürburgring was run in heavy rain; fog lifted just before the start. A crowd of 300,000 watched Nuvolari lead but, when the fog came back, Rosemeyer – who, legend insists, could see through fog – powered his Auto Union past the Alfa Romeo and won it by more than 2 minutes, making it won twenty-four, lost four.

On 15 July the United States Olympic team left New York for Germany on the SS *Manhattan*. There would, literally, be no turning back. The Nazis now felt they could solve one outstanding problem without fear of consequences. Gretel Bergmann, the outstanding Jewish women's high jumper, was informed by letter that she was not good enough for the team but could buy tickets to watch if she wanted. There had been Rudi Ball at Garmisch-Partenkirchen, whose presence had been tolerated for strategic reasons, and there would be Helene Mayer, the half Jewish fencer, in Berlin. That was all.

By then Max Schmeling had been in the United States for some five weeks preparing for his heavyweight fight against Joe Louis. Schmeling was, of course, a former world champion and Louis, a ferocious destroyer of opponents, unbeaten in his twenty-three professional fights. Of them, only four had gone the distance and his victims included Hans Birkie from Hamburg, beaten on a technical knockout[8] at Pittsburgh in 1935, Primo Carnera (the Italian 'Ambling Alp'), who lasted six rounds, American King Levinsky, who lasted 2 minutes and 21 seconds, and Max Baer, who lasted four rounds. Reportedly both Levinsky and Baer were frightened men when they stepped into the ring.

Schmeling would not be. 'Why should I be afraid?' he would say. 'This boxing is my business, my trade, my profession. I have been hit before and I did not like it, I admit, but I was not scared then and I will not be scared when Louis hits me.'[9]

The general feeling about the fight, however, was that Schmeling represented just another opponent on the Louis ascent to a world championship fight against the current holder, James J. Braddock.

The Nazi propaganda seems to have shared this view and was certainly not, at this stage, trying to create a struggle between an example of the Aryan master race and a representative of an inferior race. No doubt this was tempered by the perception of what could befall Schmeling when Louis got his hands on him. The *Reich Sports Journal* wrote of 'not much enthusiasm' for the fight and 'criticised those Germans who had organised an excursion to attend'.[10]

Arno Hellmis, German journalist and radio commentator who always referred to Louis as 'the Negro', wrote:

The racial factor is placed strongly in the foreground, and it hoped that the representative of the white race will succeed in halting the unusual rise of the Negro. In fact, there is no doubt that Max Schmeling, when he enters the ring on Thursday evening, will have the sympathy of all white spectators on his side, and the knowledge of this will be important moral support for him.[11]

Perhaps sections of the American press, though, wanted a political fight. Schmeling was asked if Hitler had sent him good wishes but brushed the question aside by saying that Hitler was a politician and why would he spend time coming to watch the boat depart? Certainly some American journalists – who knew that Schmeling had been fighting in the United States from 1928, was a good man and had an American Jewish manager – created the inevitable (and tedious) labels which boxing seems to need. One dubbed him the 'Heil Hitler Hero', which is so corny and contrived it becomes non-political.

The politics would begin after the fight.

Schmeling thought he had found a weakness. He had watched hours of film and noticed that when Louis thrust in a jab he dropped his left hand – and left himself open. He would not be open for long but Schmeling would not need long. There seems no doubt that Schmeling prepared very thoroughly and Louis perhaps less so.

The fight was to be at the open-air Yankee Stadium and on the day of it heavy rain forced a postponement. Next day Schmeling quickly found that the Louis punches hurt and Louis found, after three cagey rounds, that Schmeling could punch too. In the fourth round, he landed a right-hander to the head and Louis went down for the first time in his professional career. He never recovered and took more and more punishment until, in the twelfth round, a combination of punches sent Louis down again and he was counted out. Hellmis, hoarse, bayed into his ringside microphone 'out … out … out … out …' in time to the count.

Langston Hughes, a celebrated African-American writer, was at the right and wrote: 'I walked down Seventh Avenue and saw grown men weeping like children, and women sitting in the curbs with their head in their hands. All across the country that night when the news came that Joe was knocked out, people cried.'[12]

The reaction by Schmeling and in Germany was the opposite.

Schmeling was quoted by a German reporter as saying: 'At this moment I have to tell Germany, I have to report to the Führer in particular, that the thoughts of all my countrymen were with me in this fight; that the Führer and his faithful people were thinking of me. This thought gave me the strength to succeed in this fight. It gave me the courage and the endurance to win this victory for Germany's colours.'[13]

By radio – presumably courtesy of Hellmis – Schmeling was able to speak to his mother and wife and 'in a lower voice, as if self-conscious in the crowded dressing room, he appended a *Heil Hitler*'.[14]

Goebbels telegrammed: 'Congratulations. I know you won it for Germany. We are proud of you. Heil Hitler.' He later wrote in his diary: 'In the twelfth round Schmeling beats the Negro with a knockout. Wonderful, dramatic, exciting fight. Schmeling fought for Germany and won the whites v blacks - and the whites was a German.'

Hitler himself sent Schmeling's wife flowers with a message attached: 'For the wonderful victory of your husband, our greatest German boxer, I must congratulate you with all my heart.'

The Hellmis commentary achieved a fame of its own within Germany and soon enough cinemas were showing film of the fight.

Schmeling had delivered Goebbels a priceless gift. Goebbels would know exactly what to do with it.

A day after the fight, the Japanese became the first team to arrive in Berlin for the Olympic Games. They had spent twelve days on the Trans-Siberian railway and, once they were settled in the Olympic Village, the Berliners found their behaviour slightly eccentric. No doubt this was a significant discovery. The rest of the world did not necessarily look like Germany but the rest of the world was coming to Germany.

That same day the Torch Run began from Olympia. By the time it was delivered to the Olympic Stadium for the opening ceremony on 1 August it would have covered 3,075km through seven countries.

There were two Grands Prix – Hungary and Milan – in quick succession. A crowd of 100,000 came to the tight track in gardens in Budapest and saw Rosemeyer lead but slow, so that Nuvolari (Alfa Romeo) stole by to win it: won twenty-four, lost five.

In Milan, Varzi persuaded Auto Union to enter a car for him – Mercedes did not go – but the Sempione Park circuit was tight like Budapest, favouring the more nimble Alfa Romeo, and after a hectic duel Nuvolari won it: won twenty-four, lost six.

Fred Perry had made a complete recovery by Wimbledon and was determined to take a third championship there before turning professional. He reached the semi-finals in straight sets and even there Budge took only one off him.

Von Cramm moved through his first three rounds in straight sets, too, but against Enrique Maier – leading Spanish player and a friend – he went to 10-8, 6-2, 2-6 and finally 6-2 to reach Jack Crawford in the quarter finals. It was the first time they had met on grass and anti-climactic: the court was slippery, making movement more difficult for a man of Crawford's size, and everything went wrong for him in what *The Times* called a 'dismaying collapse'. Von Cramm had him 6-1, 7-5, 6-4.

Bunny Austin in the semi-finals provided long, fast-moving rallies but von Cramm countered with superior speed, a variety of services and he worked wider angles. He won it 8-6, 6-3, 2-6, 6-3 and that meant Perry in the final.

It was even more anti-climactic than Crawford. When von Cramm first served he pulled a muscle and Perry murdered him. Von Cramm had to be persuaded to allow an announcement explaining to the crowd, some of whom had slept out overnight, why he had played as he had and apologised 'for not being able to play better'.

That was the beginning of July, a month which distilled the potent and almost bewildering combination of the political and the sporting: on 11 July, Hitler recognised Austrian independence; that day at Randall's Island, New York, Jesse Owens qualified for the United States Olympic team by winning the 100m and 200m sprints, adding the long jump; on 19 July, General Franco arrived in the southern port of Cadiz, a springboard for conquering Spain; on 25 July Hitler recognised the Italian occupation of Abyssinia; a day later the German Grand Prix was run at the Nürburgring.

The British driver T.P. (Thomas) Cholmondeley-Tapper caught the atmosphere:

I was not surprised to see a crowd of mammoth proportions on the bright, cloudy morning of the race. All night long [the nearby village of] Adenau had seemed in continual uproar, as thousands streamed through on their way to the course, and when I left my hotel a solid throng was moving slowly towards the Nürburgring, but my pass and the notice on the car I was driving, ensured that I was waved through halted traffic by the Nazi soldiers who were on duty everywhere. German enthusiasm for the sport of motor-racing is, in my experience, quite unmatched and almost fanatical. Some 350,000 people had come to witness the battle for the Grosser Preis, and like mushrooms after a shower or rain, hundreds of little tents had appeared overnight alongside the fourteen-mile course.

There was a theatrical air about the pit area, with innumerable flags and bunting bright against the dark green pines, and officials resplendent in many-hued uniforms. My pit was conspicuously naïve in equipment: a few cans of petrol, an odd spanner or two and my two spare wheels contrasted unfavourably with the high-powered efficiency of the big firms, but when eventually the twenty competing cars were lined up in front of the grandstand, and 'Deutschland über Alles' ponderously echoed through the crowd, I was proud to see the Maserati, the only spot of English green amid a predominantly red and white field. Once again I endured an uncomfortable interlude while surging thousands gave the mechanically militant Nazi salute, and then we prepared our cars for the start.[15]

The race was straightforward, Rosemeyer beating Stuck by almost 4 minutes although during it Lang, leading, pitted to give his Mercedes to Caracciola. The crowd did not like that and hissed and booed until a loudspeaker announcement told them Lang had done it because he needed medical treatment. He had split a finger.

That was won twenty-five, lost six. That was also Sunday 26 July, with the Olympic opening ceremony on the following Saturday.

The Torch Run, which that Sunday was coming 265.1km through Bulgaria, had been organised with military planning, rehearsals and precision. In that sense it stands as symbolic of the whole Nazi approach to the Olympics. Each of the 3,075 runners – allocated 1km each – had a specially manufactured torch so that its flame would not go out, and of course back-up if it did. Each of the 3,075 sectors had been examined, tested. A special German radio broadcasting unit tracked the progress, creating a mounting sense of anticipation within Germany and particularly Berlin:

Herr Klingeberg, Director of the Sport Department of the Organizing Committee, and Herr Carstensen of the Propaganda Ministry covered the entire route

Outside the Olympic Stadium in Berlin, 1936.
(Courtesy of Josef Jind ich Šechtl)

Youths demonstrating at the Berlin Olympics, July
1936. (Wikimedia Commons)

Whether or not the Nazis would allow Jews
to compete in the Olympics was a subject of
international discussion leading up to the Games.
(*The New York Times*, 7 June)

YIELDING BY NAZIS ON OLYMPICS LIKELY

Resolution Assuring Right of Jews Slated for Adoption by Committee Today.

UNITY OF OPINION SEEN

Berlin's Fear Games Might Be Held Elsewhere Regarded as Factor in New Attitude.

Wireless to THE NEW YORK TIMES.

VIENNA, June 6.—A resolution establishing the right of Jews, whether Germans or not, to participate in the Olympic Games will be introduced at tomorrow's open session of the Olympic Games Committee here, and it is virtually certain to be passed.

In a preliminary conversation today so much unity of opinion was realized that Dr. Theodor Lewald, head of the German Olympic Games Committee, told your correspondent:

"While I don't wish to comment on the situation in advance, you can say that in a preliminary discussion we have agreed about the questions before us relating to the next Olympic Games and the conditions under which they will be held. A satisfactory conclusion will be reached."

Colleagues of Dr. Lewald are Litter von Halt and the Duke of Mecklenburg-Schwerin, also members of the German committee, and Dr. Karl Diem, member of the Reich Committee for Athletics, represents the German Government.

Reich Seen as Yielding.

The Olympic Fire in
Berlin, 1936. (Courtesy of
Josef Jind ich Šechtl)

Berlin, 1936. (Courtesy of
Josef Jind ich Šechtl)

Hitler watching the opening ceremony of the
Winter Olympics, Garmisch-Partenkirchen,
Bavaria, February 1936. (Wikimedia Commons)

Hitler saluting the Games
with Baillet-Latour, Garmisch-
Partenkirchen, Bavaria, February
1936. (Wikimedia Commons)

German high jumper Elfriede Kaun at the Olympic trials in Wuppertal, 1936. (Wikimedia Commons)

Ball gymnastics, Germany, 1933. (Wikimedia Commons)

Pentathlon awards ceremony at the Berlin Olympics, 1936. (Wikimedia Commons)

A sculpture commemorating Jesse Owens and his four gold medals at the 1936 Olympic Games. The German sculptor, Branko Medencia, had to seek special permission from the Olympic Committee to use Olympic rings on the statue. (Courtesy of the Jesse Owens Museum/ Charlie Siefried)

Hitler being shown the Tatra T77 engine at the Berlin Motor Show, March 1934. (Wikimedia Commons)

Motorcyclists lining up at the Saxtorp Grand Prix, Sweden, 1937. (Courtesy of Nowotny)

Robin Hanson driving a Maserati, Donington Grand Prix, 1937. (Courtesy of James Hamilton)

Percy Maclure driving a Riley, Donington Grand Prix, 1937. (Courtesy of James Hamilton)

"Hapgood thought standing at attention should have been sufficient," *Says HENRY ROSE from Berlin*

Henry Rose, *Daily Express* correspondent, commented, 'my lasting impression is of eleven England professional footballers lined up in the centre of the field giving the Nazi salute'. (*Daily Express*, 16 May 1938)

Villa booed by Germans, refuse Nazi salute

From HENRY ROSE
BERLIN, Sunday.

ASTON VILLA football team were booed off the field by 110,000 people at the Olympic Stadium in Berlin this afternoon, after they had defeated a German eleven (ten of them were ex-Austrian internationals) by three goals to two.

They had irritated the crowd all through the match by playing the offside game.

The booing grew when, towards the end of the match, Massie, Villa's Scottish international right half, came in collision with Schmaus, the German left back.

Schmaus was carried off the field on a stretcher, but was able to return.

After the match the German players lined up to give the Nazi salute. The Villa team, with the exception of Allen, the captain, and one or two others, ran off the field.

Allen tried to call the players back, but they refused to return. Finally Allen joined the rest and the band tried to drown the din of booing.

It was an unfortunate end to a bad game. The view of Football Association officials who watched the game was that all the good work of the previous day, when England had defeated Germany 6 3 in the international in a friendly atmosphere had been completely destroyed.

LATEST
CENTRAL 8000

Weather: showery (see Page 11)

In contrast, Aston Villa refuse to give the Nazi salute in their game against Germany on the same day, being booed off the field. (*Daily Express*, 16 May 1938)

German boxer Max Schmeling, 1938. (Courtesy of William C. Green)

HENRY ROSE in his DAILY SPORTLIGHT says

No Schmeling boycott:Gate of £200,000

WE shall soon see a return to the million dollar gate in boxing. Max Schmeling, Germany's sporting ambassador, has arrived in New York all set for his world championship fight against Joe Louis in the Yankee Stadium on June 22.

Something seems to have gone wrong with the threats by the anti-Nazi organisations to boycott the fight, for a message I received from Mike Jacobs, the promoter, last night, says that he has received advance bookings totalling £20,000 —————— lunch on board at Southampton by the steamship company.

They'd better make the most of it. They won't be drinking too much champagne on their 3s. a day allowance.

Threats from anti-Nazi organisations to boycott the Schmeling–Louis fight fell flat. (*Daily Express*, 11 May 1938)

The first boxing match between Joe Louis (left) and Max Schmeling (right), New York, June 1936. (Courtesy of *World Telegram*)

Sportler und Turner stimmen am 10. April für den Führer
Adolf Hitler!

An advert in an Austrian newspaper directly calls for sportsmen and athletes to support Hitler; a further example of Hitler's politicisation of sport. (*Neue Freie Presse*, 8 April 1938)

Germany Challenges Britain In Motor-Cycle "Derby"

STRONG OPPOSITION TO GEORG MEIER

Will No. 1 Be First Again?

WHO will win to-day's Senior T.T.? The blue riband of the motor-cycle racing season, this will be the 77th Tourist Trophy race held in the Isle of Man, and it brings to a conclusion the 28th meeting since the first race 32 years ago.

Six nations will be represented in the field of 47 riders and machines—Great Britain, Germany, Italy, Finland, Australia, and South Africa.

The Isle of Man is also represented, and Ireland is to the fore with six competitors.

EVERYTHING O.K.? — Scrutineer Reuben Harveyson examining the "works" Norton presented by J. H. (Crasher) White as a preliminary to to-day's race.

ROYAL VISIT

Great Britain, Germany, Italy, Finland, Australia and South Africa competed in the Isle of Man TT races, just months before the Second World War broke out. (*Isle of Man Examiner*, 16 June 1939) personally in September, 1935 and arranged all of the details of organization. The torches were distributed in March, 1936, and thus all of the preparations for the success of the event were completed at an early date. The relay run over a distance of 1885 miles was carried out exactly according to schedule without a mishap of any kind.[16]

The planning can be illustrated by just one more example among many:

> The season tickets for the various sports were placed on sale on June 1st, 1935, and by July, 1935 the first million Reichsmarks in entrance money had been received, the second million being attained in January, 1936. At the beginning of February, 1936 the single admission tickets were placed on sale. The attempt to open a public sale in April, 1936 at the Headquarters of the Organizing Committee had to be given up because of the huge crowds which assembled, thousands standing in line from the earliest hours of the morning. At our request the Deutsche Bank und Disconto-Gesellschaft placed its principal banking rooms in the centre of the city at our disposal for this purpose, and on June 15th, 1936 the public sale of tickets was inaugurated there. In the meantime, however, the total receipts from the sale of tickets had already reached 4,000,000 Reichsmarks and finally attained a figure of 9,000,000 Reichsmarks, the Stadium and other centres of competition being sold out for practically every event except a few preliminary competitions.[17]

When the athletes from various countries arrived in Berlin many of them found a military atmosphere in the city. Marty Glickman, the American sprinter, would remember arriving by train and someone discreetly coming up to him and asking if he was Jewish 'because I am, too'. It had to be discreet because the platform was full of people in uniform.

Doris Carter, Australian high jumper, remembered:

> It was very obvious that Hitler was preparing for war – more than every second person wore a uniform of some sort. But we were led to believe that they were very afraid of the Russian Bear and had to prepare to be ready for any invasion from that direction. Hitler of course, was very cunning. He was, as we learnt later, really facing in the opposite direction, and he planned accordingly. We heard that Hitler could travel from the Reich Chancellory to the stadium via a tunnel – we walked through tunnels from the dressing rooms to the arena. All these were prepared for air raid shelters for the Berliners if needed.[18]

Dorothy Odam, British high jumper, remembered: 'We woke every morning to the sound of marching feet. When I got to the window, I could see young people with shovels held like rifles over their shoulders. I learned that they were the Hitler Youth. When we went shopping we were greeted "Guten Morgen. Heil Hitler!" We replied, "Guten Morgen. King George!"'[19]

Pat Norton, Australian swimmer, remembered:

> The Sports fields were guarded by Nazi SA Troopers. Their uniforms were very forbidding to see for the first time. The tunics and trousers are black, with black boots and leggings. The tunics are belted with red armbands with the Nazi swastika emblazoned on them, but it is the black helmets that add a sombre picture to this. They come low down on the forehead, level with the eyebrows, giving the wearer a sinister look. I became used to them after a while, but I did not like them. Added to this if one were to pass them (which was quite often) a snappy Nazi salute and a *'Heil Hitler'* would greet you. For quite a while I did not know what they were saying as they ran both words into one another, *"ile 'itler."*[20]

All this happened while the Nazis were trying to demonstrate to visitors that they had reached a peace-loving, unmilitaristic country. Perhaps the structure and nature of the country the Nazis were creating precluded it ever being anything but militaristic. Hitler himself would open the Games in full military uniform. As he entered the stadium, most of his entourage were in full military uniforms. Uncounted numbers in the crowd were in full military uniforms, too. The whole crowd were primed to give the Nazi salute, and did repeatedly throughout the Games.

Anything anti-Semitic, however, had been taken down and there is no doubt that Germany was on its best behaviour.

> Ordinary people were longing to meet foreigners – a pleasure scarcely ever granted them – and as a result visitors found themselves almost overwhelmed with friendliness and hospitality. Often the reception was made still warmer by an element of relief: many Berliners had secretly feared that people would shun the Games, put off by the excesses of the regime, so that they were overjoyed when foreigners actually arrived.
>
> Newcomers were bombarded with helpful advice. People arriving by sea at Bremen discovered an Olympic office established there, ready with help and information. Those approaching Berlin by train found representatives of the German Transport Office on board, and anyone who had not yet secured accommodation was able to make a booking during the final stages of the journey. Those coming by car were similarly cosseted, being met on the outskirts of the city and given advice about the best route to their destination. In Berlin itself the visitors found official interpreters everywhere …[21]

Foreign visitors were awestruck by the Olympic Stadium and the other Olympic buildings nearby, set in their own parkland and fed by a special, extensive railway station. The athletes were awestruck by the Olympic Village, set in the countryside to the west of Berlin, with its facilities (including special menus for each country) and houses (each named after a German city) for the athletes.

No doubt Germany was making an even more favourable impression because so many people had come expecting to find a concentration camp – and now found themselves among a population which looked fit and happy, in an impressive city bent on looking after their every whim, with an Olympic Games unfolding on a scale never seen before; and Germanic thoroughness made it all work.

Goebbels' initial instinct had been correct. The visitors were living through the greatest propaganda coup of all time.

Who really noticed the athletes who were not there, like the American hurdler and Jew Milton Green who, troubled and not sure what the implications were, took advice from his rabbi in Boston and decided to boycott. Newspapers showed no particular interest, he said nothing publicly and felt nobody knew he was boycotting.

Judith Deutsch, *the* Viennese swimming champion in 1935 and a Jew, was inevitably selected to represent Austria but boycotted, with fellow swimmers Ruth Langer and Lucie Goldner. Deutsch said, 'I refuse to enter a contest in a land which so shamefully persecutes my people.' Boycott or not, the Austrians did not appreciate Deutsch saying that and banned her anyway.

Werner Seelenbinder, a German boxer and wrestler, became a committed communist and had already been in trouble for refusing to give the Nazi salute at the 1935 German championships. He was persuaded to compete in the Olympics so at the medal ceremony he make a rude gesture rather than give the salute – but in the wrestling he finished only fourth.

As is in the nature of it, these people and their principles were lost in the background. There was a great deal happening in the foreground, most famously when Jesse Owens won the 100m, 200m, long jump and as a member of the 4x100m relay. Of that, more in a moment.

Owens, with a running action like a piston, won the 100m in a time of 10.3 seconds, which equalled the Olympic record. Hitler was there to witness it. Hitler did not, however, invite Owens up in order to congratulate him but left the stadium. This was interpreted as Hitler, enraged that a black man had beaten the white men, stormed out.

The background was important and almost nobody knew what had happened there the day before. Baillet-Latour pointed out to Hitler that he either had to congratulate every gold medal winner – not just the Germans – or none. Hitler reasonably pointed out that he had a country to run and would therefore not be doing the congratulations (although he had a private box behind his balcony at the stadium and would congratulate some of the German winners there without any publicity).

Far from storming out, Owens would say that, when he passed in front of Hitler's balcony, Hitler 'arose, waved his hand at me, and I waved back at him. I think the writers showed bad taste in criticising the man of the hour in Germany.'[22]

This is confirmed by John Woodruff, the American athlete who was there and saw it.[23]

Owens and Ralph Metcalfe, the American sprinter who had finished second in the 100m, were, according to the *Daily Express*, 'conducted towards Hitler's box so that they could salute him from a distance'.

Whether Hitler was inwardly enraged but hid that publicly is unknown. He has been quoted as saying (by von Schirach, who was on the balcony with him) that the Americans should be 'ashamed of themselves letting Negroes win medals for them. I shall not shake hands with this Negro.'

It leads to a strange story which surfaced in the British press in 2009, saying that a German reporter, Siegfried Mischner, claimed Owens carried a photograph in his wallet of Hitler shaking his hand before he left the stadium. Mischner further claimed that he had witnessed this, that it took place behind a stand so the world's press missed it, and that in the 1960s Owens, who still felt writers were showing bad taste, tried to get him – Mischner – and the German press to correct what really happened.

The decades of silence were explained by Mischner as a response to the post-war consensus that Hitler had behaved very badly towards Owens, and that this must continue.

What is not explained exists as simplicity itself. If Owens' sense of fair play demanded that the correct version be finally known, why did he not take the photograph out of his wallet and show it to the world? The world would have been very interested, as it remains.

Hitler certainly did storm out of Germany's second soccer match. They had beaten Luxembourg in the first, 9-0, but now lost 2-0 to Norway. Not only did Hitler storm out but, as it seems, he never went back to another soccer match in his life.

FIFA met during the Olympics and, although the next – in fact the second – World Cup was due in France in 1938, Germany applied to be host in 1942 (Brazil would subsequently apply too). No decision was ever made.

Traditionally the track and field climaxed with the relay races but the Americans faced a particular problem. They had too many good sprinters – six, in fact: Owens and Metcalfe, Foy Draper, Frank Wykoff, Marty Glickman and Sam Stoller. The last two were Jews.

Owens evidently felt that three gold medals were enough and his place should go to one of the others. He was told in no uncertain terms to shut up, and when white officials told the black men that in 1936 they did shut up. Owens and Metcalfe picked themselves, leaving the other four. Draper and Wykoff got the other two places.

For the rest of his life, Glickman insisted that:

anti-Semitism was the basic reason I believe that Sam and I didn't get to run in the Olympic Games. Here were the great black athletes who couldn't be kept off the winning podium – they were marvellous – but here were two rather obscure Jewish American athletes who could be kept from the winning podium so as not to further embarrass Adolf Hitler.[24]

If Glickman was right, Hitler had hijacked the United States relay team in the sense that he was picking half of it.

Gretel Bergmann, at home, understandably showed no interest in the Games or in how the jumper substituted for her fared. Dora Ratjen seems, according to the latest research, to have been born with uncertain genitalia but concealed this at the Olympic training camp by never showering with the other girls. He was ordered to room with Bergmann because she was Jewish and as a result under the strict Nazi laws he would not dare to let his hormones (if he had them) lead him to lay a hand upon her. She never saw him change out of his clothes either.[25]

The Nazi thinking must have been that if they entered him for the women's high jump he would have to win and bring even more glory to the Reich. Nor necessarily did Ratjen find himself in a position where he could refuse. As a member of the Hitler Youth he had do what he was told or else. In the women's high jump he finished fourth.

Helene Mayer won silver in the fencing and at the medal ceremony gave the stiff arm salute.

The man who built and organised the Olympic Village, Captain Wolfgang Fürstner, was a regular soldier and heavily involved in the German army's fitness programme. The Olympic Village proved an outstanding success but, some weeks before the Games began, Fürstner – a *Mischling* – was replaced by Lieutenant Colonel Werner von und zu Gilsa. Fürstner loyally made no complaints (in public, anyway; nobody knows what he might have said in private) and served under Gilsa.

Shortly after the Games, a banquet honoured Gilsa's contribution to making the Games a success. This, it seems, was too much for Fürstner who returned to his barracks and shot himself. Goebbels ordered the German press to report this as a car crash and the truth only emerged when foreign journalists heard about it and investigated.

William Shirer, broadcaster and journalist, gave a beautifully balanced summary:

The Olympic Games held in Berlin in August 1936 afforded the Nazis a golden opportunity to impress the world with the achievements of the Third Reich, and they made the most of it. The signs '*Juden unerwuenscht*' (Jews Not Welcome) were quietly hauled down from the shops, hotels, beer gardens and places of public entertainment, the persecution of the Jews and of the two Christian churches temporarily halted, and the country put on its best behaviour. No previous games had seen such a spectacular organization nor such a lavish display of entertainment.

Göring, Ribbentrop and Goebbels gave dazzling parties for the foreign visitors – the Propaganda Minister's 'Italian Night' on the Pfaueninsel near Wannsee gathered more than a thousand guests at dinner in a scene that resembled the Arabian Nights. The visitors, especially those from England and America, were greatly impressed by what they saw; apparently a happy, healthy, friendly people united under Hitler – a far different picture, they said, than they had got from reading the newspaper dispatches from Berlin.

And yet underneath the surface, hidden from the tourists during those splendid late-summer Olympic days in Berlin and indeed overlooked by most Germans or accepted by them with a startling passivity, there seemed to be – to a foreigner at least – a degrading transformation of German life.[26]

Hitler had hijacked the Olympic Games and recast it in a Nazi image. The hijacking did not end in Berlin on the final day of the Games either. The idea of a custom-designed stadium as the centrepiece became a necessity which endures to this day, and a custom-designed athlete's village, too. The Torch Run captures the Olympic idea so exquisitely that people are surprised it only began in 1936. Berlin set out a template which indicated that, if a host country has the will, the Games can be constantly expanded. They have been. The 4,066 athletes from forty-nine countries in 1936 had become about 10,500 from 204 by Beijing, 2008.

Hitler achieved something else. He brought a specific, political, *un*Olympic creed to the Games, shamelessly exploited them in the biggest propaganda exercise the world had ever seen – and got away with it. This is why Berlin 1936 will always belong to him or, if you prefer, will always be shared between him and the sharecropper's son.

The Grands Prix season continued regardless of the Olympics, and in fact the *Coppa Ciano* at Livorno was run on the second day of the Games. Mercedes did not go but Auto Union entered three cars. Even they could not defeat Nuvolari – won twenty-five, lost seven.

Mercedes did not go to the Coppa Acerbo either and Auto Union had problems of their own. Varzi was now becoming a morphine addict and a search party tried to find him in Rome. He came to the track but was in no state to race. In practice Stuck's front wheel came off at big speed and the car plunged into a cornfield. Stuck jumped clear and now he was in no state to race, either. Nuvolari's Alfa Romeo suffered engine problems and Rosemeyer won it – won twenty-six, lost seven.

In Switzerland, Caracciola took pole from Rosemeyer and Varzi, and thereby hangs a true motor-racing tale. Caracciola led and used some direct methods to keep Rosemeyer behind him. Fists were shaken and Caracciola was told by signs from the Clerk of the Course that he would be black-flagged (ordered immediately to the pits) if he did not let Rosemeyer through. Rosemeyer won it – won twenty-seven, lost seven.

In Italy, Nuvolari forced his Alfa Romeo into the lead but Rosemeyer sailed by on lap three – won twenty-eight, lost seven.

During September, the German army carried out its biggest exercises since 1914.

The German soccer team journeyed to Glasgow to play Scotland. Since the Olympics, they'd drawn 1-1 with Poland in Warsaw, beat Luxembourg 7-2 in Krefeld and Czechoslovakia 2-1 in Prague.

The *Glasgow Herald* wrote:

Efforts have been made by trade unions and other sections of the community to make the match a mater of politics, but it is to be hoped that enthusiasts who patronise the game will remember the words of the captain of the German team when he arrived at Renfrew Aerodrome on Monday: 'We come here as sportsmen, not as politicians.'

When the Germans played England at White Hart Lane … last season, a campaign similar to that now being experienced in Glasgow was waged, yet the game was played before a sporting crowd, and little or no trouble was experienced.

Several hundred German enthusiasts are expected to arrive at Queensferry this morning [Wednesday] by steamer. They will, it is understood, motor direct to Ibrox Park, and will return to the steamer immediately after the game.

A crowd of 60,000 waited 15 minutes for the German team to appear – they were held up in traffic – and then watched the German team come out in the Nazi colours of white shirts with red collars and cuffs, and black shorts. They had Nazi eagles on their shirts. 'The players lined up and gave a Nazi salute to the main stand to "loud applause", turned and saluted the opposite side, and again repeated the salute during both national anthems. The Scottish team refrained.'[27]

Scotland won 2-0, although it was evidently a disappointing performance. Jimmy Delaney of Celtic scored the goals although the crowd made up their minds that Fritz Szepan was the real star and dubbed him 'Saucepan'.

Dr Erbach of the German Football Association made all the right noises afterwards. 'I hope you will appreciate that we Germans can stand a defeat without bitterness and without resentment.' Or, as the *Glasgow Herald* summed up Erbach's speech: 'The game had proved that it was possible to fight without hatred.'

The German team flew to Dublin on the Thursday to play Ireland at Dalymount Park on the Saturday. They gave the Nazi salute again and, reportedly, some in the crowd returned it – although whether this was showing approval or disapproval is not clear. There was no doubt about the result. Ireland won 5-2 in front of 28,000 spectators.

In November, Germany and Italy drew 2-2 in Berlin and coincidentally Mussolini used the word 'Axis' for the first time to denote the bond between Germany and Italy. A friendship treaty had been signed a few weeks before.

Dick Seaman was invited by Alfred Neubauer to test a Mercedes at the Nürburgring in November. To Seaman it represented a chance to secure a place in the team for 1937 but at the same time that would open him up to accusations of complicity with the Nazis. He took advice from friends and one of them explained that sport 'has no frontiers' and Seaman set off for the test.

He was impressive and Neubauer summoned him again. Unfortunately the telegram was sent to Seaman, Ennismore Gardens, and his mother, thinking it was for her, opened it. She was horrified to see what it was and sought to dissuade Seaman because of the political climate.

Seaman, however, travelled to Monza for the second test. After it, Seaman wanted to sign, Neubauer wanted him to sign but Hühnlein had to adjudicate for the obvious political reasons, not forgetting that taking money out of Germany was tightly controlled.

Seaman must have sensed he would not be able to avoid becoming a political symbol, however passive he felt about politics.

Notes

1   Hart-Davis, *Hitler's Games*.
2   Ibid.
3   Quoted in Hart-Davis.
4   Hart-Davis, op. cit.

5   Wallechinsky, *The Complete Book of the Winter Olympics*.

6   Shirer, *The Rise and Fall of the Third Reich*.

7   Reuss, *Hitler's Motor Racing Battles*.

8   Technical knockout, awarded by the referee when he judges that one boxer cannot continue.

9   Myler, *Ring of Hate*.

10 Ibid.

11 Quoted in Myler.

12 McLaren, Joseph (ed.), *The Collected Works of Langston Hughes*, vol. 14 (University of Missouri press).

13 Quoted in Margolick, *Beyond Glory*.

14 Ibid.

15 Cholmondeley-Tapper, *Amateur Racing Driver*.

16 Official German Olympic report.

17 Ibid.

18 Daniels & Tedder, *A Proper Spectacle*.

19 Ibid.

20 Ibid.

21 Hart-Davis, op. cit.

22 *Daily Telegraph*, 11 August 2009.

23 Author's interview with Woodruff.

24 *The Nazi Olympics: Jewish Athletes (Part 2)*, YouTube.

25 Author's interview with Margaret Lambert. She referred to Ratjen as 'him/her/it' and at one point asked if she was embarrassing me talking about this difficult subject. I said, 'No, but it's making my eyes water thinking about it.'

26 Shirer, op. cit.

27 homepages.strath.ac.uk/.../Swastikas%20over%20Ibrox.html.

6

TORMENTED TENNIS

Auto Union were persuaded to compete in two races in South Africa, the charming but narrow and frightening seaside circuit at East London on 1 January, and Cape Town on 16 January.

It happened like this: Brud Bishop, a shrewd motor-racing promoter, met Baron Klaus von Oertzen at a party. The baron was the Auto Union representative in South Africa. Bishop made a sales pitch: bring some Auto Union racing cars, race them and it will create enormous interest – not least in the DKW models which were part of Auto Union. The baron agreed.[1]

They sent two cars by ship, to be driven by Rosemeyer and Ernst von Delius. The scope of what the Germans were doing is revealed by what they took: eight mechanics, a scientist, a tyre specialist, a timekeeper and manager, and, in equipment, 500 plugs, 146 tyres of various sizes and sixty wheels.

Rosemeyer's wife, Elly, flew him down in her Taifun[2] and it was a journey from another time: Belgrade, Athens 'after some rough moments over the Balkan mountains', Cairo, Khartoum, Nairobi and Johannesburg – eight days.

The races were handicaps and the Auto Unions had no chance as they were so heavily punished. Under the handicap, Rosemeyer (pole, scratch) started 52 minutes and 53 seconds behind the first man to go, and even Rosemeyer could not regain that over 211 miles, especially since the Auto Unions had experimental tyres which began to disintegrate. He finished fifth and that made the scoreboard won twenty-eight, lost eight.

Auto Union now debated whether it was worth going on to Cape Town but went and Rosemeyer started from scratch again, von Delius 2 minutes and 6 seconds in front of him. The organisers decided to use national flags to send each driver away from the grid, so that both the Germans were shown the swastika. By the time Rosemeyer was shown it, the drivers who had gone first had already covered nine laps. Von Delius won, beating Rosemeyer by 25 seconds – won twenty-nine, lost eight.

On 31 January Germany launched a long, important season of international soccer by drawing with Holland 2-2 in Düsseldorf. The team had a new coach, Sepp Herberger, who had joined the Nazi Party shortly after Hitler came to power. Herberger would become a legendary figure after the war but his role before it is less clear. Author Niels Havemann[3] has concluded Herberger 'never had anything to do with ideologies but he was willingly used for the inhuman ideology'.

Herberger, from a poor background – he started work at 14 – played for a team called Waldhof Mannheim at 17 and three times for Germany between 1921 and 1925 after service in the First World War. He became assistant manager to Dr Otto Nerz in 1932 and this endured to the Olympic Games, Germany's performance there against Norway and Hitler's disgust. Herberger took over from Nerz as *Reichsfußballtrainer*.

The long hand of Hitler would reach out and take hold of him. Herberger spent 1937 assembling and honing a team to redeem everything in the World Cup and then Nazi politics swept it aside. In January 1937 neither he nor anybody else could have imagined that.

That month, Hitler guaranteed the neutrality of Belgium and Holland, and banned any German from receiving a Nobel Prize.

In February, the German ambassador to Britain, Joachim von Ribbentrop, gave the Nazi salute to King George which was literally gesture politics but the main preoccupation of the day was the savage civil war in Spain, in which Germany was actively involved.

That month, Mercedes sent Seaman a draft contract. Hitler's permission had been needed, and sought, for him to join the team.

That month the Davis Cup draw was made in London too. In the first round of the European Zone, Germany were drawn against Austria.

The soccer team played twice, beating Luxembourg away 3-2 and France 4-0 in Stuttgart. They had four more 'friendly' matches before they would begin qualifying for the 1938 World Cup in June.

The attraction of getting the German Grand Prix cars to take part in the Vanderbilt Cup, a major motor race, at New York on 5 July was obvious enough but brought all the potential political problems. That aside, the Vanderbilt did clash with the Belgian Grand Prix in the sense that they were six days apart, and in an era of sea travel that was not enough time to get back.

Two American negotiators arrived in Berlin and on 19 April and, faced with specific demands by the ONS, were happy to give assurances that there would be no 'political protests' against the Germans, although how anyone could guarantee that Americans would not indulge in political protesting if they so desired is not at all clear. According to Auto Union, one of the negotiators, a Mr Abbott, said:

> that the Germans would without doubt be greeted with great enthusiasm by the organisers and by the Christian community, especially German-Americans, and could count on a gala reception. In addition, he would arrange for the police to take all precautionary measures to ensure that from the moment they landed, up

to the start of the race, any incidents would be avoided. Such incidents could only originate among New York's Jews, whipped up by the press. However, all good Americans would distance themselves from this Jewish posturing, just as they had always done. He and his company, and everyone concerned with the race, had rejected the Jewish machinations in the strongest terms. This was confirmed by Mr Sparrow, who sharply condemned the incitement by the press.

As a 'protection against acts of sabotage' – to guard the cars – the German Embassy would hire the Pinkerton detective agency.[4]

That April the Luftwaffe bombed the undefended Spanish town of Guernica on market day. It remains an outrage and a terrible vision of what was to come.

The hunt for homosexuals in Berlin intensified with Gestapo informers hard at work. It left von Cramm vulnerable although he had been told, discreetly no doubt, that Göring the tennis lover was protecting him. Von Cramm refused to join the Nazi Party, however, and it made protection problematic. On the word of an informer in Hanover he was taken in for questioning although he denied all accusations.[5]

The next month he was ordered to play *only* in the doubles at the French championships in Paris despite the fact that he had an outstanding record in the singles there. The decision was not taken by the German Federation but the highest level of government.[6]

In the singles, Henkel's play 'stressed the present strength of Germany', as *The Times* correspondent wrote, 'with G. von Cramm, the holder, absent'. Henkel had been 'almost unperceived under von Cramm's shadow'. Henkel, the third seed, duly won by beating Bunny Austin 6-1, 6-4, 6-3. Hilde Sperling won the women's and von Cramm and Henkel the doubles. They beat the South Africans Norman Farquharson and Vernon Kirby 6-4, 7-5, 3-6, 6-1.

Germany met Austria in the Davis Cup second round in Munich – both countries had had a bye in the first round – and Germany swept through 3-1.

Manchester City won the First Division and toured Germany. A crowd of 70,000 watched them play a German eleven at the Olympic Stadium. The City players were asked, for diplomatic reasons, to give the Nazi salute.

Inside-forward Peter Docherty remembered:

We were expected to give the salute … but we decided merely to stand to attention. When the German national anthem was played, only eleven arms went up instead of the expected twenty-two! Most of their players seemed to be in the German Army already and were sent away to special camps to prepare for the games. The entire stadium was swarming with armed guards, all wearing *Swastikas*. We knew we'd be expected to give the Nazi salute before the kick-off but when the time came we just stood to attention. Afterwards, we were treated with enormous kindness, though, and the Germans just seemed to want to send us away with a favourable impression of their country but you couldn't fail to see the military preparations everywhere. The whole country seemed to be one huge armed camp.

Manchester City lost 3-2 and won only one of their five matches, drawing two and losing the other two during the three weeks they were in Germany.[7]

The *Manchester Evening News* confessed that City had rather lost sight of the tour (meaning it had not been covered: abroad was still a long way away) and carried an interview with Sam Barkas, the captain. The reporter set the scene: 'Sitting in the cosy parlour of Barkas' home in Levenshume, after he had returned from a long walk in the sunshine …'

Barkas said, 'I am not going to pretend that English football teams making tours of the Continent do not have a very pleasant time, but at the same time these tours are not picnics.' He described the routine in a German city on a non-match day. The players got up about 9 a.m., had breakfast and went on a pre-arranged visit. They might be free after lunch or there may be another pre-arranged visit. Evenings were invariably given over to official entertainment and the players went to bed between 10 and 11 p.m.

It was all delightfully innocent and Barkas did not mention Nazi salutes, armed guards or swastikas (during the war he served as a sergeant in the RAF).

The Grand Prix season began at Tripoli on 9 May with both German teams there in force: von Brauchitsch, Lang, Seaman and Caracciola in Mercedes, Hasse, Rosemeyer, von Delius, Fagioli and Stuck in the Auto Unions. The lottery prize money still exercised a powerful attraction.

Dick Seaman was making his debut. Stuck took pole but Caracciola led, although the lead would be shared as the race unfolded. Mechanical problems, sand and tyre wear guaranteed that. Seaman got as high as second but Lang won it, beating Rosemeyer by 9.6 seconds – won thirty, lost eight. Caracciola and Fagioli indulged in a duel so intense that after the race Fagioli stormed the Mercedes pits and flung a wheel hammer at Caracciola, narrowly missing him.

Both German teams were fully represented in Berlin for the Avus race, although Stuck had taken an Auto Union to the Rio de Janeiro Grand Prix (lured by an enormous prize, as were Ferrari, who sent two cars and one of them beat Stuck on a tight, twisting circuit). It meant that German cars had now been raced on four continents, Europe, North and South America and Africa. Rio made it won thirty-one, lost eight.

At the Avus, the north curve was now the bricked banking (43.6 degrees, known as the 'wall of death') and, because of its two long straights, the circuit allowed enormous speeds. The German teams adapted their speed record cars; there had been extensive testing and 'the result was the most spectacular entry of sheer speed in the pre-war era'. Moreover, the Nazis turned it into 'a great propaganda show. The event stood under the patronage of … Goebbels and the NSSK-Motor Brigade Berlin was ordered to carry out the organisation.'[8]

After two heats a final was run over eight laps and Lang won it from von Delius – won thirty-two, lost eight. Lang averaged 261.6kmph (162.6mph) and Rosemeyer set fastest lap at 276.3kmph (171.7mph). Rosemeyer's car ran on only thirteen cylinders, his goggles were smeared with oil, but that lap remains the fastest ever driven in a formula race. The race itself was the fastest in all motor racing so far, and it would not be beaten until 1958.

Schmeling was due to fight James Braddock for the World Heavyweight Championship, although Braddock had already ducked a meeting the previous year. In this spring they had signed for 3 June and Schmeling undertook serious training at Speculator, a small village in the Adirondack mountains. Schmeling ignored rumours that Braddock has signed to fight Louis and would not be there on 3 June. Indeed he was not.

In farcical circumstances Schmeling went to the New York State Athletic Commission on the day of the fight, was medically examined and passed fit and weighed. He was ready. Braddock was nowhere to be seen.

Goebbels noted in his diary: 'With the Führer this afternoon. Question if we, ourselves, in the event that Braddock chickens out, should declare Schmeling world champion. The Americans are the most corrupt people on earth.'[9]

Germany beat Italy 4-1 in the Davis Cup European Zone quarter finals in Milan.

The Grand Prix cars went to the Nürburgring for the Eifelrennen race, Mercedes with five drivers and Auto Union with four. In practice a bird hit von Delius in the face and he crashed, wrecking the car. In the race the Mercedes suffered from problems with their plugs and Rosemeyer won it from Caracciola – won thirty-three, lost eight.

In direct contrast, the contorting and short track at Sempione Park, Milan – with two right-hand hairpins – prevented the German cars from exercising their power, and only one Auto Union went, driven by Hasse. Ferraris finished first and second – won thirty-three, lost nine.

Germany beat Belgium 4-1 on grass in the European Zone semi-finals in Berlin.

Budge was top seed for Wimbledon, followed by von Cramm, Henkel and Austin. Von Cramm only dropped a couple of sets in the early rounds, one against the Japanese Jiro Yamanashi. (Prenn reached the fourth round.) Then it got harder: five sets against Jack Crawford (Henkel reached these quarter finals too, losing to the American in five sets), four sets against Austin (the third of which Austin won 14-12) before meeting Budge in the final.

Von Cramm was no match for him and the game barely lasted an hour, although von Cramm did have chances and could have led 4-2 in the first set and 5-4 in the second. Budge won it 6-3, 6-4, 6-2.

The German Grand Prix drivers sailed on the SS *Bremen* for New York and the Vanderbilt Cup. Rosemeyer and von Delius would drive the Auto Unions, Caracciola and Seaman the Mercedes. In her recollections of the trip, Rosemeyer's wife Elly mentions no unpleasantness and other sources indicate an absence of problems of that kind. Instead the American press concentrated on the cars and the race. In fact the American organisers even asked the German teams to paint swastikas on the flanks of their cars. Rosemeyer beat Seaman by 51 seconds – won thirty-four, lost nine.

Rosemeyer had been made SS *Obersturmführer* when he won the Eifelrennen the year before and was now promoted to SS *Hauptsturmführer* (captain). When Rosemeyer got back to Berlin he was mobbed at the railway station and Himmler sent congratulations, including the promotion. Rosemeyer's wife would point out that 'being in the SS he had to have a uniform but he never, ever wore it' – not even when Goebbels hosted a reception for him after the Swiss Grand Prix victory in 1936. Goebbels evidently made it into a joke.

While they were coming back, the other drivers gathered at Spa for the Belgian Grand Prix. Von Brauchitsch crashed heavily in practice. Evidently he missed a braking point and his Mercedes somersaulted into a field but landed upright. In the race, Stuck led but the speeds were crucifying tyres and a constant pattern of pit stops kept the race fluid. Hasse broke the lap record and in the end cruised home from Stuck – won thirty-five, lost nine.

The German Davis Cup team beat Czechoslovakia 4-1 in Berlin, which meant, two weeks after Wimbledon and on the same centre court, they would meet the United States in the Davis Cup Interzonal final.

Norah Gordon Cleather, secretary at the All-England Club, would write[10] that German players had been prominent before the First World War and after it but:

> my most arresting memories of their appearances on the centre court at Wimbledon concern not only the representatives of the Fatherland, but their flag.
>
> It is putting it mildly to say that to me that red, white and black standard, emblazoned with the sinister symbol of the crooked cross, looked out of place flying on our flagstaffs in company with the Union Jack and the friendly, rather faded, green and purple colours of the All England Club. Even in the middle 'thirties, when to most people a world war was nothing but a hideous nightmare of the past, it seemed to me to represent something menacing. In spite of its smart newness and its decorative value, it struck a discordant note, and the unaccustomed atmosphere of tense, regimented discipline that came to Wimbledon with the German teams of that period seemed, even then, to synchronise with the unfurling of the Swastika.
>
> The first occasion on which the Swastika fluttered over Wimbledon was during a Davis Cup final between the American and European Zones.

Ms Cleather suggested, or rather claimed 'it was known', that the German players played with a threat hanging over them: failure would make them liable for military service. She concluded: 'The very natural result of this "persuasion" system was that a distasteful feeling of apprehension pervaded the whole team even before the match began.'

Piquancy was added to the tie by the fact that the Germans had hired Bill Tilden, the American, as their coach; and further piquancy (although the general public were presumably completely unaware of the situation) that Tilden had a notorious appetite for young boys and was, as a consequence, more than just homosexual like von Cramm: he was promiscuous with it.

On the first day, the German ambassador to Britain, Joachim von Ribbentrop, attended and his presence allied to the Nazi flag generated its own atmosphere (although, as Jon Fisher points out,[11] in upper class English circles there was a certain sympathy for the Nazis as well as empathy for von Cramm, and this produced a 'palpable pro-German sentiment'). Von Tschammer und Osten flew from Berlin on the morning of the match and Ms Cleather observed that he brought with him 'an air of robot-like inscrutability that seemed queerly out of place on the carefree lawns of Wimbledon'.

Von Cramm began the tie by destroying Bryan Grant 6-3, 6-4, 6-2, but Budge responded to that by destroying Henkel 6-2, 6-1, 6-3 to level it. Intriguingly, in the doubles on the second day Budge and Gene Mako beat von Cramm and Henkel 4-6, 7-5, 8-6, 6-4.

Ms Cleather:

> saw Henkel look up appealingly during the match at von Tschammer und Osten. 'Their eyes met for one pregnant moment and then I saw Henkel flinch under [von Tschammer und Osten's] disdainful gaze and turn away like a dog that knows it will be whipped. It was a small incident, but frighteningly revealing and altogether alien to the sunny, smiling scenes so closely associated with lawn tennis as we like to know it here.'

On this third day, Henkel beat Grant 7-5, 2-6, 6-3, 6-4 to level the tie again.

It set up the final singles between Budge and von Cramm as the decider. Much rode on the match, not least the fact that the winners would face Britain in the challenge round for the cup itself, and Fred Perry had turned professional. Without him, either Germany or the United States would win easily.

It may be that von Cramm felt the apprehension very keenly. Some time before, he had confided in Bill Tilden that the Nazis had him under observation and to keep them at bay he *needed* to take the Davis Cup – then one of the most famous sporting trophies in the world – back with him.[12] This would produce a mythology almost as misleading as that of Hitler and Jesse Owens at the Olympic Stadium. No doubt the presence of the swastika and von Tschammer und Osten contributed, however unwittingly, because of the chill they brought with them – Ms Cleather would describe him watching the match 'with an expressionless, glassy stare'.

Both von Cramm and Budge were at the height of their powers but von Cramm played better in the Davis Cup than he did in the Wimbledon championships – even though he was a thrice-beaten finalist – because he was 'very highly strung' and the day off between the semi-finals and the final used to 'play havoc with his nerves'. There was no day off in the Davis Cup.[13]

Although unlikely, he and Budge became firm friends and each admired the other's tennis. 'Gottfried was always a joy to be with. Anyone who ever really knew him could not help but feel close to him.'

They were dressed in cream flannels and von Cramm wore his Rot-Weiss blazer. Teddy Tinling, to become famous for designing tennis costumes, led them from the players' locker room towards the court where Queen Mary and nearly 15,000 spectators waited. Among them were, apart from von Ribbentrop, comedian Jack Benny and newspaper columnist Ed Sullivan as well as von Tschammer und Osten.

Budge and von Cramm were accompanied by the non-playing captains, Walter Pate and Heinrich Kleinschroth. Ms Cleather was not impressed by the latter. All the German players were not popular in their ways, and one particular pre-First World War star who was still playing at Wimbledon in the late:

> twenties and afterwards came to England regularly as captain of the German teams was Heine Kleinschroth. Kleinschroth had the most irritating manners; for instance, we used to have huge bowls of fruit salad for lunch at Wimbledon in those days and he had an infuriating habit of picking out all the strawberries before we even sat down to eat.

On the way to the court, according to Budge, von Cramm was called away to the telephone and, according to the mythology, it was Hitler reminding him it would not be a good idea to lose the match. Von Cramm concluded the conversation by saying, '*Ja, mein Führer*'.

The mythology was created by Budge, who wrote in his autobiography:

> As Cramm and I were leaving the locker room, the telephone rang and Cramm was called back, and it was Hitler calling him to wish him good luck, in this particular match. Of course it was quite exciting because the fellow who had charge of getting the players out on the court on time had both of us by the arm, he wouldn't let Cramm go, and Cramm was saying, '*Yes Mein Fuehrer*,' this and that, and it got to be quite a tense moment. However, we finally did get out on the court.

As Jon Henderson points out,[14] Budge fabricated the tale of the phone call to liven up his account of the Davis Cup contest, and admitted as much when confronted by von Cramm after the war. There are two ironies here. The first is that the contest needed no livening because seasoned witnesses proclaimed it the best ever played, certainly up to then, anyway. The second is that evoking the very name Hitler was enough by itself to create, in the reader, an array of sinister images.

In fact, one report claims von Cramm did receive a telephone call and, although it was not from Hitler, he never disclosed who it was from. It did not last long enough to delay the start of the match. Another report suggests that Hitler listened to the match on the radio.

Budge broke von Cramm's serve to lead 5-4 in the first set, which ordinarily might have been decisive but von Cramm, inspired, returned four winners on Budge's serve and, four games later, broke Budge's serve to take the first set 8-6. Budge felt he was playing as well as he had ever done and although he was hardly making any mistakes, von Cramm was making fewer. Von Cramm confirmed that by taking the second set, 7-5.

Ms Cleather noted that even when von Cramm won the first two sets 'no smile of pleasure or encouragement' crossed von Tschammer und Osten's face. 'The spectators, too, sat in tense, hushed silence almost as if they sensed the particular consequences that for von Cramm turned on the result.'

Budge rallied and took the third set 6-4. There followed what was quaintly called an intermission; a customary rest break. The players returned to the court at 6.30 p.m. and von Cramm's touch deserted him. Perhaps the intermission had, on a minor scale, affected his nerves in the same way the day off during the Wimbledon championships did.

Budge won the fourth set 6-2, the first and only easy set in the whole match. Von Cramm's touch returned in the fifth set and he led 3-1 then 4-1.

At this moment Tilden rose and made a distinctive gesture towards Henkel with the clear meaning of 'It's in the bag for us!' – 'us' being, of course, the German team Tilden was coaching. One report suggests that Ed Sullivan was so enraged he shouted 'You dirty son of a bitch!', jumped up, tore his jacket off and made for Tilden. He was restrained and Tilden was unimpressed.

Ms Cleather noted that at this crisis Pate, the American captain seated, as tradition demanded, by the umpire's chair, had his hands clasped as if in prayer and his eye cast up to the heavens. Certainly Pate would say that 'no other player – living or dead – could have beaten either man that day'.

The score moved to 5-4 then 6-5 but von Cramm lost his service in the thirteenth game so at 7-6 Budge served for the match and the tie but he needed six match points to get there and fell on the last of them but still got the shot in.

Von Cramm was fulsome in his praise, saying this was the best tennis he had ever played and the best man won. Subsequently Budge reciprocated when he wrote: 'I never played better tennis, nor did I ever play anyone as good as Cramm.'

However, not long afterwards, von Cramm lost the fifth set in an early round of the German championship, which Henkel won, beating McGrath 1-6, 6-3, 8-6, 3-6, 6-1, and this was as the Nazis wished it: Henkel the Nazi taking over from von Cramm the non-Nazi.[15]

Inevitably, the German Grand Prix at the Nürburgring attracted the full German entry: five Auto Unions and seven Mercedes drivers, although only two practised. Rosemeyer did 9 minutes and 46.2 seconds in qualifying (fastest times determined the grid) and the lap became an enduring monument to the Nazis' monumental assault on Grand Prix racing. It stood until 1957.

At the pre-race briefing Korpsführer Hühnlein explained to the drivers that public displaying of affection, i.e. kissing your wife or girlfriend in the pitlane, was to be considered as non-Aryan behavior and had to be stopped. After hearing brass bands and seeing endless motorcycle parades, the spectators finally saw the cars lining up on the grid for the 11am start. Just before ... all the drivers led by Rosemeyer climbed out their cars and ran to the pits to give their wives and girlfriends a long kiss to the delight of the spectators.[16]

Clearly Hitler's monumental assault on Grand Prix racing had not dehumanised the drivers.

Caracciola won the race which climaxed with Rosemeyer, third, putting together an immense chase to catch von Brauchitsch for second place, taking 15 seconds a lap from him – which, of course, on a circuit the length of the Nürburgring was easily possible. He could not quite make it – won thirty-six, lost nine. Von Delius crashed heavily and subsequently died.

Caracciola did remain human. He would remember that after Hitler came to power:

> I saw him several times when the racing cars drove up at the Chancellery prior to the opening of the Automobile Show in Berlin. He never forgot to inquire about my injured leg and always congratulated me on my victories.
>
> In 1937 I had won the Grand Prix of Greater Germany and with it the coveted Adolf Hitler prize. It was a great, heavy bronze trophy – head with windblown hair and lightning darting at each side of it. I suppose it represented a god of speed or of the wind. The trophy was given to me after the race … Bernd Rosemeyer stood next to me. He was chewing on his cigarette and spitting out flecks of tobacco. Never before had I seen him so disappointed and dejected.[17]

Hühnlein seems to have forgiven the kissing insubordination because he made a point of expressing his appreciation to Rosemeyer for an outstanding drive.

Two races followed in quick succession (if that is not a terrible pun): Monaco, where Caracciola took pole from von Brauchitsch and Rosemeyer. Lang had influenza and did not drive, and neither did Seaman, who had crashed at the Nürburgring, breaking his nose and a thumb. The race devolved to von Brauchitsch and Caracciola, and team manager Neubauer signalled von Brauchitsch to let Caracciola through. Passing the pits, von Brauchitsch stuck his tongue out at him – and won it.

Lang did not drive again because he had a kidney inflammation and Seaman crashed into a house at the *Coppa Acerbo*, Pescara. His car was badly damaged and there was no spare so he did not drive either. Caracciola led at the start but Rosemeyer moved past him. Caracciola pressured. Rosemeyer pulled away but hit a kilometre stone, lost a wheel, recovered and caught Caracciola who had an engine problem. Rosemeyer beat von Brauchitsch by 1 minute and 41.8 seconds – won thirty-eight, lost nine.

Herberger's preparations for World Cup qualification were moving smoothly. From beating Belgium 1-0 in Hanover and Switzerland 1-0 in Zürich, the team travelled to Breslau to play Denmark. The name Breslau remains evocative because up to the war it was a major city in the Germany industrial complex of Silesia and, after it, the city became part of Poland, renamed Wroclaw.

Just how German it was in early summer 1937 is demonstrated by the name of the stadium where the match was played: *Schlesierkampfbahn im Sportpark (Herman Göring)*. The Germans ran amok on the pitch, scoring after 8, 32, 40, 44, 47, 65, 71 and 77 minutes in front of 40,000 spectators. Five of the goals were scored by Otto Siffling, another from Waldhof Mannheim and a creative centre-forward who, as one description puts it, played with ingenuity and imagination. Siffling had played in the 1934 World Cup and would obviously be going to France to play in it in 1938.

The 8–0 victory quickly became so famous that the German team were known as the 'Breslau Eleven'.

The impression of the German soccer team's gathering power was confirmed when the team beat Latvia 3–1 in Riga. The World Cup qualifying match against Finland in Helsinki was four days away: 26 June.

Only 6,619 spectators were at the Pallokenttä Stadium, Helsinki, that Tuesday. They saw Ernst Lehner give the Germans the lead after 6 minutes and Adolf Urban seal the match with a second after 60 minutes. Herberger had taken the first step towards France, bringing glory to the Reich and, as a Nazi, showing the Führer that his – Herberger's – beloved soccer was something of value.

The Swiss Grand Prix retained its central importance and the German teams were fully represented. The race was wet and Stuck led but Rosemeyer locked brakes and skidded off. Willing spectators pushed him back on but that was illegal and he retired. Caracciola got past Stuck who fell back. Towards the end Lang closed on Caracciola but was signalled to ease off and he obeyed. Caracciola won it by 49.4 seconds – won thirty-nine, lost nine.

Herberger's side took another important step towards France. They played Estonia at another place with a name evocative of the time, the Horst Wessel-Stadium in Königsberg – Horst Wessel the Nazi martyr, of course, and Königsberg the Prussian city next to the Baltic States and therefore not far from Estonia. How many of the 15,000 crowd were Estonian is not clear. What is clear is that after the war, while Breslau was becoming Wroclaw, the fair city of Königsberg would be becoming Soviet and known as Kaliningrad. Estonia took the lead through winger Georg Siimenson but Ernst Lehner (50 minutes), Josef Gauchel (53), Lehner again (65) and Gauchel again (86) made the match safe.

In September, a full complement of German cars went to the Italian Grand Prix at Livorno on the west coast not far from Pisa – perhaps because the Italians felt the circuit, which was very twisty in places, would give Nuvolari a better chance in his nimble Alfa Romeo. He had beaten the Auto Unions there in 1936. One of motor racing's most curious tales was unfolding, however. Achille Varzi arrived and begged for a drive with Auto Union, assuring the team that he had given up drugs, as well as Ilse.[18] With some reluctance Auto Union agreed.

The start of the race was delayed because the crowd invaded the circuit. Caracciola led with Lang behind him and that was the story of the race. Caracciola won by 0.4 of a second – won forty, lost nine.

After the race Stuck was sacked by Auto Union.

The Czechoslovakian Grand Prix, at Brno, was fifteen laps of the 29.1km circuit (18 miles). It was narrow, overtaking was not easy and the drivers did not like it:

> About half the circuit was on the national highway and the other half on local
> district routes. On the latter the surface was very rough, bumpy and hilly. Due to

the extreme length of the circuit, practice was limited and so a thorough knowledge of it was hard to come by and this, coupled with its difficult nature, made crashes frequent. Crowd control was poor.[19]

And 310,000 came to watch the race.

Lang led from Rosemeyer who made a mistake on the second lap – he missed a turning and 'seemed on his way to the city of Brno'.[20] He turned and continued in second place. Rosemeyer began to catch Lang and Caracciola began to catch Rosemeyer. Then Lang went off, killing two spectators and injuring twelve more. Neubauer was told to get Lang out of Czechoslovakia immediately. Rosemeyer crashed and buckled a wheel. It gave the race to Caracciola, who beat von Brauchitsch by some 45 seconds – won forty-one, lost nine.

By now, after four full seasons, the two German teams had established their superiority beyond all doubt but they were prisoners of the Grand Prix calendar, obliged to demonstrate this superiority in the same places: Monaco, Tripoli, the Avus, the Nürburgring, Berne, Monza, Spa and Brno. The spectators there knew the Silver Arrows and the Silver Arrows knew the circuits. Familiarity could never breed contempt with machines of this power glimpsed annually, but the initial shock – no other word will do – of experiencing it for the first time could not be recaptured either.

A garage owner from Derby (and a member of the Derby and District Motor Club) called Fred Craner had an interesting idea. Not far away, the imposing Donington Hall nestled into extensive grounds in the countryside. It was owned by the Shields family. Craner – a dynamic, persuasive and earthy man – persuaded Shields that by using the roads and linking them a circuit could be built. Racing began in 1933 with motorcycles and the cars came two years later, contesting what was known as the Donington Grand Prix for national drivers.

Craner decided to take the ultimate step. He would invite the German teams and hold a full-blown Grand Prix. Craner contacted Dick Seaman, who felt sure the teams would come if the money was right. Craner made sure of that but could not persuade the governing body, the Royal Automobile Club, to allow him to call the race the British Grand Prix. It remained the Donington Grand Prix.

Something far more than a motor race began to unfold. The British drivers were well-bred chaps – amateurs, of course – full of derring-do (the 1935 race was won by 'Mad Jack' Shuttleworth) to the point where they risked being caricatures. Mostly they had ERA (English Racing Association) cars, which were sit-up-and-beg vehicles, mingled with Rileys, Maseratis and Alfa Romeos. A direct comparison: the Audis had 6,006ccs, the Mercedes 5,660 and the ERAs 1,488.

Donington was heartland England, within easy reach not only of Derby but Leicester and Nottingham. The teams which Hitler financed, and upon which he kept such a watchful eye, were about to show the heartland what Germany could do: long convoys of lorries bringing cars and spares up from the Channel ports, the size of the teams, the mechanics in their immaculate overalls, the attention to detail – even press packs – produced an impression of implacable professionalism. The professionals, armed with all the ammunition they needed, had come to confront the chaps with a terrible truth: being a chap, mad or otherwise, was not going to be enough.

It was not so much a prelude to war as what war would really look like when it broke out. Being a chap was not going to be enough there, either.

As it happened, the Donington circuit had a long straight – ideal for demonstrating the ultimate speed that the German cars could reach – followed by a downhill-horse-shoe-uphill to a crest. On that crest the power of the cars launched them so that they had all four wheels off the ground. It was so spectacular that photographs of it have lost none of their potency today. The impact in October 1937 was almost overwhelming and reduced strong men to babbling.

Von Brauchitsch took pole, lapping the 2 miles 971yds in 2 minutes and 10.4 seconds, and the fastest non-German was a Siamese prince, 'B' Bira, who took his Maserati round in 2 minutes and 25 seconds. A difference of almost 15 seconds would translate over the eighty laps to 20 minutes, and this in a sport intended to be decided by the smallest of margins.

An immense crowd watched Rosemeyer win it from von Brauchitsch, Bira again the first non-German but, to be classified, he needed to finish within 15 minutes of Rosemeyer and did not. He was what is known as 'flagged off'. It might have been a humiliation in the minds (and imaginations) of 50,000 spectators had it not been full of German power. The scoreboard read won forty-two, lost nine.

Nor did Britain show its best face. There was confusion over playing the German national anthem afterwards and some bookmakers (who had gotten the odds horribly wrong) fled rather than pay out to the German mechanics who had taken bets.

Von Cramm and Henkel sailed on a world tour, starting in the United States. In Boston they won the US doubles championship but, at Forest Hills, von Cramm went down to Budge in the final (Henkel only reached the second round). Von Cramm, however, took Budge to five sets.

The two Germans travelled to Chicago to play exhibition matches and on to Los Angeles for a tournament called the Pacific Southwest, much patronised by the Hollywood fraternity. This time the fraternity planned to demonstrate what they thought of Hitler and his anti-Semitism (many Jews had found great fame and fortune in the film industry) by waiting until von Cramm came on court. Some 200 of them planned to rise as one and leave.

They did not seem to have realised that von Cramm's wife was partly Jewish, or understood von Cramm's views of the Nazis. When the demonstrators did see von Cramm he won them over by his presence alone and they stayed. Groucho Marx said, 'I felt ashamed of what I had planned to do.'

Three weeks later Germany beat Norway 3-0 in Berlin and, in November, beat Sweden 5-0 in Hamburg in the final World Cup qualifying match watched by 55,000 spectators (Siffling and Schön two goals each). In 1937 the team had played eleven times and won them all. If they gazed towards France and the supreme examination the following June they must have been as confident as the Grand Prix teams had been going all over Europe, especially Donington.

The soccer players were wrong, although to know how wrong they would have to have been able to read Hitler's mind. They could not, and neither could anybody else.

Notes

1   www.forix.com/8w/au-sa37.html.
2   Taifun (Typhoon), a Messerschmitt, used for record attempts and forerunner of the German fighter.
3   Havemann, *Fussball unterm Hakenkreuz* (*Soccer Under the Swastika*).
4   Reuss, *Hitler's Motor Racing Battles*.
5   Fisher, *A Terrible Splendor*.
6   Ibid.
7   youandyesterday.com/.../Derby_County:_Players_saw_Nazi_war_preparations.
8   Snellman, *Golden Era of Grand Prix Racing*.
9   Fisher, *A Terrible Splendor*.
10 Cleather, *Wimbledon Story*.
11 Fisher, op. cit.
12 Ibid.
13 Cleather, op. cit.
14 Henderson, *The Life of Fred Perry*.
15 Fisher, op. cit.
16 Snellman, op. cit.
17 Caracciola, *Racing Driver's World*.
18 Ilse, the wife of fellow driver Paul Pitsch. Varzi had an affair with her and she introduced him to morphine. He became an addict.
19 Nixon, *Silver Arrows*.
20 Snellman, op. cit.

7

BOMBED

Gottfried von Cramm spent the winter in the United States. From Los Angeles he and Henkel sailed on the Japanese ship *Tayo Maro* for the Far East. In Tokyo, von Cramm made a speech about German-Japanese relations without mentioning Hitler or the Nazis. The process of deification was so complete that even sending a letter without signing it *Heil Hitler!* represented risk. To ignore Hitler in a public speech represented an act of great moral courage, or folly.

In Australia, where he would play Budge in exhibition matches in Sydney and Melbourne, von Cramm made a pass at the man ghost-writing his column for the *Sun-Pictorial* in Melbourne and reportedly provoked controversy when he and Henkel went on the beach topless, then illegal in Australia. He may have imagined he was safe so far from Germany because, apart from the pass, he was making ill-advised statements about Germany including criticism of the military service which every young person had to serve and, reportedly, even making a derogatory remark about Hitler himself.

There was an organisation (the National Socialist Organisation of Foreign Germans) in Australia and they must have been reporting von Cramm's exploits to the Gestapo in Berlin. Certainly, Tilden even felt von Cramm *wanted* something to happen to resolve the situation rather than linger in this twilight world.[1]

Budge was quoted as saying of von Cramm: 'He was an honest man and he offered what he thought was constructive criticism.'

Whatever the Nazi government wanted it was not that.

Von Cramm played in the Australian Open at Adelaide and beat an Australian, Viv McGrath, in the quarter finals 6-2, 3-6, 4-6, 7-5, 6-0, but lost in the semi-finals to another Australian, John Bromwich, 3-6, 5-7, 1-6. In the men's doubles von Cramm and Henkel were beaten in straight sets by Bromwich and Adrian Quist, a doubles specialist from South Australia.

By now von Cramm was getting messages that returning to Germany might not be a good idea, and he also received a letter from former lover Manasse, saying he was not in Portugal but living in Paris. It would give von Cramm a chance to meet him again in May during the French Open.

On 28 January, Bernd Rosemeyer prepared a world record attempt on the Frankfurt–Darmstadt autobahn. Historian Leif Snellman has set the scene:

> During the 1930s the German National Socialistic regime had recognized the propaganda value of speed record attempts on '*die Autobahnen*,' the new German highways. But by 1938 the speeds had gone up by 115kmph in just three years and were coming close to the limits of human reaction. The road was just 8 meters wide and the track went under several bridges with central pillars. With such a speed as the German cars now reached the driver only had to turn the car one degree and he would have a wheel up in the grass in less than 1.5 seconds. The race for speed had reached what [another historian] Chris Nixon calls 'lunatic extremes'.[2]

This was made worse because, as in the Grands Prix, Mercedes and Auto Union were in direct competition and the annual record attempts provoked enormous interest because they were forcing back human frontiers. To give this context, Britain's first section of motorway (the equivalent of an autobahn), the Preston by-pass, did not open until 1958.

That morning Caracciola in a Mercedes smashed the road speed records for 1km and 1 mile, beating what Rosemeyer had done the previous October.

Auto Union prepared to respond with their car, designed using a wind tunnel. A run in fact comprised two runs – out and coming back – with the average time counting. Rosemeyer was not on the pace outbound but reached 429.9kmph (267.1mph) inbound. He complained that in the cold air the engine had not reached its optimum temperature; the team made adjustments and he tried again. He reached some 432kmph (268mph)[3] when the Auto Union left the road, rolled and somer-saulted several times, destroying itself. Rosemeyer, flung out, was found 100m away in some woods, and died a few moments later.

'Caracciola's run in the morning of 28 January 1938 remains to this day the fastest ever made by a car on a normal road.'[4]

On 5 February, a week after the crash, Auto Union finally wrote to Elly. 'Dear and highly esteemed Lady' it began and ended, 'Dear, brave Ms Rosemeyer, we renew our loyalty into loyalty'.

Rosemeyer's funeral, at the Dahlem Cemetery in Berlin:

> was a macabre show of the best the Nazis could stage for a national hero, dead for the glory of the Party and Germany: SS and Auto Union shared the scene, with Daimler-Benz's top drivers and managers also duly showing. Beethoven's funeral march and the SS loyalty hymn *Wenn alle untreu werden* gave the last farewell to the coffin in a triumph of Nazi salutes. The guard of honor was provided by the elite corp Leibstandarde Adolf Hitler.[5]

A heavyweight called Ben Foord fought Schmeling in front of 30,000 and lost on points. Subsequently, after England's soccer problems with the Nazi salute in the Olympic Stadium, Henry Rose of the *Daily Express* wrote: 'I recall that when Ben Foord was in Hamburg for his fight with Schmeling he gave the Nazi salute at the weigh-in and when he took the ring.' Rose did not mention this in his coverage of the fight itself, although there was an intriguing short story beside the report:

Hitler Hears Radio Tribute
Berlin, Sunday

Adolf Hitler, in between this morning's anniversary parades and tonight's goose-stepping torchlight parade, listened to the broadcast of the Schmeling-Foord fight.

It was a vivid broadcast, and even the smack of the gloves could be heard.

Towards the end Hitler heard his German announcer say: 'Foord has staged a come-back. He is a great man, brave, tough, plucky. Under the heaviest punishment from Max, the South African's knee has not once touched the floor. He has proved himself a great fighter.'

Schmeling was looking towards the return fight against Louis and said he 'needed' a twelve-rounder to prepare himself for that.

Hitler prepared to absorb Austria into the Reich. In February the pressure grew as he told the Austrian Chancellor, Kurt von Schuschnigg, to free all imprisoned Nazis and appoint a Nazi minister. Göring visited Vienna. Hitler demanded that the Germans in Austria had the right of self-determination and, at the end of the month, Austrian troops had to surround the town of Graz to prevent a march by Austrian Nazis. Some 20,000 did march.

The Mercedes and Auto Union drivers were summoned to the Berlin Motor Show and presented to Hitler. They drove the racing cars from the Brandenburg Gate along the wide, arrow-straight road through the Tiergarten, which, as a demonstration of German power, must have been extraordinary. At the opening of the show Goebbels and Hitler made long speeches. Hitler paid tribute to 'the many daring young racing drivers who risk their lives to win prizes, not for love of their machines but for the honour of Germany'.[6]

Seaman was British …

On 4 March, von Cramm reached Munich after a three-week voyage from Australia. He was due to meet his fellow tennis players in Berlin within days at a reception to be given by von Tschammer und Osten but that had been cancelled.

He went home and the next evening, after dinner and with the whole family present, two Gestapo agents arrived in a black Mercedes. They said they wanted to discuss his Australian trip but really he was under arrest. He was taken to the Gestapo's headquarters on Prinz-Albrecht-Strasse in Berlin[7] and it seems that, in a cell there, he suffered a nervous breakdown or something very close to that, while outside his formidable mother marshalled whatever resistance she could. Inside, under duress, von Cramm confessed to having had a homosexual affair from 1931 to 1936.

The soccer World Cup seedings were announced in Paris: Germany, France, Italy, Czechoslovakia, Hungary, Cuba, Sweden and Brazil. The draw:

5 June, Marseille	Italy *v.* Norway
5 June, Paris	France *v.* Belgium
5 June, Strasbourg	Brazil *v.* Poland
5 June, Le Havre	Czechoslovakia *v.* Holland
5 June, Rheims	Hungary *v.* Dutch East Indies
4 June, Paris	Switzerland *v.* Germany
5 June, Lyons	Sweden *v.* Austria
5 June, Toulouse	Cuba *v.* Roumania

It was made in a salon at the Ministry of Foreign Affairs, the same salon in which the Briand-Kellogg Pact had been signed in 1928 by countries vowing never go to war with one another again.

The Swedish newspaper *Dagens Nyheter* wrote:

> Of course, Sweden could have had a much better draw than against Austria but our sister country of Norway has even more reason to complain. They face the world champions of 1934 and the Olympic champions of 1936, Italy. Austria is no longer in the same class as it was some years ago no longer the 'Wunderteam' but one should beware. We are unlikely to survive the match against Austria.

Schuschnigg called for a vote on Austrian independence. Hitler reacted vehemently, demanding it be cancelled, threatening military intervention and calling for Schuschnigg to be replaced by a Nazi, Arthur Seyss-Inquart. He was and German troops poured across the border. Austria was ceasing to exist which at one level was a major international political event and at another would have consequences for Austria *v.* Sweden in Lyons.

The newspaper *Svenska Dagbladet* wrote:

> Austria is the continent's strongest team, stronger than Germany's. How Germany will now proceed with its football team will be interesting to see. If you put together a German-Austrian team it may be, at least on paper, an eleven that probably only England's best professional teams are capable of beating. And England are not included in the World Cup.

The *Dagens Nyheter* was speculating that Sweden wouldn't get a walk-over and might end up playing Switzerland or even Portugal. The *Göteborgs Handel-och Sjöfartstidning* wrote (naughtily):

> The thing is, Austria has ceased to be an independent kingdom. Sindelar and his cronies may thus not represent their real country in a World Cup tournament and

we have a walkover. It has been speculated that Sweden would have a different opponent than the Austrians, who for the time being are German, but it is not clear yet.

On 14 March Hitler entered Vienna in triumph.

That day von Cramm appeared in court, 'the gloomy old Moabit courthouse on Lehrterstrasse',[8] in central Berlin. His case would be heard in secret, and not only because the Nazis were not anxious for the world to see their system of justice in action but because von Cramm was immensely popular.

Don Budge organised a protest by leading American sportspeople (including Joe DiMaggio and Helen Wills Moody), sending it as an open letter to the German government. Meanwhile von Cramm's mother did all she could by working the family's connections. None of it would count for anything in the Third Reich's legal system, because to run it Hitler had appointed a Nazi called Roland Freisler, who was not concerned with legal niceties – like evidence, innocence and guilt – but rather what was best for the Third Reich.

Von Cramm had a lawyer, Carl Langbehn, defending him. Langbehn joined the Nazi Party in 1933 and knew Heinrich Himmler because their daughters went to the same school. Langbehn, however, viewed with mounting disapproval what the Nazis were actually doing. He faced a judge called Spohner, famed for trying homosexual cases, refusing to entertain appeals and who was not concerned with legal niceties either. Like Freisler he regarded them as nuisances.

Langbehn had, immediately, the problem of von Cramm's confession but artfully argued that von Cramm and Herbst had only indulged in mutual masturbation and ceased even that in 1935, when a Nazi law – known as paragraph 175 – forbade homosexuality in any form. Langbehn persuaded von Cramm to claim Manasse had blackmailed him. There was, however, another charge against him, that he had illegally taken money out of the Reich to give to Manasse (one report says 20,000RM). This was a serious offence and von Cramm was found guilty under paragraph 175 and sentenced to a year in Moabit, minus the two months he had already served.

This was international news. The *Daily Express* reported under a Berlin, Sunday dateline (they had staff reporting in the city) how von Cramm began his sentence:

A warder wakened him at 7 a.m. Von Cramm made up his bed, strapped it to the wall, then stood at his cell door waiting until it was opened for him to go to the prison washhouse. Back in the cell, he put on his blue drill prison uniform and breakfasted on black coffee and rye bread. Later he exercised for half an hour in the yard with other prisoners, was taken back to his cell, and stayed there for the rest of the day. He was given newspapers and books to read. In two or three weeks he will be allowed exercise time in the afternoons as well as mornings. He does not have to work.

Ms Cleather commented acidly:[9]

It was the successful partnership between Hilde Sperling and von Cramm that first brought the latter into prominence at Wimbledon. With von Cramm's good looks and charming manners, he was always an extremely popular player and he had many tennis successes the whole world over. The Americans in particular were his devoted admirers. They liked him so much that when trouble overtook him and the Nazis threw him into jail in 1938, the Americans rigidly banned the German tournaments for a time. I always thought it was a typical example of German diplomacy to lock up one of their very few representatives who gained universal popularity.

She mentioned that a 'characteristic habit of the German teams was to put ice-water in the tea-pot' and 'with the exception' of a few players 'the Germans were usually a very trying lot'.

The *Anschluss* threatened another tennis player, Adam Bawarowski, the son of a wealthy Viennese living in Poland. Now Bawarowski fled to Poland and in 1939 was playing for Poland. He remains, however, almost anonymous – like so many of Hitler's victims.

It threatened Richard Bergmann, a Viennese table tennis player with one of the greatest defences. He won the world title in 1936 but now fled to England, where he would represent Britain, winning the world title again.

On 20 March, Germany beat Luxembourg 3-1 at Wuppertal and drew 1-1 with Hungary at Nuremberg on the same day. I am indebted to the German Football Association: 'As a matter of fact, it is true. Actually, it happened several times in the 1930s due to the fact that the German National team did not have a B-Team or U-21 so the head coach used all national matches to invite and test talents from all over the German Reich.'

Something much more significant was only two weeks away.

On 3 April, Austria played Germany in a reunification match – officially a 'reconciliation match' – in the Praterstadion, Vienna. It was intended to be a celebration but afforded the Viennese, and particularly Matthias Sindelar, a chance to make nationalist and political statements. The Austrians played under their new name, *Ostmark*,[10] and Germany under *Altreich* (Old Reich). The names alone were evocative.

If Austria was (or more correctly had been) a team in decline they were still artists compared to the more mechanical Germans. If, as seems likely, the Germans were seeking a victory to give them a propaganda coup it was not going to be easy.

Sindelar, a social democrat, really did dislike the Nazis, who moved quickly to ostracise the old chairman of Austria Vienna, the club Sindelar played for. Sindelar told him: 'The new chairman has forbidden me to greet you, but I, Herr Doktor, always will.' The Gestapo had already recorded in their files that Sindelar was 'very friendly to Jews' – as well he might be in cosmopolitan Vienna – and when he purchased a café from a Jew (who had been forced to sell) he paid the going rate rather than taking advantage. In the café he would be censured because he was extremely reluctant to put up Nazi posters.

A theatre critic, Alfred Polgar, has described Sindelar's style of playing:[11]

In a way he had brains in his legs, and many remarkable and unexpected things occurred to them while they were running. Sindelar's shot hit the back of the net like the perfect punch-line, the ending that made it possible to understand and appreciate the perfect composition of the story, the crowning of which it represented.

The stadium was full, including a VIP section of uniformed people with swastikas on their arms.

To disentangle myth from reality is all but impossible so long afterwards but contemporary reports suggest Sindelar had several chances in the first half and missed them all, sometimes by rolling the ball past the post as if he might have been saying, 'Could have put it in if I'd wanted to'. The suggestion remains that he was enjoying himself mocking the people with the swastikas because he would turn away and shake his head as if he might have also been saying, 'Believe that if you want'. Darker still, had the Austrians been told it would be very sensible to lose the match? The second half contradicted that because midway through it Sindelar pounced on a rebound and then his friend Schasti Sesta scored with a looping free-kick.

To disentangle the myth from reality at that moment is more possible because either Sindelar or Sesta – or both? – went to the VIP stand and danced a dance of triumph in the most public way.

What long-term damage this might have done to Sindelar's career is obscure because he would be invited to play for the new, united German side. He refused. The coach, Sepp Herberger, subsequently said: 'I almost had the impression that discomfort and rejection, linked to the political developments, had prompted his refusal. I felt I understood him. He appeared liberated when I told him so.'

Wolfgang Maderthaner, the biographer of Sindelar, has put this match into context:

> Football became the first vehicle to express resistance, it became a means of politics but this is an historical irony: it was designed by the Nazis as a means of politics but it became a means of resistance too. There was this big game, kind of a farewell game. The game was meant to be a symbol of the fraternity of the two nations … the VIP sector … was full of Nazi functionaries and they did a dance for them. So this was a kind of expression of self confidence, kind of an expression of the underdog against the big German Reich. This was something the Nazis never forgave Sindelar for.[12]

The *Neue Freie Presse* newspaper in Vienna was circumspect. It carried these headlines:

Swastika over the Stadium
TRIUMPH OF THE VIENNA FOOTBALL SCHOOL

> The 60,000 crowd stood with arms raised in the salute singing the German national anthem and the Horst Wessel Song. They were all for Hitler.
> The final verdict on the match was that the fast men had chances they did not make use of because their opponents were Austrian. If they had been English it

may have been entirely different. The teams did not fight as they would have done against other opponents.

The Swedish newspaper *Dagens Nyheter* wrote: 'Zurich, Friday (4 April). From the International Football Association (FIFA). The Austrian Association has announced that it is dissolved and the administration taken over by the German Association. The Austrian Association ceases to be as independent body and its membership of FIFA is nullified.'

The Grand Prix motor-racing season began at Pau but Auto Union's new car was not ready and they did not go.

Nuvolari drove an Alfa Romeo and crashed in practice. The car was flexing 'under cornering loads and causing the fuel tank, mounted just above his knees, to start to leak … petrol seeped out and caught fire. Nuvolari had to steer the blazing car into the trees and bale out, narrowly escaping with his life.'[13] He vowed never to drive for Alfa Romeo again, and never did.

Mercedes took two cars in what has been described as a shakedown (the term used to denote the first running of a car to see what might be right and wrong with it) but it all went wrong. Both cars had slipping clutches and plugs which oiled up, and that on a street circuit where pole would be taken at an average speed of almost 60mph. Lang lost control of his car and it rode into straw bales so hard that it was withdrawn.

That left Caracciola for the race and he led from Dreyfus and a driver called Maurice Trintignant. Because Pau was a street circuit, Dreyfus could exploit Delahaye's car and amazingly get past Caracciola, who did re-pass him. Oil and rubber were beginning to coat the surface of the track, giving Caracciola a surfeit of power. At half distance he pitted for fuel and the constant brake-accelerate-change gear tormented his old leg injury. Lang took over the Mercedes but Dreyfus was long gone and the Delayaye allowed him to run to the end without stopping for fuel. Dreyfus won by just under 2 minutes, a genuine sensation and perhaps deeply satisfying to Dreyfus, a Jew – and that made it won forty-three, lost nine.

The German soccer team drew 1-1 with Portugal at Frankfurt, the World Cup only six weeks away. In between they would play a 'friendly' against England which, like the reconciliation match against Austria, takes its place as a political event heavily overlaid with nationalism. The match was to be played at the Olympic Stadium, already, of course, a symbolic Nazi stage.

The symbolism was being taken to the United States too. On 9 May the SS *Bremen* docked in New York after a six-day trans-atlantic crossing. Max Schmeling was on it but his wife and mother were not. Goebbels had forbidden them to accompany him[14] to make sure he returned to Germany rather than, as some friends would urge him to do, take American citizenship. Schmeling would not have done because he was a proud German, but that did not mean being a Nazi.

The mood in New York had altered in the two years since he beat Joe Louis. Because a hostile reception awaited him on the quayside, promoter Jacobs took the newsmen out to the *Bremen* on a tugboat so they could do their interviews in, literally, calmer waters. Schmeling caught the change of mood then because although naturally he was asked about boxing other questions – about Hitler, about race, about whether he considered himself a representative of the master race – came at him like jabs. On the quayside several hundred people jeered and called out abuse. One banner exhorted Schmeling to go home and another demanded a boycott of the fight.

Schmeling travelled to his hotel by a roundabout route but confronted more demonstrators there. Whenever he left the hotel he faced abuse and people giving mock Nazi salutes. He now understood how political the fight had become. He retreated to his training camp in the small village of Speculator in the Adirondack mountains he knew so well. The quietness and remoteness of Speculator had also, in its time, attracted other boxers like Gene Tunney and Max Baer to do their training.

Promoter Jacobs had journalistic contacts and now used them. He fed Henry Rose of the *Daily Express* in London with information. In the 11 May issue Rose wrote:

> Something seems to have gone wrong with the threats by the anti-Nazi organisations to boycott the fight. A message I received from Mike Jacobs last night says he has received advance bookings totalling £20,000. Jacobs has received a telegraphed ultimatum from the non-sectarian anti-Nazi League demanding that Schmeling contribute his share of the purse to the German Refugees Relief Fund or else face a boycott against the fight.

Schmeling trained hard but even at Speculator he could not escape the politics completely. 'Whether I wanted it or not, I was a showpiece for the Nazis. Up to the day of the fight I received thousands of hate letters signed "Heil Hitler" or "Hit Hitler." I didn't know what to do – only two years earlier this same city had cheered me wildly.'[15]

While Schmeling trained so diligently, England prepared to play Germany at soccer in Berlin.

The Berlin newspaper *Der Angriff* started the build-up many days before with long feature articles on German soccer through the years. Interest was so great that 400,000 people wanted to see the match and the 'Strength Through Joy' organisation – *Kraft durch Freude*, a Nazi leisure organisation which was part of the German labour front – had 20,000 tickets for its members.

England were traditionally a powerful side, so powerful they disdained to enter any World Cup because they judged the domestic competitions more important. The Germans approached the match from the other direction, lending it great importance. It was obviously a good test to be meeting England in Germany's final match before the World Cup. They had not been beaten for sixteen matches, making England even more of a relevant test. Some 400,000 people applied for tickets.

The Germans trained specially in the Black Forest for two weeks while the England team arrived with no preparations, their season just having finished. The FA Cup final, between Preston North End and Huddersfield (Preston won 1–0) had been on 30 April and two Huddersfield players, midfielders Charles Willingham and Alfred Young, would be in the team. It was, however, relatively inexperienced with only two players, skipper

Eddie Hapgood (Arsenal, full-back) and Cliff Bastin (Arsenal, winger), bringing real international experience. Left-half Don Welsh (Charlton Athletic) and centre-forward Frank Broome (Aston Villa) were debutants.[16] Broome retained a vivid impression of Germany: 'What struck me was how the military was everywhere.'

The *Daily Express* reported under a Berlin, Thursday dateline: 'Our party arrived here shortly before five o'clock this evening, after a tiring 12-hour train journey following the boat crossing in brilliant sunshine. The reception at the station was just the reverse of what was expected. I was staggered at the tranquillity. No crowds. No cheers.'

England secured an agreement that Germany would not pick Austrian players, in effect denying them the fruits of the *Anschluss*, although one did play, Johan 'Hans' Pesser, a striker with Rapid Vienna who had represented Austria eight times, scoring three goals. The agreement hinged on a match the next day when Aston Villa, on tour, were to meet a combined German and Austrian side.

The controversy at the Olympic Stadium would be over whether to give the Nazi salute, just as it had been for countries in the Olympic march past two years before. This would now confront the England team when they lined up for the national anthems before the kick off. They either had to give the salute, provoking outrage at home, or not give it, provoking outrage here.[17]

Others – Nuvolari and Seaman – would find positions of compromise with their arms, using them like flippers to escape the dilemma, and they were able to do this in the melee and crush after a Grand Prix, a swell of people washing round them. No such option would be open to the England footballers with the eyes of 105,000 upon them and, standing there in line, no place to hide.

Having swallowed Austria, Hitler was now eyeing Czechoslovakia, a country he did not consider a country but a bastard creation of the aftermath of the First World War – 'it is a lie, not a country' – and he had the perfect tourniquet. Across the north of Czechoslovakia, bordering Germany, stretched the Sudetenland, full of ethnic Germans who spoke German and behaved like Germans. The tourniquet would tighten until he could liberate them.

Europe seemed balanced between great powers and who could say what might upset the balance, especially with a man like Hitler? The matter of the salute was therefore considered so sensitive that the British ambassador, Sir Nevile Henderson,[18] reportedly ordered the team to give it (Henderson does not mention this in his book, and with the world darkening day by day it must have been an irritant).

Sir Robert Vansittart, chief diplomatic advisor at the Foreign Office, contacted Stanley Rous, secretary of the Football Association, to make the situation absolutely clear. 'It is really important for our prestige that the British team should put up a really first-class performance. I hope that every possible effort will be made to ensure this.'

This reads like diplomatic code for 'no misbehaving and smile, smile, smile'.

The Football Association replied in the only way they could: 'Every member of the team will do his utmost to uphold the prestige of his country.'

The *Daily Express* carried, under a Berlin dateline, a story headlined: 'England players may give Nazi salute.' Mr C. Wreford Brown, a London solicitor and Football

Association member, was quoted as saying: 'We regard the matter as so important that we are holding a special conference in the morning to decide.' The reporter felt the players would give the salute, especially if Hitler was in the stadium.

Historian Simon Kuper has written:[19]

Meanwhile British officials were trying to work out whether the team was going to give the Nazi salute. This was a common diplomatic problem in the 1930s, a decision every sports team playing Germany had to make ... The English could have avoided saluting. But war between Germany and Britain seemed very possible just then.

Rous 'favoured a salute for different reasons'. He had seen the march past at the Olympics and seen 'the German crowd jeer the British team for only giving Hitler the "eyes right"'. In fact, as we have seen, the British team was greeted by absolute silence. Rous thought a salute would put the crowd in good temper.[20] More than that, he would subsequently say of the players' reaction: 'All agreed that they had no objection, and no doubt saw it as a bit of fun rather than of any political significance.'

To put it mildly, and even knowing that the England players – who may not have been political animals – had no way of knowing there would be a hideous war, this seems disingenuous. Whether the England players were capable of appreciating the importance and sensitivity of what they were doing is another question altogether. Clearly Ambassador Henderson could and acted on that. He would have been entitled to make a judgement that giving the salute would be a lesser evil than not giving it.

Anticipation for the match was so keen that the first of sixty-three special trains began arriving the day before.

Like the reconciliation match, disentangling myth from reality is all but impossible so long after. Some reports suggest Henderson gave the instruction to salute in the dressing room but one factor mitigates against that. The team would have been selected before, giving Stan Cullis of Wolves time to refuse and be quietly dropped.

Hitler, who had been visiting Mussolini in Italy, would not be present at the match although that scarcely mattered since, the Nazis would have argued, it was the principle which mattered.

The teams lined up and both gave the full salute.

Henry Rose in the *Daily Express* reported that Hapgood thought standing at attention should have been sufficient. Rose felt the players were not happy about the salute. 'Hapgood looks along the line. There is a shuffle, and orders being orders, hands are raised. They are lowered as one anthem finishes (I detect relief) and raised again with some diffidence.

'There was a good deal of talk about it among the players before the game, and there has been a good deal since. There was no unanimity about the decision of the committee in charge that the salute should be given.'

Then England crushed the Germans. Bastin volleyed in after 16 minutes and although the Germans responded 4 minutes later when inside-right Rudi Gellesch (FC Shalke 04) equalised, Jackie Robinson (Sheffield Wednesday, inside-right) gave

England the lead again 6 minutes after that from a corner, and 2 minutes later Welsh's pass opened up the defence and Broome made the score 3-1.

With 3 minutes to half time, Stanley Matthews (Stoke City) trapped a high pass and waltzed past three defenders, as he would do against generations of defenders, making him one of the greatest right-wingers of all. Goalkeeper Vic Woodley (Chelsea) did not clear properly just before half time and Josef 'Jupp' Gauchel (Neundorf, centre-forward) scored. That made it 4-2.

Just 4 minutes into the second half Robinson produced a low drive which, reportedly, goalkeeper Hans Jakob (Jahn Regensburg) wasn't expecting. At 77 minutes Presser capitalised on confusion between Woodley and Bert Sproston (Leeds United) to score his second and Germany's third.

However, 3 minutes after that Len Goulden (West Ham, inside-left) hit a shot so fiercely from some 30yds that it flew just under the crossbar and tore the netting.

Ulrich Linder, author of *Strikers for Hitler*, has said: 'To lose to England at the time was nothing unusual because basically everybody did. For Hitler the propaganda effect of that game was more important than anything else.'

The suggestion is that because this match was played so normally it opened the way for British Prime Minister Neville Chamberlain to meet Hitler in Munich in September and reach an agreement over Czechoslovakia (which resulted in Hitler tearing Czechoslovakia apart). This is a difficult argument to sustain because the future of the world, no less, was in play and that could never depend on a friendly soccer match, however tempting it may be to think it did.

The salute by the English players would haunt them although even that has controversial dimensions. After the war, when the full Nazi horrors were laid bare for all to see, Hapgood – who served in the Royal Air Force – would say: 'I've been V-bombed in Brussels before the Rhine crossing, bombed and rocketed in London, I've been in a shipwreck, a train crash, and inches short of a plane accident, but the worst moment of my life, and one I would not willingly go through again, was giving the Nazi salute in Berlin.'

The day after the England match, Aston Villa did meet a German eleven, also in front of 110,000 people at the Olympic Stadium, but did not give the salute. Eric Houghton, long associated with the club, remembered that 'they said we'd got to give the Nazi salute, so we went to the centre of the field and gave them the two finger salute and they cheered like mad. They thought it was all right. They didn't know what the two fingers were.'

However, Jimmy Hogan, the Aston Villa manager, told Henry Rose of the *Daily Express* that, although the team were not anxious to give the salute, they 'yielded to the suggestion of the Football Association to do so'.

David Downing, in his book *The Best of Enemies: England v Germany,* tries to disentangle the mythology: 'After the match most of the Villa team hurried off the pitch, but attempts were made to get them back on in order to join the Germans in the Nazi salute as the FA had "requested".'

At the final whistle the German players lined up to give the salute. The Aston Villa captain, Jimmy Allen, and 'one or two others'[21] remained on the pitch. Allen tried in vain to get the rest of the players to come back on and give the salute. The *Daily Mirror* headlined, 'ASTON VILLA MEN IN SCENE AFTER BERLIN GAME', reporting: 'Several Villa players seemed to hesitate and it appeared to the crowd that they had objected to going back.'

Downing sums up:

> The German crowd whistled and booed, their anger at Villa's offside tactics and an appalling foul by [Alex] Massie now compounded by the implied disrespect to their beloved Führer. The Foreign Office was furious with the FA, and the FA was furious with the Villa players. Arms were twisted, and after the second and third matches of the tour, in Dusseldorf and Stuttgart, the Villa players obediently performed the dreaded salute.[22]

By contrast, the Grand Prix at Tripoli on 15 May seemed almost quiet. The new 3l cars were on display, although Auto Union were not ready. Mercedes sent cars for Caracciola, von Brauchitsch and Lang. Because there were only thirteen entries the organisers added seventeen Voiturettes – lightweight cars limited to 1,500ccs – to have a full complement for the lottery, tickets for which the Italian public spent a fortune and which financed the race. Having two classes of car with such a discrepancy in performance was inviting disaster, however.

Lang recalled that a marshal showed him a yellow flag, meaning slow, danger ahead. The track was covered with thick cactus leaves and roots. It had been lined with sandbanks and the cactuses planted in them to give them firmness. Somebody must have ploughed through.

On lap eight, Eugenio Siena in a Grand Prix Alfa Romeo caught up to a Voiturette Maserati and braked violently. He lost control, skimmed a sandbank and rammed a house. He was killed immediately. Lang meanwhile led in his Mercedes, taking that lead from Carlo Trossi's Grand Prix Maserati. On lap thirteen the Hungarian László Hartmann (Voiturette Maserati) cut a corner in front of Giuseppe Farina's much faster Alfa Romeo Grand Prix car. They flipped and skidded down the track upside down. Both drivers were thrown out, and Caracciola and Lang only just missed them. Lang would describe how it happened in a 180mph corner and, in a moment from a nightmare, he only just managed to slot the Mercedes between them.

The Mercedes of Caracciola and von Brauchitsch had engine problems, leaving Lang to win it – won forty-four, lost nine.

Germany beat Norway 5-0 in the Davis Cup in Berlin from 20 to 22 May and this, inevitably, became a political event because Germany selected Austria's leading player, Georg von Metaxa, even though the competition's rules stipulated that if you had played for one country you must wait for three years before you could play for another. Reportedly[23] only Poland protested and this was ignored. Von Metaxa played.

He won his opening singles in five sets, then he and Henkel won their doubles in three sets before von Metaxa won his second singles, this time in three sets. He dropped only one game.

Between 26 and 28 May, in the Davis Cup Germany beat Hungary 3-1 in Budapest, von Metaxa winning one singles and losing the other but, again, he and Henkel won in the doubles. Germany would now play France in the semi-finals in July, again in Berlin.

The irony was that von Cramm was physically close in his plain cell (bed and wooden stool) in Moabit prison, where his exercise was an hour a day walking in a circle round the courtyard.[24] He now lived in a world of 3,000 fellow prisoners, some of whom were badly maltreated. Mercifully, he was not. Nor could Norway and Hungary be considered serious examinations for the German team without him. France would know if he was being missed and, if he was, by how much.

The soccer World Cup in France has been called the 'Forgotten Cup' because it was not manipulated or financed by the French government. Spain was being dismembered by the civil war, Uruguay – still brooding over how many countries had *not* come to them in 1930 – were boycotting, and Argentina were brooding because the World Cup ought to have alternated between the two big continents (South America and Europe) but here it was in France after Italy 1934, and the Argentines were not coming. The news 'provoked rioting outside their federation's offices in Buenos Aires'.[25]

Just before the competition began, the French President Albert Lebrun welcomed the various federations at the Elysee Palace in Paris and said that the World Cup was 'the occasion of a rapprochement between peoples' (which one cynic says he cannot possibly have believed himself).

The original sixteen countries facing the four knockout rounds were now, of course, fifteen. Austria had qualified by beating Latvia 2-1 but withdrawn because under FIFA rules you could not have 'two Federations for one country'. Austria had played a preparatory match against France and the Germans annulled it. As one French source says: 'From this moment on, the Third Reich would impose its rules even on European football.'

La Libération newspaper, reviewing the competition many decades later, carried a reflection under the headline:

> The unquiet World Cup. The noise of boots in Europe deadens the clamour from the stadiums

> The images are blurred, as if memory has made its own selection, traumatised by the horrors of what which was going to follow. It was proof that the ball doesn't weigh as heavily as cannon balls. Now there remain only yellowing photographs coming out of dusty drawers. The fascist slogans being uttered across the Rhine made a lot more noise than any coming from the stadiums. The hopes aroused by the Popular Front in 1936 [a left-wing grouping which had formed the government] revealed

themselves to be illusions from this moment on: the world war was coming with giant strides.[26]

The German and Italian teams would face anti-fascist demonstrations, the Italians in particular getting hostile barracking from the crowds wherever they played. Nine Austrians travelled with the German team, although the coach, Herberger, would have great difficulty marrying their inspired play with the German style of individual marking and rugged tactics. It would be a fundamental difference and the cause of Herberger's problems.

For their first-round match against Switzerland in Paris on 4 June he selected: Rudolf Raftl (Austrian); Willibald Schmaus (Austrian), Wilhelm Hahnemann (Austrian), Hans Mock (Austrian), Rudolf Gellesch (German), Hans Pesser (Austrian), Albin Kitzinger (German), Andreas Kupfer (German), Paul Janes (German), Ernest Lehner (German), Josef Gauchel (German).

The match was played at the Parc des Princes at 5 p.m. in front of 27,000 spectators.

One report says that the German team was pelted with tomatoes, eggs and bottles, and when the *Horst Wessel Song* (a sort of Nazi anthem named for the martyred Wessel) was played, sections of the crowd showed their displeasure by whistling as loudly as they could.

There was another dimension to the match because the Swiss were coached by Karl Rappan, an Austrian who invented a strategy called the 'bolt', which opened the way to *catenaccio* (Italian for 'door-bolt'), a way of organising the defence. Rappan's strategy was to concede the midfield and move four men back in defence with one of them – the bolt – supporting the other three.

Gauchel opened the scoring for Germany in the twenty-ninth minute, but Andre Abegglen equalised 2 minutes before half time and it stayed like that through extra time – although Pesser was sent off in the ninety-sixth minute.

The tie had to be replayed in Paris five days later. Hahnemann gave the Germans the lead after 9 minutes and Ernest Loertscher became the first player in a World Cup final to score an own goal. That made Germany two up after 22 minutes, but the Swiss did not seem to need the bolt. They scored through Wallaschek (42 minutes), Fredy Bickel (65) and Abegglen (76 and 79).

Dick Seaman now had a chalet on the Starnberger See, a lake 30 miles from Munich. There, that summer, he was invited to another chalet across the lake for a dinner party and met 18-year-old Erica Popp, daughter of the managing director of BMW. They fell in love very quickly and that brought understandable delights – he handsome, famous, striking; she pretty as a peach – as well as the necessary complications of the Englishman now being interwoven more and more closely to the life of the Reich. Mrs Seaman was not pleased.

Henner Henkel was seeded fourth for Wimbledon. Henkel was drawn in section six, the same as Daniel Prenn, now of course playing for Britain. Henkel overwhelmed a Briton, Derek Bull, 6-2, 6-0, 6-2, while Prenn lost to another Briton, Murray Delaford, 6-4, 6-4, 5-7, 1-6, 4-6. If he had won he would have met Henkel in the second round.

Another German, Rolf Goepfert, reached the third round. Henkel sailed into the semi-finals with five three-set victories but met Bunny Austin who destroyed him 6-2, 6-4, 6-0.

In direct contrast to the grass courts of London SW1, anticipation for the Louis-Schmeling fight was building and building:

> It didn't help Schmeling's case when various rumours gained wings. Hitler was going to make him Minister for Sport for the Third Reich if he won. His trainer, Max Machon, kept a full Nazi uniform, right down to swastika armband, in a closet at the Osborne Hotel. Storm troopers would join German fans sailing over on the SS *Hamburg* and SS *Europa*. A German correspondent, Arno Heilmis, informed his homeland that the Jewish governor of New York, Herbert Lehman, was part of a conspiracy to make sure Louis won. Schmeling knew he could dismiss the stories as the nonsense they were, but held back because he didn't want to cause more problems for his wife and mother, virtually held hostage by Goebbels.[27]

Evidently Louis was getting the political questions too, and expressed irritation. He wanted to beat Schmeling and did not feel that committed him to beating Germany and Hitler as well. Nor does he seem to have hated Schmeling, certainly in the ordinary sense, any more than Schmeling hated him. Louis had, more accurately, a memory to beat – his own memory of what Schmeling did to him. Rather than knock out his sparring partners (promoter Jacobs liked that), Louis concentrated on blocking and parrying Schmeling's fearsome right hand. The sparring partners fed him right-right-rights until the blocking and parrying became automatic.

'The Non-Partisan Anti-Nazi League and the American Jewish Congress urged Jacobs to cancel the fight. Jacobs offered to donate 10 per cent of the gate to groups helping Jewish refugees.'[28]

The undercurrents had surfaced, if indeed they had ever been concealed. Jacobs was Jewish and the pressure for a boycott from the American Jewish Congress grew as the anticipation grew, but Jacobs reasoned that the fight exercised such a fascination it would sell out even if the Jewish community did boycott it.

The American press were portraying the fight as democracy versus dictatorship: 'The American public now came to view Joe Louis – a black man – as *their* official representative of American strength and virtue. In the racist society of the time, that was revolutionary almost beyond belief.'[29]

On the morning of the fight a news agency quoted Louis as saying he was fighting for America 'against a foreign invader' and in Berlin the newspaper *Der Angriff* – a Goebbels mouthpiece – responded by accusing America of 'an organised campaign of lies'. They asked: 'Do Americans think so lightly of their world champion that even in the last hours before the fight they are trying to destroy Schmeling's morale with such attacks?'[30]

That Wednesday was warm and muggy but later there would be a cooling breeze. During the day Louis went for a walk and confided that he was worried he might kill Schmeling. He reached the Yankee Stadium 3 hours before he was due to fight and the crowd, which would eventually number 70,043, was already so dense that Louis had to carve a path through it to get to his dressing room. Among that crowd were members of the Non-Sectarian Anti-Nazi League, giving out handbills demanding a boycott – not of the fight but of German goods – and communists exhorting spectators to cheer Louis and (of course) boo Schmeling.

Once he was in the dressing room Louis promptly fell asleep.

His trainer woke him at 9 p.m. and taped his hands. At this point before a fight Louis would do a 10-minute stint of shadow boxing to loosen up, get the body working as he wanted it to work. Now he did a full 30 minutes as if he was priming his body to launch an all-out assault from the bell. He emerged and came towards the ring to tremendous cheering, wave after wave of it.

Schmeling, surrounded by police, was applauded, except by those close to the ring who threw banana peels and paper cups. Schmeling put a towel over his head.

The announcer, in evening dress, said, 'Fifteen rounds for the world heavyweight championship – weighing 193 [lb], wearing purple trunks, outstanding contender for heavyweight honours, the former heavyweight title holder Max Schmeling.' He came towards the centre of the ring bowing as he went while a mixture of cheers and jeers rang out – the cheers louder. 'Weighing 198 and three quarters, wearing black trunks, the famous Detroit Brown Bomber, world heavyweight champion Joe Louis.' More cheering. One report said: 'The anti-Nazi boycott failed completely. The reception given to Schmeling when he entered the ring was even better than that given to Louis.'

The bell rang.

They slow-waltzed towards each other feinting and weaving but that was almost ritualised movement, a seeking out of an initial position. Schmeling took two half-steps backwards and Louis found him with a left jab. That was after 7 seconds. Louis followed it with an immediate uppercut and a blow over the top of Schmeling's arm which did not seem to land. That was after 8 seconds.

They moved apart, prodded the air and Louis sprang at Schmeling, hammering in another left hook. That was after 19 seconds. Schmeling dipped his head and Louis hit him with both hands including another left hook, Schmeling with his arms in front of his face and body trying just to protect himself.

Twice Louis landed more left hooks, the second bucking Schmeling's head back. That was after 30 seconds. Schmeling launched his right but it brushed Louis' shoulder, and that was the first serious punch Schmeling had tried. They sparred as if they were on tiptoe, just out of reach of each other. They danced and glared. They moved together and Louis was upper-cutting with both hands, landing a right then a left then a fiercely powerful straight right. Schmeling reeled and for an instant his head had that lost-control look as if he might go down. That was after 1 minute 25 seconds. Schmeling half turned his back and Louis rained a torrent of blows on him. A right to the head and Schmeling's knees seemed to buckle. He was holding on to the ropes while, still, blow after blow battered him. One right-hand punch was almost certainly an illegal kidney punch, albeit not done deliberately. Louis was to say, 'I just hit him', but 'man did he scream'.

The live radio broadcast to Germany was cut at this moment, or at least a mythology has grown up that it was.[31] One report suggests Schmeling's cries of pain as the punches landed were audible and that he had two broken vertebrae. The Nazis clearly knew what was going to happen and did not want Germany hearing it. However, Patrick Myler, in *Ring of Hate*, says clearly: 'The Berlin Associated Press report made no mention of a power cut, deliberate or coincidental, but said that gloom enveloped the taverns where Schmeling supporters gathered for the radio transmission.'

The referee stepped forward, Louis stepped away and after a glance at Schmeling the referee waved for the fight to resume.

Schmeling stumbled forward, his guard wrecked, and a savage right to the jaw sent him down.

He rolled completely over and rose at the count of two. He stumbled forward again and now Louis was free to unleash his full armoury without fear of retaliation. Schmeling went down again. That was after 1 minute and 55 seconds. Louis landed three punches, fast as machine-gun fire, and Schmeling was down a third time. On all fours, this brave man tried to get up as the referee began the count. A white towel was thrown in from Schmeling's corner but the referee continued the count – New York State did not recognise towel-throwing – and had reached five when it was obvious to him, and to the world, that Schmeling was physically incapable of offering any further resistance. Joe Louis might really have killed him.

The fight was over. It had lasted 2 minutes and 4 seconds.

It took three men to guide Schmeling back to his corner and without in any way making excuses – he just was not that kind of man – he said subsequently that the kidney punch had literally paralysed him for a moment or two, the pain so intense he could do nothing. He would go to hospital and be there for several days.

Louis took the victory calmly, not least because that was the sort of self-control he had required through his career. If he had been seen gloating over the white men he destroyed that would certainly have damaged him – even gloating over a German.

A journalist called O.B. Keeler, writing in the *Atlanta Journal*,[32] caught the American dilemma which, it must be said, was some way towards the Nazi view of race:

> The average of white intelligence is above the average of black intelligence probably because the white race is several thousand years further away from jungle savagery. These black boys are Americans – a whole lot more distinctly so than more recently arrived citizens of, say, the Schmeling type. There should be just as much pride in their progress and prowess under our system as in the triumph of any other American. For all their misfortunes and shortcomings, they are our people – Negroes, yes, but our Negroes.

Hitler may have tried to hijack the World Heavyweight Championship but in doing so he created the circumstances where Louis, like Jesse Owens, forced Americans to define themselves or at the very least think about defining themselves. Louis' victory did not prevent the black area of New York and far beyond starting a carnival with Harlem citizens 'doing the goosestep and mocking the "Heil Hitler" salute'. People rushed from their apartments shrieking, banging kitchen utensils and blowing horns. In Detroit a banner unfurled: 'JOE LOUIS KNOCKED OUT HITLER.'

The Reuters new agency reported under a Cleveland, Ohio, dateline:

> Police used tear gas to quell a rioting crowd in the negro section here after the result of the fight was known. One man was shot and probably fatally wounded. Two police-men were stunned by flying bricks. Passengers in a tram were hurt by stones, and at one busy intersection general fighting broke out, with men using knifes and clubs.

The reaction in Germany was perhaps captured by Arno Hellmis, the Nazi boxing commentator, whose coverage of both Louis-Schmeling fights was couched in Nazi ideology. Hellmis referred to Schmeling as 'Max' and Louis as 'the negro'.

One legend (or myth) suggests that during this second fight Hellmis said on air that Jews were as unpopular in the United States as they were in Germany. Another legend (or myth) has Hellmis ending his broadcast with the words: 'We sympathise with you, Max, although you lost as a fair sportsman. We will show you on your return that reports in foreign newspapers that you will be thrown into jail are untrue.'[33]

Whether Hellmis would broach something so politically sensitive – revealing that foreign newspapers thought the Nazis were so dishonourable they were writing about Schmeling being jailed – must be problematic.

The German ambassador in Washington journeyed to New York to see Schmeling in hospital and evidently was anxious that he – Schmeling – lodged an official protest about the kidney punch. Like Henderson in Berlin before the soccer match, one must assume the ambassador had momentous events coming at him from many directions and the last thing he needed was a messy, controversial boxing row, which, in real terms, Schmeling could not win. No doubt Goebbels saw the potential in the row, however – not least in creating an excuse for why Schmeling lost – and may have been instrumental in having the ambassador go to the hospital.

Goebbels was certainly not about to let the defeat rest and his ministry started rumours that the illegal Louis punch had been landed deliberately and even that Louis had concealed lead in his gloves. There are suggestions too that when film of the fight appeared in Germany it had been censored to remove the rain of blows before the disputed kidney punch, and of course without context the punch assumed a quite different character. A boxer might aim one in a calculated move but it would be more difficult in a fluid, frantically fast flurry with his opponent twisting and con-torting. Inevitably, the Goebbels press wrote that Jews controlled boxing in New York and what could a German expect when he got there?

The fight stood as confirmation of what any thinking person already knew: Hitler was not a good loser, Goebbels was not a good loser and none of the other Nazis were, either.

The irony is that Max Schmeling was. It is how he and Louis became friends. Frank Deford, writing in *Sports Illustrated Vault*, sums Schmeling up perfectly:

> He was sometimes credulous and sometimes weak and often an example of what the road to hell is paved with. Schmeling has, however, been candid about his life under Hitler, baldly admitting to the concessions he made, to his sins of omission, to expedience in the face of evil. Neither does he deny that he liked the Führer's attention.[34]

During June, German children in Berlin painted the Star of David on Jewish shops that were pointed out to them by adults, while in Austria the Nazis tightened their grip, introducing strict anti-Semitic laws. Just as ominously, the Sudeten German party made big gains in the Czechoslovak elections.

On 2 July, Wimbledon concluded with Budge beating Bunny Austin 6-1, 6-0, 6-3, to polite applause. Wimbledon had its fifty-seventh men's champion.

The Mercedes and Auto Union teams lined up at Rhiems for the French Grand Prix. Auto Union had not contested the first two Grands Prix, of course, and their new streamlined cars were by no means race ready. They took two cars and three drivers (Christian Kautz as reserve) and during practice Hasse destroyed his car and Müller damaged his. Auto Union contemplated a complete withdrawal but the entry was already so small – nine cars – that their absence would have reduced the sixty-four laps to either a demonstration run for Mercedes or a tedious farce. As a compromise, Auto Union did withdraw their streamliners and raced two rebuilt cars from the previous season.

The circuit was drying after a shower and the French crowd applauded the German cars for literally making a race of it. Caracciola started badly, allowing the other two Mercedes – von Brauchitsch and Lang – to escape. This opening lap proved a wild one: Kautz hit a kerb at the village of Gueux and rammed a house backwards.

At the sharp-right Garenne corner, Hasse spun and stalled. He tried to restart the car downhill using reverse gear but it went into a field, not to return. That left six cars – a Bugatti was already gone with a broken oil pipe, and in the next lap it became five when a French driver dropped out. To please the crowd Alfred Neubauer allowed the three Mercedes to race each other and in the end von Brauchitsch beat Caracciola by a minute and a half, Lang inevitably third. Only one other car finished, a Talbot which had covered fifty-four laps at the end – ten behind von Brauchitsch, translating to 48 miles – and the big scoreboard read won forty-five, lost nine.

Georg von Metaxa was about to be properly tested in the Davis Cup semi-final against France on the clay at Berlin's Rot-Weiss Club. Henkel gave them a solid start, beating Yvon Petra (Vietnamese born – Vietnam then a French colony, of course – and who would win Wimbledon in 1946). Von Metaxa survived a hard match against Bernard Destremau (who would fight the Germans in the war and become a diplomat afterwards) 6-4, 7-5, 5-7, 5-7, 6-3. Henkel and von Metaxa beat Petra and Jean Lesueur in another hard match, 4-6, 6-4, 2-6, 10-8, 6-4. Petra then beat von Metaxa in three straight sets. That gave the tie to the Germans, although Destremau took the final match against Hans Redl, a 23-year-old Austrian who would have a spectacular career after the war.

Germany now faced Yugoslavia in the European Zone final in Berlin a week later.

In between, the Grand Prix cars contested the German race and, of course, Auto Union were ready for that. They had signed Tazio Nuvolari; a sensation at the time, and involving Nuvolari abandoning Alfa Romeo to drive for the opposition, although the fiery crash at Pau had removed any political or nationalistic under-tones. The German Grand Prix remains, however, deeply etched in the political and the nationalistic. The line-up: Auto Union – Nuvolari, Stuck, Hasse, Müller; and Mercedes – Caracciola, von Brauchitsch, Lang, Seaman (Mercedes brought seven cars, four for the race and three as reserve).

Von Brauchitsch took pole with a brave, flamboyant lap almost 6 seconds faster than Lang, then Seaman and Caracciola, with Nuvolari the fastest of the Auto Unions 15 seconds slower. The starting lights failed and the cars set off in a ragged surge of very great power, Lang leading from Hasse and Nuvolari attacking. Soon the Mercedes formed a phalanx at the front, Nuvolari spinning and damaging the Auto Union.

Von Brauchitsch led from Seaman and when von Brauchitsch pitted, Seaman, who had been running close behind him, inherited the lead. Von Brauchitsch complained that Seaman was so close he was unsettling him.

On lap sixteen von Brauchitsch made his second pit stop, Seaman following in some 10 seconds later. During the stop von Brauchitsch's car caught fire when fuel overflowed. Seaman was ordered back out on to the circuit; cryptically he had said, when he sat in his car motionless, that he had been told to follow von Brauchitsch and that was what he was doing. So Seaman emerged in the lead again. Von Brauchitsch was ordered out, too, when the fire had been doused.

Rudi Uhlenhaut would say,[35] 'Neubauer was later blamed by a Nazi SS man for sending von Brauchitsch out again, as he crashed not long after leaving the pits, the implication being that the car was badly damaged by the fire and ought not to have been allowed to continue.' Uhlenhaut added that he had checked the car himself and it had been fine: von Brauchitsch made a driving mistake on his first lap back on the circuit.

The received wisdom is that Hühnlein saw all too clearly that he would have to tel-egram Hitler after the race, as he did after every race, and explain that an Englishman had won the German Grand Prix in a German car in front of 300,000 Germans, thus taking the prize Hitler had himself awarded the race. Hühnlein therefore ordered Neubauer to order von Brauchitsch out, and if Neubauer had refused he would have placed himself in a very dangerous position.

Carraciola had a stomach upset – possibly Neubauer had just acquired one – and Lang took over his car, bringing it home 4 minutes and 20 seconds behind Seaman, making it won forty-six, lost nine.

Seaman was garlanded – an enormous floral affair which engulfed him – and people all around gave the Nazi salute, including Hühnlein, while Seaman half-raised his right arm.

Hühnlein chose his words to Hitler with exquisite care:

My Führer, I report: The 11th Grand Prix of Germany for racing cars ended with a decisive German victory. From the start the new German racing construction of Mercedes-Benz and Auto Union dominated the field. NSKK Storm Leader Manfred von Brauchitsch, leading from the beginning and giving admirable proof of his courage and ability, was deprived of victory by his car catching fire while refuelling. The winner and consequently the gainer of your proud prize, My Führer, was Richard Seaman on a Mercedes, followed by NSKK Chief Storm Leader Hermann Lang, also on a Mercedes, Hans Stuck and Tazio Nuvolari on Auto Union cars. Heil, My Führer.

Soon after, Mrs Seaman journeyed to Munich to see her son and, however much his friends pointed out to her how delightful Erica Popp was, all her misgivings remained – though mingled with a grudging acceptance that Popp was delightful.

Germany met Yugoslavia in the Davis Cup European final and Henkel over-whelmed Franjo Puncec, a Croat who had reached the semi-finals in the French Open. Von Metaxa, however, needed five sets – the fifth going to 12-10 – before he beat Josip Palada, who had also reached the semi-finals in France and whose career would last until 1956. He was in no sense a leading player, however.

Henkel and von Metaxa won the doubles, beating Franjo Kukuljevi (another Croat who had been an international since 1930) and Puncec 1-6, 7-9, 7-5, 6-4, 6-4. Henkel demolished Palada but Redl was brushed aside by Kukuljevi 6-4, 6-3, 6-2.

Germany would face Australia in the Interzonal final in Boston in August.

In July, Hitler attacked 'degenerate' art, while in Rome Mussolini began to follow the anti-Semitic Nazi laws. In Germany, Jews had to carry special identity cards.

The *Coppa Ciano* at Livorno was a minor race in the overall context. Auto Union did not go but Mercedes did, and von Brauchitsch beat Lang only to be disqualified because spectators gave him a push when he had hit straw bales and stalled. Farina in the Alfa Romeo next was 48 seconds away. Caracciola won the *Coppa Acerbo* a week later – won forty-eight, lost nine.

At Longwood Cricket Club in Boston, between 18 and 20 August, Australia over-whelmed the German Davis Cup team 5-0. Redl did not play, leaving Henkel and von Metaxa facing two singles each and the doubles. The Australians won all five matches in straight sets and in fact the only seriously close set was between Henkel and Adrian Quist, which Quist won 8-6.

Time magazine wrote:

… the Australian Davis Cuppers (Quist & Bromwich) were at Longwood – prov-ing their proficiency by taking all five matches from the German team of Henner Henkel & Georg von Metaxa (an Austrian acquired by anschluss to replace impris-oned Baron Gottfried von Cramm). After losing their third straight match, the German team received a cable from the German Tennis Federation 'requesting' them to discontinue further competition in the U. S., [and] return home 'to be saved from too much tennis' (meaning, presumably: Aryan humiliation).[36]

Returning home meant they would miss the US Open. Hitler, Goebbels and the Nazis did not like failure.

Von Cramm seems to have been a model prisoner because he was given small jobs to do in Moabit prison and, while others were not allowed newspapers or books, he could listen to the radio. He heard the Davis Cup defeat.[37]

The absence of von Cramm scarcely needs elaboration, as the Nazis themselves must have realised. Without him, German tennis and the German Davis Cup team were simply not the same. He would be released in October and resume his career, although the conviction haunted him through 1939.

At Bremgarten for the Swiss Grand Prix, Seaman took pole from Lang and Carraciola, Stuck the fastest Auto Union next (having been rehired by the team). Race day was wet, making the snaking, tree-lined circuit particularly dangerous. Seaman led because Lang had so much wheel spin his Mercedes didn't move. As the rain hardened Seaman drove like a master to lap eleven, when he came upon two back-markers absorbed in their own struggle. They baulked him and Caracciola knifed past to win, Seaman second – won forty-nine, lost nine.

Hitler was increasing the pressure on Czechoslovakia and, between Bremgarten and the European Athletic Championships, the Sudeten Germans began talks with Czech president Eduard Beneš. In fact, the European championships were divided, the men in Paris and the women in Vienna. In Paris the men were strong, winning the 800m, the 4x100 and 4x400 relays, pole vault, long jump (Lutz third), the discus and hammer.

In Vienna, the highjumper Dora Ratjen broke the world record with 1.67m (5ft 5.75in), but 'afterwards, it came out she was not a man and not a woman. I heard this from the discus winner, Mauermayer. I was in touch with her for a while and she wrote me that Ratjen was "in between"', Gretel Bergmann would remember:

I know how he got caught – the shaving. He was on a train coming back from Vienna [and the European championships]. At Magdeburg[38] two women saw this person in women's clothing with a five o'clock shadow and you know in Germany to denounce somebody was a great sport. So at the next stop these two women got the police and the police pulled her/him off the train and took him to the police station. Then he was told, or she was told – I don't know [chuckle] – *it* was told that there would be a medical examination. *Then* he admitted he was a male. His genitalia were set back, evidently. The funny part of it, I always say, is that there were three girls in that family already and when Dora was born the midwife told the parents 'you have another girl' because there was this *thing* that wasn't quite right down there. And that's how they brought him up as a girl. But if you wipe a baby's bottom you know whether it's a boy or a girl![39]

Ratjen was subsequently disqualified.

The German women were as successful as the men (4x100 relay, long jump, shot put, discus, javelin). In Hitler's time the German teams had become second only to the United States and, if the Berlin Olympics were an accurate form guide, in front of the United States. At the Europeans, they led the combined table with thirty-two medals, Sweden next on thirteen and Finland eleven.

Emmy and Leo Steinweg married in a civil ceremony in July 1933 because they had been told that marriages between Aryans and non-Aryans would soon become illegal. That August an SS friend told Leo that he should get out of Germany within days because in November there would be even more persecution of the Jews. On 1 September, Leo left for Holland, leaving Emmy to wind up the business. Presumably he thought he would be safe there.

On 4 September the IOC awarded the 1944 Olympic Games to London. A day later France mobilised troops to man their great defensive wall against Germany, the Maginot Line, as the tension over Czechoslovakia grew. The day after that Beneš offered self-government to the Sudetenland. The Sudeten Germans responded with mass rallies and the chant of reunification with the Reich. That was 8 September and the Grand Prix teams were gathering for the Italian Grand Prix at Monza.

There, the Italian governing body announced that cars would be restricted to 1.5l engines for their major races in 1939, which Neubauer of Mercedes took to be a way of preventing the Germans from harnessing their power. Grand Prix racing would probably be run with the 1.5 formula in 1940 and 1941.

Lang put the Mercedes on pole from von Brauchitsch and Caracciola, Müller the fastest Auto Union driver, Nuvolari on the second row. Lang led but Nuvolari moved up on him and at lap eight went by, Lang's engine down on power. Seaman, who would be running second, suffered engine trouble too, and von Brauchitsch suffered mechanical problems. Nuvolari won it from Farina in an Alfa Romeo – won fifty, lost nine.

Mercedes had been so confident of winning that they had ordered a 'celebration dinner' for seventy. That had to be cancelled but Neubauer decided he would have one anyway to celebrate Seaman's engagement to Erica Popp. Popp would remember that Neubauer had gone for a 'quiet dinner alone with his wife. It turned into a riotous evening and the crowning glory was our visit to The ambassador's nightclub afterwards, where Dick and I taught everyone the *Lambeth Walk*. They all thought it was great and we were *Oi'-ing* all over the place.'[40]

Seaman went to London and, under heavy questioning from his mother, confessed that he and Erica were more or less engaged. Her parents were coming too, in order to sort out the marriage settlement. Mrs Seaman retorted that when she had finished with Erica's father the wedding would be off.

After Monza, Mercedes moved quickly to meet the new 1939 regulations, setting up a special, secret unit to build the cars they would need.

Martial law was declared in Czechoslovakia to try to control the German Sudetens.

Fred Craner had persuaded the German teams to come and race in a Grand Prix again, due on 1 October. The race meant the British public would see the might of Mercedes and Auto Union measured for the second successive year against an assortment of, among others, little sit-up-and-beg British ERAs, a Riley and an MG to be driven by splendid chaps who were amateurs, including the bandleader Billy Cotton. The Germans would be giving a demonstration of what war would look like; even their convoys from Germany to Donington were arranged with military precision.

As the pressure on Czechoslovakia mounted day by day, war suddenly seemed imminent.

En route to Donington, Lang and his wife drove into Strasbourg. They were stopped at a crossroads by a traffic policeman. They waited and waited because, it appeared, the policeman was giving priority to everyone else and ignoring them. Eventually they were waved through and Lang could barely believe it when, as he moved past the policeman, he heard him say (presumably in Alsatian-German patois, which Lang could understand), 'good luck for your next race'.

They went to Strasbourg's railway station because a nearby bank exchanged money. The whole area 'teemed with people. Large numbers of men with suitcases and bundles or boxes streamed towards the entrance, accompanied by women and children.' Lang murmured to his wife that this looked like a full-scale mobilisation. He overheard a telephone conversation between a bank employee and (apparently) his wife – in the patois – in which he asked her to bring warm underclothes and socks because he had to report to the railway station within half an hour.

'France has mobilised against Germany,' the employee added. As Lang returned to his car a well-dressed, elderly man brushed against him and asked where he was going. Lang explained: England via Paris. In essence the man said, 'I wouldn't do that, I'd go straight back to Germany', and melted into the crowd. Lang talked it over with his wife and they decided to continue.

Outside Strasbourg they became 'involved in a whole stream of cars and horse-drawn vehicles. All were packed out with bags, cases and bundles, and perambulators, and full up to bursting point with people. Next to the drivers, bedding had been pushed in, so they could hardly move. This exodus looked almost like a panic.' By Sarrebourg, halfway between Strasbourg and Nancy, even Lang's wife – a courageous women, he insisted – was getting nervous and every village from there on 'presented the same picture: men hurrying to the station with their cases, women and children running alongside, crying, and other groups standing about arguing and reading the fresh call-up notices on the walls'.[41]

Seaman arrived in London with Erica and asked his mother to consent to their marriage immediately, by special licence 'so that', as Seaman explained, 'if war breaks out Erica need not return to Germany. She will be a British subject by marriage and can remain in this country, even if I am called up to fight in the army or air force.'

Mrs Seaman pointed out that if war did begin, Erica would not be allowed to return to Germany 'for years' and if Seaman was called up, she – Mrs Seaman – would be left with a 'young German wife in England, probably with a baby. A German grandson would be anathema to me and I should be the object of suspicion with the Home Office and the police.'[42]

On the Tuesday before the race, Hitler was giving ultimatums about Czechoslovakia and the situation deteriorated so sharply that both German teams were ordered to leave Donington for the Channel ports and Germany. If angry mobs stormed their convoys they were to burn the racing cars. In fact the situation calmed and both convoys were stopped – one at Leicester, the other at Market Harborough – and returned to the circuit.

Ladislav Hecht, the Slovakian Jew who was a leading player for the country, fled to the United States with only days to spare.

As Prime Minister Chamberlain prepared to fly to Munich to meet Hitler, the teams were told to leave again, and this time they did return home. Chamberlain flew back to London with an agreement that promised 'peace for our time'.

The next day, the day the Donington race should have been, German troops poured across the Czechoslovak border into the Sudetenland.

Von Cramm was released on 16 October after six months for 'good behaviour'.

The German teams did return to Donington and the race was run on 22 October. The power, speed and noise of the Mercedes and Auto Unions had an almost mesmerising effect on the huge crowd, which went to see them. At one point in the circuit, cresting a rise, the cars were flying through the air, all four wheels a long way off the ground. The impact of this can be gauged by two statistics. Lang took pole with a time of 2 minutes and 11 seconds, and the nearest Briton was Arthur Dobson (ERA) with 2 minutes and 24.6 seconds. In a sport which measures time in fractions of a second this was a whole dimension of difference.

A reporter for *Motor Sport* magazine wrote:

At the pits we see again the amazingly thorough organisation; every lap timed, copious notes made of every piece of work undertaken and cars continually given flag signals by their respective chiefs. At the depots, one's breath is again taken away by the astoundingly complete equipment. The tyre-store, in charge of Continentals' imposing representative [Continental, a make of tyre], is a wonderful sight, and Mercedes alone brought more than eleven hundred gallons of special fuel. When the cars are warming up the fumes and noise overcome one surprisingly quickly.

On race morning the Duke of Kent, who was to start it:

arrived almost unnoticed but the public address system played the National Anthem and the crowd realised royalty must be present. A great cheer echoed round the parkland and thousands rushed to the railings to see [the owner of Donington Hall, Gillies] Shields and Seaman being presented to the Duke. Then the Duke got into the Lagonda – on the back seat – and Seaman took the wheel, gave him a slow lap of the circuit so that its main points could be explained. A couple of other saloon cars followed, Hühnlein in one.

The duke was introduced to Hühnlein, a chunky, plumped figure encased in a heavy coat and with binoculars round his neck. He shook the duke's hand, retreated a step, stood stiff and gave the Nazi salute. The Reich really had come to the English Midlands.

Nuvolari won the race from Lang, Dobson the leading non-German six laps (more than 18 miles) behind. While Hühnlein and several Germans around him gave the Nazi salute, Nuvolari adopted the Seaman compromise position and used his arm as a flipper. The big scoreboard read won fifty-one, lost nine.

A Midlander in a heavy accent said of the cars 'ah'm dumfounded'. There would be a great deal more to be dumbfounded about in 1939.

On 9 and 10 November the SA unleashed *Kristallnacht* (the Night of Broken Glass) against Jews in Germany, killing ninety-one, ransacking shops and torching synagogues. It provoked shock round the world, especially neighbouring Holland. Germany were due to play them on 11 December in Rotterdam's Stadium De Kuip.

The newspaper *De Nederlander* wrote that 'the German pogrom [*Kristallnacht*] has most severely affected public opinion in our country'. And later: 'An international football match has in the course of years grown to be more than a game of football. Particularly in the dictatorship countries, they have become semi-national events' – propaganda exercises:

> Therefore we think it is at least necessary to consider the desirability of the match going ahead. The football part would become of secondary importance if rival supporters 'meet' in the grandstands. It goes without saying that under those circumstances there are serious chances of unpleasantness which will benefit nobody.

The Mayor of Rotterdam, Pieter Oud, agreed and banned the match, much to the fury of the KNVB (the Dutch FA) and the Dutch National Socialist Party.

The KNVB responded by saying the match would be played and committee member Karel Lotsy (a future chairman) even said that since Hitler took power German players always behaved correctly. The *Horst Wessel Song* would not be a problem and, to avoid offending Germany, the match should be played as if it was just another match. Lotsy added that sport and politics must be kept separate.

The ban stayed and now a fierce parliamentary debate began. The National Socialists used it to point to the 'Jewish danger' that threatened Holland, and it found an echo in the German News Agency, which claimed the ban was a 'decision yielding to the irresponsible Jewish-Marxist elements, with only one aim: to injure the relationship between the Netherlands and Germany'.

The newspaper *Telegraaf* pointed out that 'the Netherlands – not only Jews and Marxists – condemns the persecution in Germany'. The National Socialists kept up their attack on Oud, saying he wanted to antagonise Germany. 'The motive – fear of riots – is simply ridiculous. There are no riots in Rotterdam if the government does not want them.' The National Socialists feared the ban would adversely affect the relationship with Hitler, but other members of the parliament jeered them and called them traitors.

Holland would play Germany normally – or rather West Germany – in Düsseldorf, but in 1956.

We are still in December 1938, however. At Caxton Hall, London, Seaman and Erica were married. Mrs Seaman did not attend and never saw her son again.

Notes

1   Fisher, *A Terrible Splendor.*
2   Snellman, www.kolumbus.fi/leif.snellman/rose.htm.
3   To read a figure like 268mph is easy; to visualise the actuality of it much more difficult – especially when you have to imagine the (comparatively) primitive tyres, brakes and body strength. It is almost four times the legal maximum on British roads (70mph) today. The distance from London to Paris is 212mph, which Rosemeyer would have covered in 48 minutes. In Japan, the Bullet Train covers the 120 miles between Hiroshima and Kokura in 44 minutes, averaging 164mph and making it the fastest scheduled train service anywhere. Rosemeyer would have beaten it by 17 minutes.
4   Snellman, op. cit.
5   www.kolumbus.fi/leif.snellman/zana.htm.
6   Nixon, *Shooting Star.*
7   These headquarters lay where the Berlin Wall would run and are still there, with a museum on site, though there is so little of the original left – some cells – that they look more like Roman remains than the domain of monsters and monstrous acts.
8   Fisher, op. cit.
9   Cleather, *Wimbledon Story.*
10 Wikipedia says: 'Ostmark (English: 'Eastern March') was the name used by the Nazi propaganda to replace Austria after the Anschluss … the name *Austria* was forbidden and at first replaced by "Ostmark", referring to the 10th century *Marcha orientalis.* The change of name was meant to blank out the millennium of separate Austrian history.' Gabriella Strauss, a friend and Austrian, advises me that 'Eastern March' sounds correct to me and I would put the German Ostmark and the translation in parentheses.
11 Quoted in Jonathan Wilson, *The Guardian,* Tuesday 3 April 2007.
12 *Fascism and Football,* BBC4, Tuesday 23 September 2003.
13 Owen, *Alfa Romeo.*
14 Myler, *The Ring of Hate.*
15 Schmeling's autobiography quoted in Myler.
16 www.englandfootballonline.com/…39/…/MS216Ger1938.html.
17 'For decades, whenever the match was recalled, on radio or television or in print, the testimony of the England players was sought. The problem is that they were unreliable witnesses. Members of a patriotic generation, who after 1945 knew the

horrors of Nazi Germany as they could not have done in 1938, they were aghast at what they had done. Their version of salute and match were invented after the fact'. In Simon Kuper's book *Ajax, the Dutch, the War*.

18 Henderson, *Failure of a Mission*.

19 Kuper, op. cit.

20 Quoted in www.twofootedtackle.com/.../to-z-of-football-n-is-for.html.

21 *Daily Express*.

22 Quoted in www.twofootedtackle.com/.../to-z-of-football-n-is-for.html.

23 Fisher, op. cit.

24 Ibid.

25 Glanville, *The Story of the World Cup*.

26 www.liberation.fr/.../0101246174-les-quinze-coupes-du-monde-revisitees-3-france-1938-la-coupe-d-un-monde-inquiet-les-bruits-de-bottes-en-e.

27 Myler, op. cit.

28 www.jewishvirtuallibrary.org/jsource/US-Israel/louis.html.

29 sportsillustrated.cnn.com/vault/article/magazine/.../index.htm.

30 Quoted in Myler.

31 As Patrick Myler points out in *Ring of Hate*, after the war many Germans said they had in fact heard the whole fight and a 13-year-old, who happened to be Jewish, distinctly remembers beseeching Schmeling to get off the canvas.

32 http://www.thehistorychannelclub.com/articles/articletype/articleview/articleid/282/fists-of-freedom.

33 Quoted in Myler.

34 *Sports Illustrated Vault*, 3 December 2001, 'Almost A Hero'.

35 Quoted in Nixon, *Shooting Star*.

36 http://www.time.com/time/magazine/article/0,9171,789171,00html#ixzz110WmlS9C.

37 Fisher, op. cit.

38 Some reports suggest Ratjen was literally uncovered at Cologne. For more on this man see chapter nine.

39 Hilton, *Hitler's Olympics*.

40 Nixon, *Silver Arrows*.

41 Hilton, *Hitler's Grands Prix in England*.

42 Nixon, *Shooting Star*.

8

LAST LAP IN BELGRADE

On 29 January 1939 the German soccer team travelled to Brussels and beat Belgium 4-1. That is an ordinary sentence to write and, as it seems, the match was ordinary enough, just the first of the fifteen Germany would play between then and 3 December against Slovakia at Chemnitz.[1] By that December the world would have been at war for three months and Belgium had five months to live as an independent country.

Germany would play Yugoslavia (3-2), a country Hitler dismembered; Luxembourg (1-2), a country he would occupy; Italy (2-3), a country he would befriend, then occupy and ultimately fight; Ireland (1-1), a country he intended to invade; Norway (4-0), a country he would occupy; Denmark (2-0), a country he would occupy; Estonia (2-0), a country he would occupy; Slovakia (0-2), a country he would occupy; Hungary (1-5), a country he would make an obedient satellite; Bulgaria (2-1), another satellite; and Bohemia/Moravia (4-4), which he would make Nazi-administered territories, as we shall see in a moment.

With the advantage of hindsight, surveying all this without seeing shadows creeping across it is very difficult, but the spectators at these soccer matches could have no real understanding of the storm that would follow the shadow, or what it would do to them, whatever their forebodings. The reason is simplicity itself. No storm in all human history had resembled the one which was coming, in either extent or brutality.

The Jews had had forebodings for years, which was why so many fled Germany taking with them what they could carry, and that foreboding deepened in January. They were forbidden from becoming dentists, vets or chemists, from driving, from going to the cinema or theatres. This intensified through February and was reaching a point where ordinary life became impossible. It intensified further into March, although by then Hitler's gaze was intently upon Czechoslovakia as well.

Many other Jews did not flee and paid the ultimate price.

The Slovakian Jewish tennis player Ladislav Hecht saw the shadow. He set off for the United States and a new life three days before the Nazis, fomenting riots, made a series of demands which represented an ultimatum to Prague. The German army went in on 14 March, and a day later – in Prague – Hitler proclaimed that Bohemia and Moravia were annexed to the Reich. This explains the soccer match between the two 'countries' – the match, incidentally, would be in November, the incorporation by then well established as the new status quo.

The tennis player Bunny Austin saw the shadow. In the February issue of *Tennis Illustrated* his seventy-six-page book on moral rearmament was fully discussed. It quotes Austin as writing of the crisis the previous autumn: 'War threatened my wife, my daughter, my parents and all I cared about with destruction. It seemed uncanny to think of putting my baby daughter in a gas-proof tent.'

Austin concluded:

In the despair of the crisis a new hope was born – a new hope contained in the two words 'Moral Rearmament,' which have caught the imagination of nations, and, gathering momentum, have circled the world. But what of to-morrow? 'To-morrow' and 'Crisis' are words in danger of becoming inseparably linked. Moral Rearmament must become the rule of individual and national life. We must be the 'laughing, living, loving, willing obedience to restore God to leadership' and through Him to remake ourselves, our nation and the world.

The book contained a supporting letter signed by leading British sportspeople, including cricketers Jack Hobbs and Len Hutton, fellow tennis player Dan Maskell, boxer Len Harvey and soccer player Eddie Hapgood.

Von Cramm was playing in an international tournament in Egypt 'after a year out of competitive tennis', as *Tennis Illustrated* put it cryptically.

Now Hitler had Austria and Czechoslovakia. His gaze was moving intently towards Poland.

British Prime Minister Neville Chamberlain told the House of Commons that Britain and France would defend Poland against an aggressor. Hitler responded by denouncing this and annulling the 1934 naval treaty with Britain. It was more nuanced, however. The port of Danzig stood in a corridor between Germany and Poland as a free city. It had Polish and German origins and Hitler intended to bring it into the Reich. In March, Poland rejected that. Hitler could now increase the pressure as he wished like a tourniquet, tightening and tightening.

In April his gaze remained firmly on Danzig and, by extension, Poland – and Germany would not be playing soccer against them in 1939.

The Grand Prix season was already riven by politics of its own. The Italians, tired of the German domination, had announced that all their races, including Tripoli, would be confined to cars of 1,500cc. Because of the immensely popular lottery held annually before the race all over Italy, Mercedes risked losing a lot of money if they did not go.

The first big race, however, was Pau in France, and Mussolini resented the fact that the French government had been supporting the anti-fascists in the Spanish Civil War. He banned Italians from going to any French race. Lang won from von Brauchitsch with Etancelin (Talbot) next but two laps – 3.5 miles – behind; won fifty-two, lost nine. That was 2 April. The Grand Prix cars would return quite normally but in another world, and never contest a championship Grand Prix there again.

One of the great conundrums of the twentieth century remains unresolved. Was Hitler a master strategist, calculating each move in advance, or was he an opportunist with an intuitive feel for human weakness in situations which he could exploit? What seems certain is that the vision he set out in *Mein Kampf* in 1924 never altered. He would destroy the Jews forever, make Germany the only serious power in Europe and seize enough land in Eastern Europe and Russia to feed and fatten Germany forever.

On 20 April, Nazis fought in the streets of Danzig with anyone who opposed them. Hitler was tightening the tourniquet.

Mercedes took three cars to Mellaha for the Tripoli Grand Prix but Auto Union were still not ready. Two of those Mercedes created a sensation because they had been conceived and built in a mere eight months to conform to the new 'Italian' regulations. Tripoli was part of the Italian empire of course. Carracciola had tested his car at Hockenheim but Lang's car actually needed to be finished on the boat to the race.

The Alfa Romeos and Maseratis fell away in the intense heat so that Lang won again, this time from Caracciola with Emilio Villoresi (Alfa Romeo) one lap – 8 miles – behind. The race would be run again in 1940 but only Alfa Romeo and Maserati of the factory teams entered. The race was never held again after that, another casualty among so many – won fifty-three, lost nine. That was 7 May.

On the same day Germany began their Davis Cup season by beating Switzerland 5-0 on clay in Vienna. The German team contained von Metaxa and Henkel, described in a British magazine as an ardent Nazi.

Because the Eifelrennen nestled into the bosom of Germany at the Nürburgring, the big Grand Prix cars came back and in strength: six Auto Unions and five Mercedes, with three Maseratis completing the field. To demonstrate the 1,500cc cars to the crowd, Caracciola and Lang did laps of honour before they clambered back into their big beasts for the real business.

Lang won from Nuvolari's Auto Union, Caracciola third. Caracciola would accuse the Mercedes team of favouring Lang, 'sabotaging' his pit stop and more. The leading Maserati finished ninth, more than 14 miles behind Lang – won fifty-four, lost nine.

That was 21 May. Racing would return quite normally as the Eifelrennen but not until 1949 and as a sports car event. The Grand Prix cars would pass this way again, but never as the Eifelrennen.

The German Davis Cup went to Warsaw to play Poland in the second round but, after the singles, the Germans claimed Henkel was too tired to play in the doubles and asked for a postponement – his singles match had gone to five sets, 6-4, 6-8, 6-4, 3-6, 6-3. The Poles countered by saying the Germans had defaulted and they wanted a walk-over. They were granted this but agreed to a postponement when the Davis Cup committee appealed to them to renounce it in the interests of sport. The crowd were already unhappy and had been calling 'we want Germans on the court, not Austrians' – referring to Metaxa and Menzel.

Eventually Germany went through 3-2.

Germany and Italy signed a 'pact of steel', binding them to fight together.

In Danzig, Nazi paramilitary organisations trained and SS instructors were being smuggled in as tourists before Hitler tightened the tourniquet again.

Germany dealt comfortably with Sweden (4-1) in the Davis Cup quarter finals in Berlin.

On 1 June, the SS *Fenella* from Liverpool docked at the Isle of Man, bringing the BMW motorbike team to contest the world famous Tourist Trophy races. Another German team, NSU, arrived two days later and a third, DKW, completed what in effect was an invasion force.[2] An author, Roger Willis, has said:

> a group of German riders came *en masse* ... Everyone was told they were just motorcycle racers, not Nazis ... [but] 1939 at the TT was a complete Nazi propaganda operation organised on paramilitary lines ... The whole thing was run by a leading Nazi Party official on the Isle of Man who was masquerading as the representative of the German equivalent of the Auto-Cycle Union.[3]

There were eight German factory riders, six of them NSKK members and the others (Siegfried Wünsche and George 'Schorsch' Meier) in the army. This was heavy stuff. Ewald Kluge, a member of the Nazi Party as well as the NSKK, was 'hailed as an Aryan superhero by the Nazi propaganda machine',[4] who had had a bronze monument of him and his bike erected on the Avus circuit. The monument also included Ernest Henne, who had set a world bike record on a BMW the year before (173.9mph).

The day after their arrival the BMW riders – Meier, Jock West and Karl Gall – practised. At Ballaugh Bridge, Gall crashed, went face down for about 30yds and received what would prove to be fatal injuries.

George Brown edited the *Isle of Man Weekly Times* and was writing some trenchant words about how 'of course we don't want German or Italian riders to win', adding that British riders on German bikes should be ashamed of themselves. 'There is more than a chance that the countries these famous British riders represent will be at war with Britain before the years is out.'[5]

Brown was also part of the BBC commentary team for the TT week and Erwin Kraus, an *Obergruppenführer* in the NSKK – Hühnlein's no. 2 and on the Isle of Man known as 'Herr E. Kraus' – complained officially about what Brown had written. The DKW press chief explained 'the protest was lodged because we took exception to remarks about Herr Hitler'.

The BBC reacted quickly. Victor Smythe, their North Regional Director of Outside Broadcasts (who was on the island), rang Brown to say that all his BBC contracts were now cancelled. This was followed up by a letter from J.S.A. Salt, Programme Director of the BBC for North Region. In part it read: 'we felt it would be most inadvisable at the present time for us to be associated with an element of political controversy in what we feel should be regarded purely as a sporting event.'

Meier won the Senior TT from West by 2.5 minutes and the team, except West, gave the Nazi salute. West fiddled with his gloves in, we must assume, a high state of embarrassment. At least he could nurse the consolation that Dick Seaman and Tazio Nuvolari had both faced the same problem and compromised with their semi-salute gestures.[6]

The day after Meier won, Goebbels spoke in Danzig and tightened the tourniquet himself by declaring that the city 'has become an international problem overnight'. He omitted to mention that he, Hitler and the other Nazi leaders had made it into an international problem and it certainly had not happened overnight.

The British Davis Cup team went to the 'handsome setting' of the Rot-Weiss Club in Berlin straight from the French Open in Paris and managed some practice on the slow clay. *The Times*, in masterly understatement, said the tie had 'in the circumstances aroused peculiar interest'. This, and the harsh face of Berlin decked out in swastikas everywhere, was softened because the Yugoslav royal family were making a visit and the red, white and blue Yugoslav flag flew prominently. Britain was crushed 5-0, moving *The Times* correspondent to write that:

> a tribute is due to a German audience for the dignified manner in which they accepted these sorry events. They must have been a bitter disappointment to people who seemed to wish for nothing more thasn some good lawn tennis – and, of course, a victory for the Greater Reich. The stands were packed both days in a beautiful sunny setting and, so far as this most international of games go, no team could have wished for a more friendly or more sympathetic reception.

Tennis Illustrated wrote that 'crowds of over 5,000 gave the British players a cordial welcome'.

Meier was busy. He won the 500cc race at Assen in Holland and would go on to win the Belgian at Spa, becoming the first man to lap a Grand Prix circuit on a bike at more than 100mph.

Gottfried von Cramm's conviction for homosexuality tracked him to London where the Wimbledon committee decided that, as a former convict, they could not let him play in the championship. However, Queen's Club, which hosted the traditional pre-Wimbledon tournament, did after what has been described as a heated debate. *The Times* correspondent noted, almost cryptically, that von Cramm was 'making a brief return to the English scene as the guest of Sir Louis Greig, chairman of the All-England Club'.

Von Cramm, 'noticeably thinner and paler',[7] destroyed American Elwood Cooke in half an hour and then destroyed Bobby Riggs – the leading American now Budge had turned professional – 6-0, 6-1. He met Ghaus Mohammed of India in the final and beat him 6-1, 6-3.

Von Cramm's absence devalued Wimbledon because on this form he would have been favourite to win it, especially after what he had just done to Riggs. *The Times* correspondent caught that mood: 'If ever a player looked as though he could go on and win the Wimbledon championship it was von Cramm. There was a studied severity about all his moves; his handling of Ghaus' fast serve was in itself an object lesson.'

As it was, Henner Henkel beat Franjo Kukuljevi, a Croatian playing for Yugoslavia, in the quarter finals, but lost to Cooke in the semi-finals 3-6, 6-4, 4-6, 4-6. That was 8 July and the tennis players would return quite normally, but in another world, in 1946.

Rain soaked Spa for the Belgian Grand Prix as the four Mercedes and four Auto Unions took their place on the grid. Lang was on the front row and Neubauer said he should lead. Lang was trying to do what Rosemeyer had described as 'the killing of the inner coward', which meant banishing fear. Müller took the lead, his Auto Union throwing back such a wall of spray that Lang, behind him, could not see where he was going.

Lang waved Caracciola through thinking he might be able to get to, and past, Müller, but he could not. Lang now waved Seaman by and, when Müller pitted, Seaman led. By lap twenty-two he had fashioned a lead of 28 seconds – very comfortable in any context – but, the rain falling harder, he maintained his pace rather than slackening it. He reached the left-hand corner leading to *La Source* hairpin,[8] went off and his Mercedes struck a tree with such force that it was almost torn apart, the car on fire. Seaman was semi-conscious and asked for a doctor in German. He died in hospital but not before he had said the crash was entirely his own fault.

Two British friends were there and attended a memorial service at a nearby English church next morning, organised by Neubauer. That evening Mercedes had a victory dinner – Lang won the race –won fifty-five, lost nine. The two Britons were not only invited but given places as guests of honour. One recalled: 'There was a place set for Dick and each course was served to his position.'[9]

Chivalry was not dead yet.

At the funeral, held in London the following Friday, Caracciola, von Brauchitsch and Lang represented the drivers, Neubauer represented the team management and two directors represented the company. Members of the German Embassy attended too. So did the leading figures in Seaman's life and in British motor sport.

Hitler sent a large wreath of white lilies, almost 6ft tall, with two streamers hanging from it, one marked 'ADOLF HITLER' and the other bearing a swastika. It was taken to the church at Ennismore Gardens for the funeral service but not, because of the political situation, to the cemetery in Putney.

The funeral remains evidence that chivalry, and basic respect for a human being, really was not dead yet and, because of the scale and dignity of the Germans who came to it, the funeral remains one of the last occasions of that. As the cortege made its way out to Putney, despite the *Anschluss* and the dismembering of Czechoslovakia and now the Danzig tourniquet, the Germans appeared most civilised. It would be interned in just a moment, with Dick Seaman.

The Grand Prix cars returned quite normally to Spa but not until 1946. They are still returning.

The French Grand Prix at Reims attracted a big entry, including Meier in an Auto Union. The Spanish Civil War finished in April, which theoretically ought to have made Mussolini relent about Italian teams and drivers not being allowed to race in France. He did not. To circumvent this, Auto Union asked for, and received, special permission to run Nuvolari – an Italian of course. Christian Kautz (a Swiss) entered in an Alfa Romeo, another circumvention.

Lang and Nuvolari wrestled for the lead and were travelling so fast that by lap five they were already lapping slower cars. Meier made a pit stop but his car caught fire, burning one arm badly. When he resumed he held the arm out to cool it but that meant steering the mighty, difficult Auto Union with the other hand. Lang had mechanical problems and Müller won it from Meier – won fifty-six, lost nine.

That was 9 July and the Grand Prix cars would return quite normally but not until 1948. Three drivers from the 1939 grid came through the war and would be there; only three.

Auto Union entered five cars for the German Grand Prix at the Nürburgring – Nuvolari, Stuck, Müller, Hasse and Meier – against the four of Mercedes. René Dreyfus had a Delahaye.[10]

Lang dominated practice and produced a lap of 9 minutes and 43.1 seconds, a sensation because it was faster even than Rosemeyer's 1937 time of 9 minutes and 46.2 seconds. A crowd of perhaps 300,000 watched as all but two of the German cars broke down or spun off, Caracciola beating Müller. That was 23 July and the Grand Prix cars would return quite normally, in 1951. Paul Pietsch, to become a magazine publisher, would be on both grids, and only Pietsch – won fifty-seven, lost nine.

In Zagreb, Yugoslavia beat Germany 3-2 in the Davis Cup European final, although *Tennis Illustrated* wrote: 'one hears rumours that the German team was not very satisfied with the attitude of the crowd. A too partisan support to the side one wants to win can be most disturbing to the concentration of the opposition.'

In the same magazine a player, G.P. (Pat) Hughes, lamented the pressure which had come to bear on Davis Cup matches with biased umpires and linesmen: 'Is it any wonder, therefore, that people question the usefulness of international sport in these sad days? Lawn tennis is supposed to be a game. It is supposed to be an enjoyable recreation, and played between countries, it is regarded as a means of bringing nations together.'

He added:

The trouble is partly political, but largely financial. In times like these, any kind of intercourse between the countries of Central and Eastern Europe is bound to have its troubles. There is something to be said, therefore, for a temporary cessation of international sport among nations which are unfriendly or unsympathetically disposed towards each other.

At Bad Ems, the German amateur golf championship was to be contested by two Britons and in the women's event another Briton was to play a Belgian. No doubt it was all accompanied by great decorum and normality.

At Cologne, the German athletics team beat Great Britain by 93.5 to 42.5, watched by a crowd of 60,000. The Germans were again proving how civilised they could be, although during the meeting lightning and rain produced confusion as spectators sought shelter. *The Times* reported: 'Every one, however, was in good humour.' Luz Long won the long jump. A couple of days later, virtually the same British team was announced to meet France in Paris on 3 September.

The organisers of the Swiss Grand Prix, faced with the problem of attracting the Italian 1,500cc and the Grand Prix big beasts, were typically pragmatic. They created heats for each with the best going into a final. Mercedes and Auto Union were there in strength, although Auto Union were without Meier, in hospital after crashing in the Swedish bike race at Malmö and injuring his back. He would describe the crash as 'very serious. This put me in hospital for the next seven months, which wasn't such a bad thing as it meant I couldn't be a soldier!'[11]

It was a wet race, making the Berne circuit potentially lethal. Lang, who had won his heat, had pole and Farina, who had won the other heat, lined up sixth. Lang led but Caracciola mounted a tremendous pursuit – the 'Rain Master', do not forget – and got to within 3 seconds of Lang at the end. That was 20 August. The Grand Prix cars would return to Berne quite normally, but not until 1947 – won fifty-eight, lost nine.

On 23 August, the Soviet Union and the Nazi government announced that they had concluded a pact. It was totally unexpected – two ideologies which hated each other – and it convulsed the political position. The pact stipulated that Poland would be divided between them (vanishing as a country) while Stalin got the Baltic States. In practical terms it meant Hitler could crush Poland then turn west towards France and Britain without a risk of the Soviet Union stabbing him in the back.

Two days later – Friday 25 August – a German battleship anchored at Danzig.

The two German Grand Prix teams had one final obligation, a race in Belgrade due to be run on Sunday 3 September. There was understandable nervousness in going so far with war seeming so imminent and both teams took only two cars. Auto Union would, however, take four drivers – Nuvolari, Bigalke, Müller and Stuck – while Mercedes took three, Lang, von Brauchitsch and a reserve, Walther Bäumer.

The only other entrant was Bosko Milenkovic, nicknamed Bata. He had been born in Vienna:

> his father being a rich merchant in Vienna, his mother being of French/German origin. During the war the family moved to Belgrade, Yugoslavia. When the father died in 1921, Bosko inherited some wealth including three houses. He studied at the high school, spoke perfectly German, French, Italian, English, and chose to live on his wealth. He played violin and became a friend of motorcycle racer Voja Ivanicevic, who played piano. Inspired by Ivanicevic, Bosko started racing with a 300cc NSU. He bought his first car in 1927.

At Belgrade he would run a Bugatti, which he rebuilt after a crash the year before.[12]

The Mercedes convoy took three days to get from Stuttgart to Belgrade and during it Hitler repeated his demands on Poland over Danzig. The French and British governments stiffened their stances.

The *Union Cycliste Internationale*, organisers of the Track Cycling World Championships in Milan, which embraced amateur and professional events, faced all manner of dilemmas and so did the British, whose amateur team had set off on Monday 21 August and reached Italy later in the week. On Saturday 26 August, the (British) National Cyclist's Union decided to withdraw the amateur track team 'owing to the international situation'. Reg Harris, to become Britain's leading cyclist, had travelled to Milan but did not compete because of the withdrawal.

On Sunday 27 August the Dane Jan Derksen won the amateur sprint title.

Next day Germany recalled all their cyclists and officials, the Danes followed and then the British decided not to send their road team, which ought to have left that day to compete in the amateur race on 2 September and the professional on the 3rd.

On Tuesday 29 August the *Union Cycliste Internationale* held a special meeting and decided to postpone the championships 'perhaps for a month' and hoped they could then be resumed where they had left off, in Milan again. In the professional sprint, Albert Richter was guaranteed third place but the two riders due to contest the final found the event abandoned.

On Thursday 31 August practice for the Belgrade Grand Prix, between 4 and 6 p.m., began. Lang and von Brauchitsch tested the Mercedes and Müller the Auto Union, exploring the 2.7km road circuit round a park in the middle of Belgrade. It went clockwise through eight left-hand corners (and one fast right kink), mostly on cobbles. At one point the cars were airborne.

During the day Danzig cut communications with Poland.

Civil defence authorities took over Wimbledon. The Red Cross, St John's Ambulance and Nursing Sisters came with doctors and air-raid personnel.

> The members' tea room became a canteen, so did the kitchens. The quiet reading room, with its air of seclusion, its overstuffed chairs and settees, became a dormitory, hideous with iron bedsteads. The two big players' dressing-rooms and one of the small ones were turned into First Aid Posts. The Treasurer's private sanctum was a Staff Office.[13]

At 4.47 a.m. on 1 September the German battleship opened fire on a Polish ammunition depot in Danzig and a ground assault began. German soldiers numbering 1.5 million were pouring across into Poland from Germany. The Second World War had begun.

Inevitably the innocent were caught.

Murray Walker, later a tank commander and fabled BBC motor sport commentator, remembers 'my father was running the British Army team in the international six-days motorcycle trial in Austria. The team had gone out in the expectation of there being a war and the War Office had promised to send a telegram in the event of things being so dire that we all needed to get back immediately.' The telegram duly arrived but after a delay of 24 hours, carrying the clear implication that the team should have left the day before. 'There was the question of whether to go to Switzerland – which you could reach quicker, but you faced possible internment – or take a chance and dash to France. And that's what we did.'

The two German Grand Prix teams in Belgrade were thrust into a dilemma, no doubt intensified by the newspaper headlines screaming that Germany was at war with Poland, and foreign visitors were decamping from the Belgrade hotels as fast as they could. Cut and run or stay? The organisers, who risked losing a huge amount of money, requested that they stay, and they did.

On this opening day of war, second practice for the Grand Prix began at 4 p.m. and would finish at 6 p.m. again. Lang went faster than the day before and, because Nuvolari and Stuck, both on the same train, had not yet arrived, Müller took the Auto Union out.

On Saturday 2 September, while the German army and Luftwaffe were in the process of smashing all Polish resistance, Nuvolari and Stuck arrived in Belgrade. The organisers put on a special familiarisation practice session for Nuvolari, starting at midday. Stuck did not take part, evidently because Müller had already done so many laps and Stuck would naturally request to be able to do the same number, over-stressing the engine, particularly if Müller got back in and had another go.[14]

In the 4–6 p.m. session the cars went faster and faster. That day the Luftwaffe were bombing Polish positions in Danzig.

At 9 a.m. on Sunday 3 September, Britain handed the German government an ultimatum that, if they did not withdraw their troops from Poland, Britain – and France – would be at war.

No word came.

Murray Walker and his father reached home just in time to switch on the wireless and hear Prime Minister Chamberlain announce that Britain was at war with Germany.

Neubauer hastened to the German Embassy to seek guidance and was told to stay and race. Once news of that spread, as Lang would remember, each driver wanted to win because they sensed that there would not be another race for a long time. A crowd estimated at 50,000 came to watch the race, which started at 4.45 p.m. Von Brauchitsch, who evidently had tried to board a plane to fly to Switzerland – Neubauer boarded it and ordered him back – was in a wild mood and on lap seven ran wide, churning stones back at Lang, whose windscreen and goggles shattered, putting shards of glass into his eyes. He pitted and a doctor took them out. Von Brauchitsch spun and Nuvolari won the race. It had lasted just 64 minutes and gave a final scoreboard from 1934 of won fifty-nine, lost nine (and no defeat at all in 1939).

Both teams had to run for home now. Mercedes heard all fuel would be confiscated in Hungary so Neubauer plotted a route east so they could get to Vienna – part of Germany of course. Lang would remember:

What awful, potholed, dusty roads! They led through endless maize fields and went on and on. We had to keep miles away from the main column and could recognise it by the enormous dustclouds in the distance. In Vienna we spent out first night in a black-out and began to realise that a part of our lives had indeed ended. We were in the throes of melancholy when Neubauer distributed the remainder of the petrol in the tanker to us, to enable us to get safely home.[15]

When the Mercedes trucks finally reached the factory in Stuttgart the German army requisitioned them.

Cycling magazine carried this final paragraph to its championship coverage:

S.T. Cozens, the British professional sprinter who stayed in Milan for his races, arrived in England on Wednesday evening last. In Switzerland he met Benny Clare, who had been warned at the Italian frontier that the championships were off. Clare returned to Belgium where he and Cozens were due to race in the 120 kiloms. [sic] Grand Prix of Blankenburg on September 7 and in the 100 kiloms. Grand Prix of Ostend three days later.

The shadow and the storm ran full across that.

In Berlin, an announcement said that the European heavyweight championship fight between Schmeling and Walter Neusel, due in Dortmund on 1 October, was cancelled. So was virtually everything else.

In Britain, *Tennis Illustrated*'s September issue appeared typed on plain paper: 'EDITORIAL ANNOUNCEMENT', and below it: 'The war having put a stop to tennis in this country, for the duration we shall publish once every three months.'

It was over.

Notes

1   Chemnitz was renamed Karl-Marx-Stadt by the East Germans after the war, and became Chemnitz again after reunification.
2   DKW, *Dampf-Kraft-Wagen*, was a company in Saxony which, in 1930, was the world's largest motorcycle manufacturer. In 1932, DKW merged with Audi, Horch and Wanderer to become Auto Union.
3   www.bbc.co.uk › Isle of Man › TT › My TT.
4   Willis, *The Nazi TT*.
5   Ibid.
6   In *The Nazi TT* Roger Willis concludes that although the BBC insisted the TT had been simply a sporting event the Germans had politicised it and the stiff-arm salutes proved that. 'The Führer emphatically had his propaganda coup.' He did,

but the stiff-arm saluting was irrelevant to that. As we have seen, they all did it the whole time, not just on the Isle of Man.

7 Fisher, *A Terrible Splendor*.

8 *La Source*, the severe hairpin at the end of the start-finish straight, still very much in use today.

9 Nixon, *Shooting Star*.

10 Delahaye, a racing car made by a French company which also made luxury saloons and trucks.

11 Nixon, *Silver Arrows*.

12 In www.kolumbus.fi/leif.snellman/dm.htm (source: '*Prve Beogradske Mezdunarodne Automobilske i Motociklisticke Trke, 3.IX.1939*' by Nebojsa Dordevic, Belgrade 1999. Translation from the Serb by Mira Krizman. Info supplied by Aldo Zana).

13 Cleather, *Wimbledon Story*.

14 By Hans Etzrodt, slightly edited by Leif Snellman in www.kolumbus.fi/leif.snellman/.

15 Lang, *Grand Prix Driver*.

9

ENDGAME

The fate of Albert Richter, the cyclist, forms a tragically apt epilogue. Hitler's chilled hand continued to affect so many sportspeople during and after the war that there are many, many epilogues – as we shall see in a moment – but what happened to Richter distils all the madness.

Some cyclists spied for Germany and at least a couple sold goods taken from French Jews, but Richter was not implicated in any of this. One cyclist threatened Richter's manager with currency smuggling in 1937 and he trod the familiar path to Holland's sanctuary. Richter, who had given the Nazi salute just enough to protect himself, did not follow although reportedly he realised he would have to.

After the World Championships in Milan in 1939, and his bronze medal there, he decided to ride one last time in Berlin, at the *Deutschlandhalle* on 9 December. Understandably his manager advised against. Richter went. He may or may not have been asked to smuggle money but what seems clear is that after Berlin he intended to take refuge in Switzerland.

He won in Berlin and on 31 December caught the train for Switzerland. At the frontier, according to two Dutch cyclists on the train, German soldiers made their way along the snowy platform to Richter's compartment. The cyclists said Richter 'fell unconscious from the train'. The soldiers found his bike in the baggage carriage, sliced the tyres and out tumbled 12,700 Reichsmarks. Richter was dragged to a lorry and taken away to a detention camp. His fate remains unclear: one version is that he was beaten to death by fellow smugglers, another – the official version – is that he died skiing, a third that he hanged himself in the camp, a fourth that he was allowed to choose between shooting himself and a firing squad (and chose the revolver), a fifth that a relative went to the camp and saw his body full of bullet holes.

The German Cycling Federation said: 'His name has been effaced from our ranks, from our memories, forever.'[1]

Stan Cullis, who had had an unhappy childhood and wanted to be a journalist, was a PT instructor in Britain and Italy during the war, playing soccer for a variety of clubs whenever he could. He resumed his career with Wolves in the 1946/47 season and then managed the club, although he was only 31. They would win the Football League championship three times, win the FA Cup and play matches in Europe – which opened the way for the creation of the European Cup. Perhaps he felt vindicated at last. His refusal to give the Nazi salute in Berlin had been a modest gesture, of course, but in reality it was a big one – and when the madness was over, Europeans were playing each other quite normally and peacefully.

He lost his job in 1964, worked as a sales rep, returned to manage Birmingham City and then worked in a travel agency. He died in 2001.

The FIFA meeting at the 1928 Amsterdam Olympic Games had created the soccer World Cup which, though perverted by Mussolini in 1934 and bastardised by Hitler with the absorption of the Austrian team in 1938, resumed in Brazil in 1950 and grew in its four-year cycle to the point where, when it went to South Africa in 2010, it was arguably as big as the Olympics, if not bigger.

Matthias Sindelar's death remains the subject of conjecture and suspicion, just as his reputation as one of the greatest footballers remains undiminished. Few believed then and few believe now the story of carbon monoxide poisoning. He was 35 and a Gestapo file stated he was a pro-Jewish social democrat.

Egon Ulbrich, a friend speaking on the BBC programme *Fascism and Football*, said a local Austrian official was bribed to record Sindelar's death as an accident – entitling him to a state funeral, which would obviously have been tremendously popular within Austria – because 'according to the Nazi rules, a person who had been murdered or who has committed suicide cannot be given a grave of honour. So we had to do something to ensure that the criminal element involved in his death was removed.'

Conjecture and suspicion? As someone has said: 'Despite various claims, the police records have neither been destroyed nor gone missing. They are still there in Vienna, and accessible.' They point to an accident. Was Sindelar Jewish? No. His family were Catholic. Was his girlfriend? Maybe.

The *Deutscher Fussball Bund* commissioned Niels Havemann, a historian from Mainz University, to investigate their role in the Third Reich, and at the book launch in 2005 the Sports Minister, Otto Schily, said 'unfortunately, a shadow is falling over Sepp Herberger [the player and manager]. He let himself become part of the Nazi propaganda.'

Havemann's research demonstrated that Herberger, who died in 1977 at the age of 80, was the same as most leading soccer figures at the time. They were led to support the Nazis not out of conviction but 'thoughtlessness, ignorance, opportunism or professional ambition'. Soccer was so popular, so big and so strong that it could have mounted some sort of resistance, but it did not.

It sounds very, very familiar.

Theo Zwanziger, the DFB president, discussed how Julius Hirsch, an international who died at Auschwitz, was now being honoured. Hirsch, a left-winger, was the first Jewish player to represent Germany, served in the army for four years during the First World War and evidently could not believe that his life might be in danger. He was deported to Auschwitz on 1 March 1943 and his date of death is not known.[2]

There's a statistical footnote which holds a profound eloquence:

22/11/1942 Bratislava *v*. Slovakia   5–2
22/11/1950 Stuttgart *v*. Switzerland   1–0

That was the gap and in 1949 the victories Allies divided Germany into West and East so the Swiss match was against West Germany. The East German *Deutscher Fussball-Verband der DDR* was not formed until 1952, when they played their first match against Poland in the Stadium of the Polish Army, Warsaw, and lost 3–0 in front of 35,000.

Hitler's grip would not be finally prised open until the Berlin Wall came down and Germany was reunited. Their first match:

19/12/1990 Stuttgart *v*. Switzerland   4–0

If the soccer World Cup shed Hitler and grew from 1950, so did the Olympic Games from London in 1948.

Of the three main members of the Organising Committee who met in the Council Chamber of Berlin Town Hall in January 1933, the mayor, Heinrich Sahm, was forced out of office in 1935. He was sent to Norway as a German envoy and died there in 1939.

Gretel Bergmann married Bruno Lambert, a doctor, when they reached America – Gretel was a nickname and she would be known as Margaret Lambert. Like Prenn she refused to return to Germany for many years and when she did she discovered she needed an interpreter. She went back because the stadium in Laupheim, where she had been forbidden by the Nazis to train, was now named after her.

She has been a voice of sanity down all these years about remembering the Nazis but not making their children and grandchildren forever guilty; she has remained youthful in attitude and language, and her life has been part of a major motion picture. And in 2009 her German record high jump of 1936 was finally restored to her.

The striking girl, who won fencing gold at the Amsterdam Games and returned from America to fence for Germany in 1936, went back to America in 1938. During the war her mother's house in Offenbach was searched by the Gestapo but a photograph of Hitler congratulating her kept them 'at bay'.[3]

She won the US national foil championships in 1941, 1942 and 1946, and taught German to American servicemen who had been occupying Germany but harboured ambiguous feelings about her adopted country. Eventually she returned to Germany and died there in 1953 of cancer.

Milly Mogulof has researched and written Mayer's life story in great detail and there is very little happiness in it.

Hans von Tschammer und Osten, the man with the name like a map reference, died of pneumonia in Berlin in 1943. Duff Hart-Davis, in his *Hitler's Games*, has written:

It is no longer possible to establish whether Tschammer und Osten supported the Party line on sport out of conviction or from necessity. Some foreign observers dismissed him as a Party hack, but others saw qualities in him. A small, dark, good-looking man, he had perfect manners and, unlike most of his colleagues in government, spoke excellent English ... At least once he made an effort to warn British friends about the true state of affairs in Germany. When he visited England during December, 1935, he spent a night at Burghley House, the palatial home of the Marquess of Exeter; there he urgently confided to his host that Hitler was planning a major war in Europe, and begged him to do anything he could to alert the British government to the danger.

'Dora' Ratjen was, as we saw, eventually outed as a man, Heinrich 'Heinz' Ratjen. Some reports suggest his gender was unclear from birth and his parents may even have brought him up as a girl. Just before the war his father officially requested that he be recognised as a man. After the war the mists of time close in. He was known as Hermann but called himself 'Heinz' and may have been a waiter in Hamburg and Bremen, where he may – again – have run his parents' bar.[4] He died in 2008.

Did Jesse Owens from Oakville, that very small place lost in gently rolling farmland somewhere along the pencil-thin, pencil-straight roads of northern Alabama, escape Hitler's chilled touch? 'Three small markers were all that honored' him in Oakville and in '1983, the Lawrence County Commission voted not to put a plaque in the courthouse square courtyard ... However, this vote ... only served to ignite passion in the hearts of those who wanted an appropriate tribute'. Before the Olympic Games in Atlanta, the torch route – created in Berlin of course – was diverted to take in Oakville. It worked. More than $2 million was raised and the Jesse Owens Memorial Park was completed days before the torch got there.[5]

The Hitler performance gave Owens an immortality he would not have had as an athlete, even the best athlete who has ever lived.[6] There is a rich irony in that. As Hitler was hijacking the world's most important sporting event he bestowed the immortality on a black man he felt should not have been there. One irony lay beyond even that. Hitler's performance would always stand in contrast to the dignity of Owens and the mythology – Hitler refusing to go near Owens, storming out of the stadium in a great sulk – would not help either. It did not happen like that at all, and was made worse because Hitler understood that the methods of mythology were not based on truth. The mythology he was creating, however, moved decisively against him – and still does.

Owens' life reflects a major, moving current in American life. As a black man in the team hotel in New York he had been forced to use the luggage elevator. After Berlin he was condemned for professionalism, and exclusion from amateur competition ended his career. To earn a living he was reduced to running exhibitions, even against horses. Interestingly he did not approve of the tactics of Martin Luther King (although he did approve of the aims). A lifelong heavy smoker, Owens died of lung cancer in 1980. In Berlin he remained a heroic figure, with even a road named after him at the Olympic Stadium.

There is of course nothing named for Hitler.

Nor is Owens remembered in Berlin only. He is still big in Oakville and I am indebted to James E. Pinion, board member and park co-director, for describing this:

The Jesse Owens Museum was completed in 1998 using Federal grants of $750,000. The Jesse Owens family participated in the opening.

The Museum presents a timeline of Owens' life as a sharecropper's son in Oakville, Alabama, his high school years in Cleveland Ohio where Coach Riley discovered and developed his talents in track, Ohio State where he became a track superstar, the 1936 Olympics in Berlin where he nullified Adolph Hitler's[7] theory of Arian Supremacy, and his life beyond the Olympics.

The Museum contains exhibits of sports and personal items donated by the Owens family and Ohio State Archives. A movie theater shows his return to Berlin in 1951 where he revisits the Olympic Stadium and recalls his achievements. Also in the theater can be seen a re-run of 'This is Your Life', a popular 1960s TV program honoring Owens and featuring his family and friends. Touch screen kiosks show 8 video clips, features of his life and sports accomplishments.

Annually, the Museum has approximately 48,000 visitors from 30–40 states and 15-20 other countries. Visitors in 2010 commented that the museum is 'a hidden treasure', 'very educational', 'Jesse Owens was my idol', 'Museum gives me chills', 'Remarkable man', 'A spiritual experience for me', 'Everyone should see', 'A great tribute to an incredible man', and (from a Berlin Visitor) 'Being here after a long life admiring Jesse Owens'.

Most visitors come due to a great respect for Owens' athletic and humanitarian achievements. Those who personally knew him have only good things to relate about him.

I never met Owens, but his wife Ruth and daughters, brother and grandchildren are some of the nicest people you can know. I'm sure the same things could have been said about Jesse. The Owens family was very helpful in developing the museum and park. They are our friends.[8]

Luz Long, the 13-year-old with a mop of hair curling down his forehead who had joined a sports club in his home town, Leipzig, and befriended his rival Owens at Berlin, served as a corporal in the German army. He was wounded in 1943 when the Allies landed in Sicily and died in a British-controlled military hospital. He is buried in the war cemetery at Motta Sant'Anastasia.

The wrestler Werner Seelenbinder, fourth in the Berlin Olympics in 1936, paid the ultimate price for his commitment to communism. He was arrested in February 1942 for acting as a courier to a resistance group, sentenced to death and executed in October 1944. Immediately after the war an urn with his ashes was buried at his club, the Berolina 03 in Berlin. As the East Germans assumed power they named schools and streets after him.

Judith Deutsch, the Austrian swimmer who refused to go to the 1936 Games, immigrated to Palestine. She was stripped of her titles and her name was removed from the records. This was not reversed until 1995 when the Austrian parliament apologised to her.

Hans-Heinrich Sievert, the decathlete who won the gold medal at the 1934 European Championships and became a symbolic hope for Aryan success in Berlin – where he was injured – served in the German army but lost a foot to a land mine in Hungary. After the war he advised the West German government on sport. He died in 1963.

Theodor Lewald died in Berlin in 1947, so did not live to see his beloved Olympics re-born in London the following year.

Carl Diem's relationship with the Nazis is ambivalent and disputed. Although his involvement with the Olympics stretched back long before they came to power he seems to have been drawn to their creed, contributing to propaganda and being tainted in other ways. The mists of time swirled round this after the war when he rejoined the mainstream as a historian of German sport. He died in 1962.

The Berlin Olympic Games, awarded to crisis-ridden Germany in 1931, remain – as they always will – 'The Hitler Games'. Because the stadium he built was on the edge of Berlin it escaped the bombing and the savage fighting when the Russians took the city in 1945. It is one of the few Nazi monuments which remain as it was. Many of the other Olympic buildings around it remain too, so that anyone wandering around can, without stretching their imagination at all, feel in close proximity to those distant days which seem always to be with us. The 2006 World Cup final was played there and the stadium only required what you might call a make-over.

Daniel Prenn, who had been ranked eighth in the world by the great American tennis professional Bill Tilden, built a new life in England after he fled Germany. He retired from tennis after losing in the first round at Wimbledon, 1939, and devoted himself to business, buying an engineering firm in the period he described as 'before my first Rolls'– a Rolls-Royce being shorthand for 'I've made it big'. He prospered, sending his son to Oxford – and the son would win Junior Wimbledon in 1955. Prenn refused to return to Rot-Weiss until 1984, when he was 80, just before he contracted Alzheimer's. He lingered until in 1991.[9]

Gottfried von Cramm, the classically blonde, elegant man who moved to Berlin and compromised his career in a homosexual relationship, faced a final humiliation by the Nazis. He was entered in a tournament in Rome but was suddenly ordered back to Germany before he could play. *The New York Times* explained that this was because the Nazis did not want him to play, and probably beat, Henner and other compatriots.

Von Cramm was drafted into the German army as a private and served initially in occupied Holland before being transferred to the Eastern Front. He got frostbite and was given a dishonourable discharge. He ran the family estates and spent time in Sweden where he did some tennis coaching. Because Sweden was neutral he took messages from the resistance in Berlin and, although interrogated by the Gestapo, they could not find anything.

He knew a Russian princess[10] who'd write about one of the bombing raids on Berlin in 1944: 'Trapped in a cellar in Wilmersdorf [a district], Gottfried had tried to read Schopenhauer[11] but could not keep a straight face, as he found himself surrounded by old ladies with towels tucked round their chins and wet sponges protruding from them like beards; this supposedly affords protection against phosphorus burns.'

After the war, von Cramm resumed his tennis career, winning the German championship in 1948 and, at 40, again in 1949. He played in the Davis Cup until 1953. Two years later he married the society heiress Barbara Hutton (they divorced in 1959). He became a leading German tennis administrator and businessman, importing cotton. He died in a car crash in Egypt in 1976.

Carl Langbehn, who had defended von Cramm in the court case, joined the Nazi Party in 1933 but grew less and less fond of it. He modulated into an active anti-Nazi and worked to try to end the war. In 1943 he went to Switzerland to talk to the Allies and when he got back was arrested by the Gestapo. He was tried, found guilty and hanged in the Plötzensee Prison, Berlin.

After the war Giorgio de Stefani, the left-hander who von Cramm beat in the 1934 French Championship semi-finals, became a prominent member of the International Olympic Committee and a moving force behind trying to get tennis into it. He was president of the Italian Tennis Federation for ten years. He died in 1992.

The Austrian Hans Redl lost his left arm in the war – in combat – but played at Wimbledon from 1947 to 1956 using only his other arm. Because of his disability the rules were stretched so that, to serve, he could use his racket to throw the ball up (in 1947 he reached the fourth round).

Bernard Destremau, who won the French Open in 1941 and 1942, managed to escape from France during the war and joined the Free French forces as a tank officer. He was wounded in combat, decorated and subsequently became a significant politician, diplomat and author. He won the Wimbledon over-45s men's doubles with Bill Talbert in 1965. He died in 2002.

Roderich Menzel was brought up in the Sudetenland and competed for Czechoslovakia, then Germany. He became an 'ardent Nazi' and during the war 'took part in English-language propaganda broadcasts from Berlin'. Von Cramm might have been allowed back into Wimbledon but Menzel was not. He died in Munich in 1987.[12]

Ladislav Hecht, who got out of Czechoslovakia with three days to spare, reached the United States and worked in an armaments factory during the war. He resumed his career after it and ran businesses. He died in 2004.

Bunny Austin was a committed Christian and a conscientious objector who went to the United States to promote world peace when the war began (and went with the blessing of the British government).[13] The All-England Club did not re-admit him until 1984.

Tennis, as we have seen, did return to Wimbledon in 1946, although early on in the war the centre court had been hit by a bomb. The 'monumental task' of restoring normality in a short time in 1946 was 'entrusted to Lt. Col. Duncan Macaulay, the newly appointed secretary. With unlimited enthusiasm he overcame a multitude of problems created by the rationing of almost every commodity, available only by licence, permit or coupon.'[14]

Hitlers come and go, Wimbledon goes on forever.

Of the German motor-racing fraternity whose cars had made the earth tremble beneath them, Manfred von Brauchitsch remains the only one who can be called enigmatic. The man who had been so handsome but haughty – coming from a strong military family – did not do military service in the war because his body had been too battered by crashes. He worked as a private secretary to a general and after the war went, thanks to the generosity of Caracciola, to Argentina to try to find work.

He returned to West Germany bitter and was arrested for spying in 1951. He defected to communist East Germany leaving a large unpaid tax bill. His wife, distraught, committed suicide. In East Germany he remarried and worked for the Ministry of Sport. He died in 2003.

Adolf Hühnlein, who was arrested trying to seize a petrol station as the Nazis staged a Beer Hall putsch in Munich in 1923, died of cancer in Munich in 1942. Ferry Porsche said of him that he was a 'humourless man who seemed to have absolutely no qualification for his job … as he had no mechanical knowledge at all' and 'always seemed to be in a bad temper'.[15]

Hühnlein was a loyal, committed Nazi who got things done. Caracciola wrote: 'He had been rather conciliatory on my part – a bumbling, good-natured fellow who had honestly believed in his national-socialistic ideal, and who got neither riches nor advantages from his position.'[16]

Because of his illness, a lot of NSKK work was taken over by Erwin Kraus, the man in charge on the Isle of Man in 1939 and who succeeded Hühnlein. Kraus was one of 'those very obscure men who held high rank in the Party. Kraus was an NSKK Obergruppenführer and head of the Technical branch of the NSKK. He survived war and was imprisoned with the other top leaders for a short time – after that, his whereabouts or his death is unknown.'[17]

Hans Stuck's father owned an estate at Freiburg, in the rolling hills and flatlands of south-eastern Germany not far from France and Switzerland – the Stucks were originally Swiss. Stuck, however, had been born in Warsaw, which was then part of the Austro-Hungarian Empire and this enabled him, after the war, to claim Austrian citizenship: important because Germans were banned from racing. He continued until 1960 and died in 1978. He married three times and the third produced a son, Hans-Joachim, who reached Grand Prix racing himself.

Rudolf Caracciola with the boyish face and button nose left an embarrassing trail of photographs in which he was pictured grinning with pleasure and giving the Nazi salute. He had lived in Switzerland since 1929. 'The fact that he was living abroad, making no contribution to the Nazi war effort, *and* still drawing a salary from Mercedes, did not go down well with the Third Reich and in 1942 his payments were stopped.'[18]

He was too old to be called up and waited the war out living on his savings before going to the United States in 1946 and accepting a drive at Indianapolis. He crashed and suffered head injuries. He recovered, crashed again and died in 1959.

The distinguished-looking young English teenager from Rugby School who became a racing driver, not a politician, established a reputation for bravery and sportsmanship. Richard Seaman, however, would always be remembered for finding himself driving for a German team in Nazi Germany, falling in love with a German and being ex-communicated by his imperious mother. If you are interested in these things, his victory in the German Grand Prix of 1938 was the first by a Briton since Henry Seagrave won in France in 1923. No Briton would win after Seaman until Mike Hawthorn, again in France, in 1953. Contrast that with the German domination between 1933 and Belgrade, September 1939.

Bernd Rosemeyer, who enraged the police in Lingen – the town on the Rhine near the Dutch border – by riding his motorbike like a hooligan, is regarded as one of the great drivers and a stone memorial stands today marking the place where he crashed in his Auto Union. It is in trees just beside the Frankfurt-Darmstadt autobahn, where the traffic passes carelessly by all unknowing.

Hermann Lang, who was born in 'humble surroundings' near Stuttgart, expressed his feelings about the outbreak of war in a single phrase: 'my world disappears.' In his autobiography he would add that 'little did I realise that almost seven years would pass before I sat in a car again. Seven years in which many a friend had disappeared. It was particularly painful to lose my dear friend Jakob Krauss [an engineer], killed in a bombing rain in 1944.' Lang resumed his career after the war and drove competitively until the mid-1950s.

The crash and fatalities on the fifth lap of the Czechoslovakian Grand Prix of 1937, however, did not release him for many years. The organisers had cleared the spectators from the area of the crash but they returned and reportedly some of them sat with their legs dangling over the ditch where the crash happened.

Lang faced a complication. Some reports suggested his car had struck a milestone on the opening lap but continued and this was a contributory factor. Lang would write: 'In the irresponsibility of continuing with a seriously damaged car, they saw a rash, nonchalant attitude to spectator safety and believed in that way to have found a firm proof of my guilt. Several witnesses were needed to prove that the claimed crash with the stone never had occurred.'

Proceedings began on fourteen counts against Lang; the war halted the hearing but it was resumed after it and Lang was not acquitted for several years.

Lang wrote about all this in his book *Grand Prix Driver*, first published in English in 1953. If you search the index you do not find entries for Hitler, Goebbels, Hühnlein or von Tschammer und Osten. Lang covered the most murderous war in human history in a single paragraph.

Georg 'Schorsch' Meier, the Bavarian who had worked his apprenticeship after he left school at 14, was not called up for active service because of the injuries he had received in the Swedish Grand Prix. He would spend the war as a motorbike instructor in the German Military Police and as a driver to Wilhelm Canaris, head of military intelligence.

'Meier made a big noise after the war about never having been a member of the Nazi Party', although author Roger Willis points out that 'as a regular soldier he was actually forbidden to join it by military regulations'.[19] He continued a competitive career after the war as well as running his BMW motorbike business and did a lap of honour during the 1989 TT, marking fifty years since he had won it. He died in 1999.

The motorbike rider Leo Steinweg, who fled to Holland in 1938 – his wife Emmy followed in 1939 – found it was 'the start of a long, agonising odyssey of flight and persecution'.[20] He was seized and taken to Auschwitz in 1942 and shot in another concentration camp, Flossenburg.

Louis Chiron, the Grand Prix driver, resumed his career after the war and at a party in Monte Carlo in 1949 he publicly accused Hellé Nice, a former exotic dancer who had been courted by millionaires and driven a Bugatti competitively, of collaborating with the Gestapo. It destroyed her, although no evidence was ever brought, and she died in anonymity and poverty.

Chiron went on to achieve a further measure of fame by starting the Monaco Grand Prix every year. He stood ahead of the grid and waved a flag. Yearly, some drivers would dream of accelerating to get Chiron before he could get away.

Achille Varzi was born rich (textiles) and raced a motorbike before moving to cars. He was so good that he established a rivalry with Nuvolari. However, he loved 'the good life' and 'began having serious personal problems, including an addiction to morphine and a difficult affair' with the wife of a fellow driver. 'During the war, Varzi overcame his drug addiction and settled down with his new wife, Norma Colombo.' At the age of 42 he made a comeback but in practice for the Swiss Grand Prix in 1948 his car flipped in wet conditions, crushing him.[21] His death resulted in crash helmets being made compulsory for racing.

Max Schmeling, who at 16 went to the cinema, saw the World Heavyweight Championship between Jack Dempsey and Frenchman Georges Carpentier and fell in love with boxing, served in the Luftwaffe and made at least one visit to an Allied prisoner-of-war camp, giving out photographs of himself. The GIs were not evidently impressed and knew what to do with them.

After the war a boxing contact in America offered Schmeling the Coca-Cola franchise for Germany. It was a gateway to wealth and he set up a foundation, giving to children's organisations, handicapped people, churches, the Red Cross and old people's homes.[22] He remained in touch with Joe Louis and once terrified him by driving on the autobahn where, of course, there was no speed limit. He died aged 99 in 2004.

After his boxing career Louis suffered what so many ex-boxers did: bad businesses, enormous tax debts and, in desperation, comebacks – even as a wrestler. When he fell ill Schmeling sent him money to pay his medical expenses. He died in 1981 and Schmeling then sent $5,000 to his widow.

Arno Hellmis, the Nazi boxing commentator, was killed covering the German invasion of France in 1940.

Rudi Ball, the Berlin Jew who stood at 5ft 4in and weighed 140lb (no kind of a physique for an ice hockey player), took part in his last World Championship in Prague in 1938, although he continued to represent Germany until 1941 and continued to play for Berliner SC until 1944. He returned in 1946, scoring eighteen goals in five friendlies before, a couple of years later, immigrating to South Africa and becoming a businessman. He died there in 1975 – and of course he had kept on playing in South Africa, making his career total more than 500 goals.[23]

Quite how a well-known Jew could continue playing in public in Berlin during the war remains a mystery and it needs to be explored because the very idea seems to draw in not just anti-Semitism but how, even with absolute power and a love of order, the Nazi attempt to either change human beings or kill them was, in the end, a mess. Ball also draws in the uncomfortable fact that the mists of time have drifted over so much of the Nazi years, obscuring so much. Hence the Ball mystery.

Irv Osterer, a historian from Ottawa, Canada, tells me:

I have being trying to solve the same riddle for quite some time. I am slowly putting together a Jewish hockey book and I did find one interesting reference in Mandell[24] which confirms that Ball only agreed to play for the Germans in the Olympics in return for allowing his family to flee the country for South Africa. Why he stayed in Germany is a mystery to me. There were nights that he was playing for Berlinner SC in front of 8,000 spectators. He could not escape public notice. One has to come to the conclusion that he must have been a collaborator of some kind.

One fellow I contacted told me that he had been in touch with Ball's nephews in South Africa and they also had no idea how he managed.

Ball does have one beautiful hockey card. It is from the German 1933 *Bravour Zigarettenfabrik Bilder und Sport* set and is card B23 from a set of 376 cards entitled *Bravour-Bilder Film und Sport*. The front of each card shows the name, title, card number and a sepia photograph, while the back of each card has trade text, written in German. The cards were given as free premiums and were inserted into packages of Bravour cigarettes.

He was as famous as that and had been for years.

Another historian, Patrick Houda of Stockholm, says:

Before assuming that Ball was a collaborator of some kind you have to take into account that there were some insane circumstances: some Jews *were* able to make it through the war in Berlin – a book written a few years ago about a Jewish Hospital showed its staff was somehow miraculously spared – but people I have talked to also believe that there had to be other reasons why he was spared. Other Jewish athletes did not fair as well.

I believe that Ball was in a Red Cross Displaced Persons camp at the cessation of the war. How he got there, who knows? – and if his family knows anything they are not talking. Also I believe that Ball's teammates may have sheltered him by threatening that they would not play without him. Remember that Ball was unquestionably the best hockey player in Europe at the time.

Ball was a key member of Berliner SC, and a longtime linemate of Gustav Jaenecke (one of the most popular German athletes at the time). Berliner SC was an immensely popular team, followed by many Germans. On most nights they played

in front of capacity crowds (late 1920s and all the 1930s), and an entire nation listened to radio broadcasts from these games. So because of his popularity, politically
it would have been an unwise move to 'liquidate' or 'remove' him from the squad.

Also remember that Ball was only a 'half-Jew' and his race wasn't much of an
issue in the beginning as long as he entertained the crowds – but it wasn't until
the 1942–43 season that he was forbidden from playing ice hockey in Germany.
(He didn't play hockey again until late 1946).

If the cyclist Richter provides a saddened but revealing epilogue, Ball provides – in
Patrick Houda's words – glimpses of great deeds against a background of the insane.

The insanity would not go away. In 2008 the magazine *Der Spiegel* carried a story
about the inauguration of a German Sports Hall of Fame but the opening ceremony,
in Berlin, was reportedly marred by criticism that some of the forty selected to be in
it had been members of the Nazi Party.

Hans Wilhelm Gäb, chairman of the board, said that:

> from the start we were aware of the problem of choosing top athletes who were asso-
> ciated with – and used by – the Nazi regime, but if we had automatically excluded all
> the athletes[25] who were successful at that time and who inevitably came into contact
> with the Nazi system, or if we had only honored resistance fighters, such a blanket
> judgment would have been self-righteous. It would have been tainted by the arro-
> gance of a generation that was fortunate enough to have grown up in a democracy.[26]

Perhaps *that* ought to be the real epilogue.

The man who strode the Olympic Stadium, his Olympic Stadium, tried to beat the
world and found the world was too strong. He tried to hijack world sport and found
the same thing too.

Notes

1   en.wikipedia.org/wiki/Albert_Richter.
2   wapedia.mobi/en/Julius_Hirsch.
3   Mogulof, *Foiled*.
4   http://www.sports-reference.com/olympics/athletes/ra/dora-ratjen-1.html.
5   www.jesseowensmuseum.org/index.cfm?fuseaction=park.
6   This is no place to get into the intermidable (and fascinating) debate about
    absolute merit, relative merit and, ultimately, Who Was The Greatest Of All? The
    passage of time brings so many changes in its wake that comparing eras is good,
    clean fun but always leading to indeterminate conclusions. However, Owens' four
    medals – and very significantly, one of them in the long jump – can only be
    matched by one other athlete in the whole history of it, Carl Lewis.

7   Adolph is the American usage and I have left it like that because it is an American writing the words. I have left the spelling alone too.

8   www.jesseowensmuseum.org/ jesseowensinfo@charter.net.

9   Fisher, *A Terrible Splendor.*

10   Vassiltchikov, Marie 'Missie', *The Berlin Diaries.*

11   Arthur Schopenhauer (1788–1860), a German philosopher.

12   Henderson, *The Life of Fred Perry.*

13   Ibid.

14   aeltc2010.wimbledon.org/en_GB/about/.../museum_history.html.

15   Alex Dekker in forums.autosport.com/lofiversion/index.php/t52950.html.

16   Caracciola, *A Racing Driver's World.*

17   forum.axishistory.com/viewtopic.php?f=45&t=6504&p.

18   Nixon, *Silver Arrows.*

19   Willis, *The Nazi TT.*

20   Reuss, *Hitler's Motor Racing Battles.*

21   en.wikipedia.org/wiki/Achille_Varzi.

22   Myler, *The Ring of Hate.*

23   www.sihss.se/RudiBallbiography.htm.

24   Mandell, *The Nazi Olympics.*

25   Athlete in the American sense – sportsman.

26   www.spiegel.de/international/germany/0,1518,551813,00.html.

10

IF ...

Nobody knows how many lives were lost between September 1939 and May 1945 as war exacted a toll on a scale never seen before. Some speak of 50 million, others 70 million, and both figures are like the speed of light, interstellar distances or quantum physics: impossible for the normal mind to accommodate.

That sportsmen and women were among those casualties was inevitable, and it was equally inevitable that the great championships would be interrupted. We need some perspective here because by definition sport is meant to celebrate being alive and consequently the opposite of what Hitler unleashed. In no sense can the Wimbledon tennis fortnight be equated to, say, the agonising, meat-grinding battle for Stalingrad, never mind Auschwitz, that ultimate horror in human dimensions, and we have not even reached Hiroshima and Nagasaki.

The perspective is that sport represents a basic, important and, to many people, an essential part of normal life. That is what Hitler hijacked, distorted, abused, altered and would surely have destroyed in the same way that he did normal German life and every place he occupied. Sport's basic importance can be gauged by how quickly it resumed after May 1945 and how, in the most difficult circumstances, it maintained its importance during the war too.

This chapter is based around a question: what would have happened if Hitler had won? However, much this has to be conjecture, there are tantalising and, I insist, fascinating clues.

Since the Olympic Games was the premier competition in the world in the 1930s, and certainly would have continued to be during the 1940s and into the 1950s, its future – or fate – needs to be addressed first.

Karl Ritter von Halt, a Nazi, replaced Lewald on the IOC's Executive Committee. He went to Belgium to tell Baillet-Latour of the cancellation of the Garmisch-Partenkirchen Games after they had been switched from Sapporo because of the Sino-Japanese war. The Nazis sought to control the IOC, or, as von Tschammer und Osten put it, 'reorganise' it. Baillet-Latour was 'the most obvious lever' for the Nazis to use 'but it is nevertheless striking that he should have been invited to act as a puppet of Hitler's Germany'. He died in 1942.[1] He was succeeded by Sigrid Edström from neutral Sweden, and whether Edström would have been able to withstand Nazi pressure on him either directly or through the Swedish government must remain problematic.

By 1942, with much of Europe conquered and 8 million German soldiers tearing the Soviet Union to pieces, saying no to whatever Hitler wanted was going to be a major step.

As events unfolded there were six Olympic casualties: Tokyo, Sapporo and Garmisch-Partenkirchen in 1940, Helsinki which was chosen to replace Tokyo when the Sino-Japanese war began, London and Cortina d'Ampezzo in 1944.

Officially the Japanese said:

So complete a satisfaction, such a great joy, is seldom felt by a nation as was experienced by Japan when her fervent and energetic wish was finally granted at the Berlin Session of the International Olympic Committee held in August, 1936. Tokyo was accorded the honour of celebrating the XIIth Olympic Games in 1940.

That December an organising committee was set up with support from the 'Ministry of Education, the Ministry of Foreign Affairs, the Ministry of War, the Chamber of Commerce and Industry of Japan, the City of Tokyo and others'.

Plans were advanced when Japan 'found itself confronted with the unforeseen Sino-Japanese incident.[2] With the passing of the months, the incident has widened its spheres and the entire nation has risen to participate in a conflict of long duration by mobilizing both spirit and resources. No other decision but the foregoing of the mission of holding the Tokyo Olympiad is conceivable under the circumstances.

'... However, the hope is not forever lost, neither the chance. The conflict will terminate in time, and peace and amity will again be restored. So, with renewed energy, we eagerly anticipate the next opportunity to stage the Games in Tokyo.' They said they intended to re-apply for 1944 but by then even thinking about an Olympic Games had become impossible as the global slaughter went on and on.

The Japanese organisers were not wrong about getting the Games to Tokyo but it would take until 1964. The Winter Games would go to Sapporo but it would take until 1972.

When Sapporo withdrew in 1938 the IOC re-allocated the Games to St Moritz (hosts, 1928), but there were problems over amateurism – a dispute over whether Swiss professional ski instructors would be able to compete as amateurs – and the Games passed on to Garmisch-Partenkirchen. Hitler invaded Poland soon afterwards, provoking the start of the war and ending the Olympics completely until three years after it was over.

If Hitler had won.

In the spring of 1937 Hitler visited me at my Berlin showrooms. We stood alone in front of the nearly seven-foot high model of the stadium for four hundred thousand people. It had been set up precisely at eye level. Every detail had been rendered, and powerful spotlights illuminated it, so that with only a little imagination we could conceive the effect of this structure. Alongside the model were the plans, pinned up on boards. Hitler turned to these. We talked about the Olympic Games, and I pointed out, as I had done several times before, that my athletic field did not have the prescribed Olympic proportions. Without any change of tone, as if it were a matter settled beyond the possibility of discussion, Hitler observed: 'No matter. In 1940 the Olympic Games will take place in Tokyo. But thereafter they will take place in Germany for all time to come, in this stadium. And then we will determine the measurements of the athletic field.' According to our carefully worked out schedule this stadium was supposed to be completed in time for the Party Rally of 1950.

The man writing these words was Albert Speer, Hitler's architect and armaments minister. The words open up a vision,[3] and never forget that German soldiers got close enough to the Kremlin to see its towers.

Hitler's plans for Russia were frighteningly specific, with most Russians expelled to beyond the Ural Mountains and the land being distributed among German settlers. The only concession would be road signs in Russian so that what remained of the local population did not stray out and inconvenience German traffic by getting run over.

The Soviet Union would have ceased to exist, rendering modern Olympic history unrecognisable. Between 1952, when they re-entered the Games, and 1988 they won 1,219 medals. That would not have happened and who knows where the medals would have gone? Germany?

If the Germans had conquered Britain in 1940 – and it was a close run thing – Hitler would have been able to concentrate his armies on the Soviet Union and that would surely have been decisive. In the moment of victory Hitler could have surveyed a map of Europe and seen, from north to south: Norway occupied, Sweden neutral but leaning heavily towards him, Finland neutral but dependent on him in case the Soviets rose again, Denmark, Holland, Belgium, France, Luxembourg and Britain all occupied with Alsace returned to the bosom of the Reich. The fascist dictator Franco would rule Spain and Portugal would remained neutral, albeit with a fascist dictator, Salazar.

Looking east he would have seen Poland destroyed to the point where it no longer existed as a country, northern Czechoslovakia returned to the bosom of the Reich and the rest of the country occupied, Austria absorbed completely into the Reich, Hungary bound in as an ally, Italy an ally, Yugoslavia to be subdued at his leisure, Greece occupied, Bulgaria and Roumania bound tightly as allies.

Looking further east he would have seen the three Baltic states as part of his eastern real estate, and the western states of the Soviet Union already occupied: Belarus, the Ukraine, Moldavia, Georgia and Armenia.

He could have done whatever he wanted with any of these places. The United States would have remained a powerful adversary but, lacking Britain as a forward base, making any physical intervention anywhere in Europe would have been problematical, if not logistically impossible. That would have applied to Germany, too, in the sense that she had no forward base from which to attack the United States. It may have been that the atomic weapons which the United States developed in time to bring Japan to the negotiating table would have been decisive against Germany too: launched from an aircraft carrier – when technology allowed – to annihilate Berlin so that no trace of Hitler, the Nazi high command, the ministers and the ministries would have remained, just a radioactive desert.

This is to forget that the Germans were working on their own atomic weaponry and if, by 1946 or 1947 – German industry not destroyed by the bombing and facing no impediment to developing the bomb – they had developed it, the world would have suddenly looked an even more terrifying place, perhaps leading to a nuclear stand-off (like the Cold War and lasting decades), perhaps leading to a moment of Hitler madness when he reached for the red phone, lifted it and said, 'Fire'.

What seems likely is that the United States would have grappled Japan to her knees and occupied the country, and at some point reached an uneasy live-and-let-live arrangement with Hitler: the stand-off (a fuller discussion of the problematic nature of this in a moment).

By then world sport would have been distorted beyond all recognition. It is not at all clear whether Hitler would have allowed any country he occupied to engage in something so potentially dangerous as a national team, risking it becoming inevitably a focus for nationalist aspirations. That begs a most interesting question: who would have gone to Berlin every four years to contest the Olympics there?

The British Commonwealth countries like Canada, Australia, New Zealand and South Africa would clearly not go near it with Britain occupied. The same would surely be true of other colonies where a British government-in-exile still ruled, and true of the United States, who only just went to Berlin in 1936, remember.

Taking those Games as a yardstick, here are the countries which could have gone to Berlin in 1948, and back to Berlin in 1952, and back to Berlin in 1956: Afghanistan, Argentina, Bolivia, Brazil, Bulgaria (sic), Chile, China, Colombia, Costa Rica, Egypt, Finland, Germany, Iceland, Hungary, Italy, Mexico, Peru, Portugal, Roumania (?), Spain, Sweden, Turkey and Uruguay.

Of the 130 gold medals won, sixty-nine were from countries which might have been absent in 1948. Subtracting the thirty-three which Germany won, you are left with a mere twenty-eight for, supposedly, the rest of the world (of course other countries, like Ecuador and Venezuela, who did not go to Berlin, might have come in).

I am indebted to Eric Morse – a foreign and strategic affairs commentator at the Royal Canadian Military Institute in Toronto and who was responsible for international sports relations at Canada's foreign ministry from 1973 to 1986 – for reflecting from a Canadian (well, North American) viewpoint. He says: 'I think the Latam [Latin American] belt would have got the Roosevelt/Truman Doctrine pretty good once it was shoved down their throats' – American pressure would have kept Latin American countries away from the Nazi-Fascist-Japanese axis. He continues:

Remember, the Royal Navy would have been for all intents and purposes intact in the East Coast and Caribbean theatres. The US could have shifted heavy weight to the Pacific and still had a respectable projection of force off Caracas, Rio, the [River] Plate.

Hitler would have won in 1942 by the skin of his teeth and only if the Japanese had not attacked Pearl Harbour. It would have been a stalemate at best since the USSR (at least, Russia) would have survived east of the Urals.

The obvious kernel of sporting resistance would have been the Empire (Commonwealth) Games, which were a modest success from the start (and have always remained so, Delhi notwithstanding). The first ones were in 1930 in Hamilton, Ontario – perfect timing and placement historically.

They would not long have remained the Empire Games since the US would have been an early joiner – after a certain amount of jacking around – and would then have taken over by main strength and awkwardness; but the Games might have become a Free World Olympics and would still have been used to showcase the freedom of the Commonwealth. They would have attracted any nation that Germany did not have a stranglehold on (perhaps including – eventually – the tiny new Jewish state of Palestine which would inevitably list Heydrich and Eichmann among its founding fathers and might feel compelled to compete in Berlin if invited. Maybe [in this chapter] we don't want to go there) ...

On the Continent, German sport, under Hitler's successors (mainly drawn from the *all-Euro SS*, as the only semi-educated class left in business) would gradually have tolerated inter-European competition – remember that by 1943 European Unity was a BIG branding thing with the Waffen-SS and a lot of them believed it – but inter-racial would have been tenser. It is hard to say how Naziism would have evolved generationally, since it had even less ideological consistency than Stalinism. However, there is also a major geopolitical question of how long a Nazi Europe could have lasted without making huge political compromises anyway, since Europe has no resources worth mentioning, and the Soviet Union beyond the Urals would have waged an endless war of attrition.

The Olympic Games, which expressly wanted to embrace the whole of humanity, could not have survived in any credible form and, whatever form it did assume, it would have been repetitive, diminished and staged only according to Hitler's wishes.

It is a provocative argument that if the French, Belgian, Dutch and British colonies had gained independence a whole array of new countries would have been available and, possibly, eager to join the Olympic movement to prove their independence but how would Hitler – do not forget Jesse Owens – have reacted to Africa coming to Berlin en masse and winning medal after medal?

We have a clue. Albert Speer recorded how, during the Olympics, Hitler was:

highly annoyed by the series of triumphs by the marvellous coloured runner, Jesse Owens. People who antecedents came from the jungle were primitive, Hitler said with a shrug, their physiques were stronger than those of civilised whites. They represented unfair competition and hence must be excluded from future Games.

The converse is no less intriguing. By the time Nazi Germany was beaten the Soviet Union had reached Berlin and was in a position to create an arc of satellite states to protect it: Poland, East Germany (a complete Soviet creation), Czechoslovakia, Hungary, Bulgaria and initially Roumania. These formed a bloc and the story of the Olympic Games from 1952 to 1988 (the last Games before the Berlin Wall came down) is largely drawn between East and West. If Hitler had won, none of that would have happened and East Germany (521 medals in Summer and Winter Games from 1968 to 1988) would simply not have existed.

I am indebted to John Woodcock, journalist and old friend, for making his own suggestions:

> The Third Reich, as conquerors, might have responded to sport, and how did the Soviet bloc respond? What if the Germans had reacted in a similar fashion to the Soviet Union? After all the Soviets apparently didn't feel threatened by their satellite states competing against them in world sporting events – they seemed to take the view that communism was the overall victor. If a Bulgarian weight-lifter beat a Russian to the gold medal it was a still a triumph for the Soviet bloc over everyone else.
>
> To make an Olympics or World Cup a meaningful contest, who's to say the Nazis wouldn't have reacted in a similar fashion? A Hungarian or Czech sprinter, say, defeating an opponent from Dusseldorf would have still represented a victory for the ethos of the Greater Reich. Well, possibly, or would you draw a distinction, in sporting/political philosophy, between the Nazis and the communists? What I'm saying is, if Stalin could tolerate winners coming from within his wider empire, why couldn't Hitler, even if meant defeat for a German?

I think the answer lies in the political philosophy. Communism was a sincere attempt, whether you liked it or not, to end the conflicts in human history by making all men and women equal, giving everyone equal shares in prosperity. When this state was reached it would be the end of history.

Hitler and the Nazis held a philosophy which was the opposite. They were the master race with, beneath them, varying degrees of inferiority, the Slavs, blacks and Jews at the bottom. Any victory by anyone from anywhere else – except presumably Spain, Italy and Japan – would have been an example of how the master race was not the master race.

If, however, Hitler planned – as he said – to hold the Olympics in Berlin forever that must have meant he accepted foreigners would come and some of them would beat Germans. The Olympic story between 1939 and 1945 is what did not happen but soccer in Germany continued right through to April 1945.

Before we reach that, a strange and perhaps revealing incident. In November 1940 the mighty German side Schalke 04 went to Vienna to play Admira Wien and –

whether this was early soccer hooliganism or profound anti-German feelings – the team coach was wrecked and the tyres of a Nazi official's Mercedes slashed.

The national side played twenty-eight matches from 1940 to 1942 but stopped after the Battle of Stalingrad in February 1943 when the German Sixth Army was surrounded and battered into submission, tilting the whole war away from Hitler. Those twenty-eight matches are fascinating because of who the Germans played and where. Germany's scores are given first.

In 1940: Hungary in Berlin (2-2) – Hungary a dominated ally; Yugoslavia in Vienna (1-2) – Austria part of the Reich, of course, making it a home match; Italy in Milan (2-3) – Italy the ally; Roumania in Frankfurt (9-3) – Roumania a dominated ally, because it had the oil Hitler needed; Finland in Leipzig (13-0) – Finland neutral but constantly threatened by Stalin's presence; Slovakia at Bratislava (1-0) – Hitler having dismembered Czechoslovakia and absorbed the Sudetenland into the Reich; Hungary in Budapest (2-2); Bulgaria in Munich (7-3) – Bulgaria an ally; Yugoslavia in Zagreb (0-2) – Hitler had not yet invaded; Denmark in Hamburg (1-0). You note that only three of the matches were away, and not far away either.

In 1941: Switzerland in Stuttgart (4-2) – the Swiss neutral; Switzerland in Berne (1-2); Roumania in Bucharest (4-1); Croatia in Vienna (5-1) – Croatia supposedly independent; Finland in Helsinki (6-0); Sweden in Stockholm (2-4) – Swedes neutral but taking care not to upset the Germans; Denmark in Dresden (1-1); Slovakia in Breslau (4-0) – Breslau then a German city, later Wroclaw.

In 1942: Croatia in Zagreb (2-0); Switzerland in Vienna (1-2); Spain in Berlin (1-1) – Spain a fellow fascist country under Franco; Hungary in Budapest (5-3); Bulgaria in Sofia (3-0) – an ally; Roumania in Bytom (7-0); Sweden in Berlin (2-3); Switzerland in Berne (5-3); Croatia in Stuttgart (5-1); Slovakia in Bratislava (5-2).

Of all these matches, the two against Denmark are the most intriguing because they are the only ones against an occupied country. Neither, significantly perhaps, was played in Denmark.

I am indebted to Søren Elbech, a Danish football historian, for background:

Certainly these matches were shrouded in controversy. They were designated 'friendlies.' However, as it was the Occupier against the Occupied you can only imagine what a conundrum it must have been.

At the beginning of the occupation Denmark quickly laid down arms and began what is called 'the period of collaboration', which was not necessarily positive. As history has been revised, particularly in recent years, it has emerged that not only was this a question of *real politik* from the side of the Danish government but also the country was spared in great part some of the hardships levied on, for example, Norway – in particular when it comes to the Jews, who were largely left to themselves in Denmark and, consequently, could escape to Sweden before Hitler Germany turned up the heat in 1943.

It was not without cost. The general population demonstrated often – by staying away from soccer matches or, apparently and very provocatively, sporting Royal Air

Force caps, or singing the Norwegian and Swedish anthems following the Danish one. But what was the Danish Football Association to do? If they played, they could be labelled collaborators but if they didn't play there would have almost certainly been repercussions from the occupying forces.

I am indebted to Andreas Werner, a German soccer historian, for exploring the topic:

> Politics had a big influence on sport during those dark pages of German history. In 1933 they changed the league system. Moreover, a lot of clubs were forbidden from competing, for example all clubs belonging to the *Deutsche Jugend-Kraf* [DJK] organisation (of the Catholic Church), clubs of the labour orgainisation and Jewish clubs. Other clubs had to merge. Their long-term aim was to have only one sports club in each city or town. The interesting thing is the countries which occupied Germany after the Second World War implemented this plan – which had not been completed earlier by Hitler.
>
> Now coming to the international games: Hitler did not treat all countries the same way. One of the occupied countries was France and some regions of the east part he considered as German. Clubs from that region took part at the German championship. In the same way, Austria was considered part of Germany and Austrian clubs played at the German championship and the German cup. After occupying Poland and Czechoslovakia you will find clubs at the German championship as well [more details in a moment].
>
> For other countries you will not find any club in the German championship. He occupied those countries but he did not annex them. Race played an important role in Hitler's ideology. I am pretty sure that he considered the people of Denmark, Finland, the Netherlands and Sweden as belonging to the same family of races as the Germans. That's why he occupied those countries without annexing them. (There are a lot of rumours of the relationship between Germany and Switzerland in those years. You will not gain any friends in Switzerland if you discuss this).
>
> If someone from the occupied countries played against Germany there were two different kind of dangers, the coming from the German occupiers. Mainly people with Jewish ancestry and people considered as partisans had to fear the occupiers. On the other hand there was danger for those who played against the Germans because they risked being seen as collaborators by their own people.
>
> I have read a report on one match against Denmark and it says the game was also played for propaganda reasons – that Germany is not only successful in the war but also in sport.

One authoritative source[4] claims: 'In comparison with other occupied countries, Danish sport had the most widespread collaboration with the Germans during World War II.' At the beginning this collaboration was regarded as a golden age and was 'far more intense than any period before or since. Banners with the Nazi swastika flew side by side with the Danish flag, while German competitors gave the "heil" salute accompanied by the Nazi *Horst Wessel* song.'[5]

Søren Elbech fleshes this out because it seems so revealing and, arguably, a guide to what might have happened after the war:

The Austrian leagues were reorganized into 'Region Ostmark' and Denmark could have become 'Region Nordermark' – the Danish league would have become a sub-set of the German league structure and the winner play against the winners of all the other Regions. The Danish international players would have been eligible for the *Gross-Deutsche Nationalmannschaft* ['Greater German team'] although of course the Germans may have learnt from their mistake of mixing Germans with Austrians right before the 1938 World Cup.

Up until mid-1941, when Germany attacked Russia and opened the second front, things went pretty much without a hitch in Denmark. Of course, there was rationing, curfews and so on but the police were still patrolling the streets and it was the German Army which was visibly present, not the SS or Gestapo (they came later, and in droves).

So the 'collaboration' was probably tolerated to a degree because it was pragmatic and worked for everyone. Outnumbered and outgunned, Danes chose to establish a tolerable way of life until the atrocities became so apparent and German rule got tougher. From August 1943 it turned very ugly and went downhill from there.

As for European Football, wow, that's a BIG question. Germany was slated to host the World Cup in 1942 – and with the propaganda machine running at full steam to portray the invincibility of the German Volk, it might have succeeded after the dud of 1938. It's a very, very big thing to think about ...

Germany applied for 1942 at the FIFA Congress in Berlin in 1936, and in 1939 Brazil applied. Who would have got it remains academic: it was another casualty of war of course.

For the record, the first Germany-Denmark match was played at the Victoria Sportsplatz, Hamburg, on Sunday 17 November 1940 in front of 28,000 specta-tors. The German goal was scored by Helmut Schön,[6] a forward whose greatest contribution would be after the war. The second match was played at the Dresdner Sportsklub Stadium, Dresden, on Sunday 16 November in front of 45,000 specta-tors. The German goal was scored by Wilhelm Hahnemann after 38 minutes and the Denmark equaliser by Kaj Hansen, who was joint top goalscorer in the 1940 Danish championship.

In Denmark the championship had been played in 1939–40 and then, from 1940 to 1945, what were called War Tournaments.

The German domestic situation was intriguing, with Germany itself and its soccer leagues divided into areas called *Gaus*. As Germany swelled through conquest, teams from Austria (in 1938 Rapid Vienna won the *Tschammerpokal* and were national champions in 1941), Poland, Czechoslovakia, Alsace-Lorraine and Luxembourg found themselves playing in German leagues. Three leagues – *Gauligen* – contained non-German clubs from regions occupied by Germany after 1940.

The *Gauliga Elsaß* comprised sixteen French clubs from Alsace, in two groups of eight. Alsace, so visually German – houses, churches, cities, even patois – had been part of Germany from 1871 to 1918 and the teams played in the German leagues. It became a French region and the clubs adopted French names. As the area was reabsorbed into Germany and the *Gauliga*, their names changed back. For example, Racing Club Strasbourg became *Rasen SC Straßburg* and SV 06 Schlettstadt became *SC Sélestat*. In 1945, with Germany defeated, the great re-revert began – which is why, today, Racing Club Strasbourg is called that and not anything else.

The *Gauliga Westmark* was located in western Germany. Three clubs – from Lorraine, and the area north of Alsace (another with an interwoven history between Germany and France), were incorporated into the Westmark but their names Germanised: FV Metz became *FC Mets*, Sarreguemines became *TSG Saargemünd* and Merlebach became *TSG Merlenbach*.

The *Gauliga Moselland* was, as its name implies, close to Luxembourg and six clubs were incorporated, again with Germanised names. The *Gauliga Schlesien* covered the Silesian region and when Germany defeated Poland in 1939 the parts of Upper Silesia which Germany lost after the First World War were reincorporated, including several soccer teams, renamed in German (Katowice became *Reichsbahn SG Kattowitz*).[7]

The Nazis knew full well how important soccer was to morale and encouraged it. Some teams even had military sponsors. As the war progressed, and the German infrastructure began to fracture under the Allied bombing, sustaining the *Gauliga* became increasingly difficult. At the same time, as the Soviet advance along a 1,000km front came towards the Reich like a giant, dark wave, more and more young men were being called up. The *Gauliga* broke up into smaller leagues producing some grotesque scores (one of 32–0) and, as the fracturing increased, the Nazis cancelled the 1943–44 championship. It was reinstated after popular protest. The final match in the Reich (and of the Reich) was played on 23 April 1945 between two Munich teams.

Germany surrendered unconditionally on 8 May. Hitler had lost. And if he had not …?

Using the fact that soccer continued in the war, and given that even the Nazis understood its importance in terms of morale, there seems no reason why national leagues should not have continued. Despite the nightmarish situation in France, championships of the north and of the south were played in 1941, 1942 and 1943.

The Italian league *Serie A* was played until 1943 when a regional championship replaced it. The league began again in 1945. The Italian passion for the game was so strong that no government was going to deny it and that could well point to a larger conclusion: the Nazis may have reasoned that allowing soccer would act as a harmless, calming influence and distraction for occupied populations. In short, a way of letting the populations release their emotions.

The World Cup – which, like the Olympics, observed a four-year cycle – was going to be held in either Germany or Brazil in 1942, as we have seen. It resumed in 1950, maintaining the four-year cycle – 1938, 1942, 1946, 1950 – in Brazil, with England taking part for the first time.

As we have also seen, Hitler invaded, absorbed or declared war on ten of the six-teen finalists in France in 1938. The countries who went into the qualifying stage to produce the last sixteen were: Germany, Sweden, Finland, Estonia, Norway, Ireland, Poland, Yugoslavia, Roumania, Egypt (withdrew), Switzerland, Portugal, Palestine, Greece, Hungary, Bulgaria, Czechoslovakia, Latvia, Lithuania, Austria, Holland, Luxembourg, Belgium, Argentina (withdrew), Brazil, USA (withdrew), Cuba, Colombia (withdrew), Costa Rica (withdrew), Mexico (withdrew), El Salvador (withdrew), Dutch Guyana (withdrew) and Japan (withdrew).

If Hitler had won, and Germany staged the World Cup in 1942, the qualifiers might well have been: Germany, Sweden, Finland, Ireland (I am assuming Hitler did not choose to occupy the country but recently revealed invasion plans of Britain include a landing in southern Ireland), Egypt, Switzerland (I am assuming Hitler did not choose to occupy the country), Portugal, Argentina, Brazil, Cuba, Colombia, Costa Rica, Mexico and El Salvador.

It would have left enough countries to hold a respectably representative competi-tion rather than a hollow propaganda exercise. Using those countries which did go to the World Cup in 1950 as a form guide, here are the ones who might well have gone to Germany in 1942 (or 1946): Brazil, Mexico, Switzerland, Spain, Chile, Sweden, Italy, Paraguay, Uruguay and Bolivia.

If the French, Belgian, Dutch and British colonies had gained independence – creating a whole array of new countries eager, no doubt, to join the World Cup – how would Hitler have reacted to Africa coming to Berlin en masse in the soccer as well as the Olympics?

I am assuming Hitler would have housed the World Cup permanently in the Berlin super-stadium. Given his nature and appetite, he must have coveted it as he coveted the Olympics, in order that the world could come and pay homage to his Germany at regular intervals. If it was held anywhere else, like South America, he could have decimated any entry by wielding his power over all the European countries to pre-vent them from going.

Beyond question, the possibilities in global propaganda of the Olympics and World Cup permanently organised by and for the Reich would have excited Goebbels, given his nature and appetite, enormously.

It is a provocative notion how the Italian public might have reacted to Hitler twist-ing Mussolini's arm so that the country could not host the World Cup ever again.

It is a provocative notion too, that if Europe's African colonies had become inde-pendent how would Hitler, up there on his balcony, react to a continent of Jesse Owenses and soccer players showing up in two four-year cycles – that is in practical terms every two years, the Olympics and the World Cup alternating – and showing their (sometimes) superior skills to the master race?

It is a further provocative notion that FIFA, snug in Switzerland, might have had something to say about all this but if they looked north they saw German soldiers, if they looked west they saw German soldiers occupying France, if they looked south they saw Italian fascist soldiers, if they looked east they saw German soldiers. A lot of

Swiss expected the German army to come across the border any day now and help themselves, as they had done in so many other places.

Silence would have been FIFA's best and perhaps only defence unless they relocated, but to leave Switzerland would have required the permission of Hitler or Mussolini.

Tennis really was genteel. You only have to look at the old films to know that. The modern power games of almost superhuman physical endurance and savage, sustained hitting were, then, gentle as well as genteel. Bunny Austin, for example, became famous for wearing shorts.

Of the four Grand Slam events, the Australian was played in 1940 and then not again until 1946, Wimbledon not played between 1940 and 1946, the United States played through but the French situation is more complicated. Roland-Garros was requisitioned as an internment camp in 1940 for Germans and Austrians who had fled the Nazis. A writer, Henry Winterfeld, who had left Germany in 1933, found himself arrested and kept there for a week, sleeping in the open.

The French Open was not contested in 1940 but was from 1941 to 1945, although the validity of each competition is still subject to dispute and they are not usually included in the all-time list of winners. The championship was evidently restricted to players of countries allied to Germany or occupied by it. Other reports suggest the Vichy regime, which ruled France as a creature of the Nazis, requisitioned the site and held a *Tournoi de France* (Tournament of France) restricted to French players. There does seem a consensus that Bernard Destremau won in 1942 and 1943, and Yvon Petra in 1944 and 1945.

The future of the Grand Slam after a Hitler victory would have been at Hitler's whim since he would be occupying two of the four countries and, like the Olympics and World Cup, have effectively exercised control over all the prominent European players. Since he intended to strip Britain of its manhood, deporting all males between 17 and 45, it is very difficult to imagine who except foreigners would have been left to play in the men's singles and doubles at Wimbledon.

If the United States had reached some sort of accommodation with Hitler, tennis might have survived as a genuine international sport. Goebbels seems to have liked watching it and so did Göring. Perhaps they would have enlarged the Rot-Weiss Club to the point where it and the US at Boston became the two pillars of the game. If there had been no accommodation, the Nazis might have run their own championship at Rot-Weiss and forbidden the Europeans to travel to the United States.

Certainly the growth of the game would not – could not – have progressed as it has. The International Tennis Federation is now made up of 205 national associations (144 full, 61 associate).

Whether the United States ever could have reached an accommodation with Nazi Germany must be doubtful once the news of the Holocaust emerged, as it was certain to do sooner or later. The total revulsion would not have been confined to the Jewish community (as indeed today it is not either). That revulsion could only be reinforced by news of the way the Germans had treated and were treating prisoners of war (working them to death) and the civilian populations of the countries they had conquered.

No doubt a German-driven European economy would have found itself in direct conflict with the United States, and that would have reflected back into sport.

I am indebted to Linda Carlson, in one sense an ordinary American and in another sense a very aware American – she fell for Grand Prix racing, has watched it in Britain as well as the United States and is fully conscious that the world does not end at the American shoreline. I asked her to muse on the accommodation, if any had come into being:

> Do I think the U.S. would have been tempted to retreat into itself in sporting terms and would it have been happy doing that? Yes, absolutely and I don't think it would have taken much tempting, either. In my opinion, the U.S. would have done this regardless of the other 'if' factors to be considered in the 'if Hitler had won the war' scenario. Americans consider their homegrown games of baseball, soccer (U.S. version) and basketball to be unique and these would have continued happily with no interference from outside.
>
> Our own versions of automobile racing would also have thrived. The U.S. has always tended to discount international sporting events in any case. There are exceptions, of course, (and I count myself among them) but most Americans would have gone about their sporting business pretty much as they always have. I also don't feel the U.S. would have wanted to be a part of the 'Olympics' if the games had become a perpetual prisoner of Hitler and Berlin. There are probably plenty out there who would disagree, however.

I hope there are. That is one of the points of this chapter.

Before we leave it, Richard Bergmann, the Viennese table tennis master who fled Austria when Hitler seized it and continued his career in Britain, was not pleased in 1947 as the world championships resumed, in Paris. He had reportedly been playing exhibition matches for money, compromising his amateur status, and consequently he could not defend his title, from 1939 – the last time it had been contested. Instead he skirted the venue with a sign proclaiming he was still the champion and challenging (for money!) anyone to take him on. He regained the title the following year.

Grand Prix racing would have resumed undisturbed, Mercedes and Auto Union producing ever more powerful cars to keep the Italians in their place, although Enzo Ferrari might have had something to say about that.

I am indebted to Eberhard Reuss, the author of the authoritative *Hitler's Motor Racing Battles*, which has been quoted so often in this book, for his musings about the future of Grands Prix racing:

> Politicians, technicians and sportsmen tend to continue their passions, or should we better say obsessions. In 1940 German and Italian officials planned to run Grand Prix races (Tripoli, Monza, Nürburgring, Deutschlandring[8] – the question was only

would they be run to voiturette or 3l Grand Prix formulae? Those plans failed, but
in 1941 with the complete European world at war, Mercedes-Benz managed to get
money from the Reich to continue the development of their record breaking car.
The thinking sounded like this: racing will be continued after war.

And so it happened – hopefully and thank God without the Nazis, but all the
others were back again sooner or later: the Italians immediately, the Germans by
1951 in Argentina – and some of the German guys formerly wore black or brown
uniforms, too ...

Mention of the Deutschlandring is instructive. The circuit, just south of Dresden, was
intended to supercede the Nürburgring:

> The new track allowed for much faster speeds and, being exactly 10km in length,
> was to have much quicker lap times. This in turn meant more fun for the one mil-
> lion spectators for which the circuit was to provide accommodation ... Parking
> space for over three hundred thousand cars was planned, all of which could leave
> the area within two hours, thanks to several direct connections to the surround-
> ing road network ... there was no doubt that propaganda played a key role. This
> was to be the track to end all tracks. On 27 April 1939, the circuit was baptised
> *Deutschlandring*. Enthusiastic supporters of the 1000-year empire quickly extended
> this into *Grossdeutschlandring*. But ironically, the circuit experienced the same fate as
> the Reich from which it had sprung. After the tarmac was laid, war broke out and
> nothing came of racing.[9]

Other sports would have had to find new shapes and structures. With Britain occupied, Lord's would no longer have been governing cricket, and whatever input the
Rugby Football Union (at Twickenham), the All-England Club at Wimbledon and
the Royal and Ancient at St Andrews had had would have been diminished or, more
likely, removed altogether.

What would the new shapes and structures have been? Perhaps the centre of cricket
and Rugby would have shifted to Australia and South Africa, and the golf doubtless to
the United States. Beyond that, even conjecture seems unwise.

From *The Independent*:[10]

> A decree of 19 December 1941 from the Vichy Secretary of State for National
> Education and Youth not only banned the Association called the French League of
> Rugby XIII, but also transferred all its assets to the National Committee of Sports.
> The net result was the destruction of records and the office at 24 Rue Drouot, Paris,
> by Axis forces, plus the seizure of playing resources by the Vichy-backed French
> Federation of Rugby XV.

No doubt Hitler would have decreed that no white man should box a black man,
which would have isolated the United States, although to the American boxing

supporter that might not have mattered much. Between 1885 and 1939 only four non-Americans held the World Heavyweight Championship – including, of course, Schmeling (1930–32). Only six non-Americans held the world middleweight title between 1884 and 1939. And so it went. The United States, embracing Mexico and the Central American states, would have had quite enough boxers and fights to disregard Hitler and Europe altogether.

I am indebted to David Oldrey of The Jockey Club for giving an overview of the situation with horse racing:

> In Britain during the War it was fairly bleak. In the First World War we continued racing on a rather bigger scale until it became politically untenable in the view of the government. It resumed but on a smaller scale – so we had been over the course. In 1939 we moved immediately to cancel a great deal of racing. Ten days into the War the St Ledger was going to be run as usual at Doncaster and it was going to be one of the great clashes between the English champion, called Blue Peter, and the unbeaten French champion called Pharis 11. It was perfectly possible to hold it but the decision was made to cancel. And they did.
>
> Blue Peter went to stud and Pharis was eventually seized by the Germans when they invaded. They stole quite a lot of horses, Pharis among them. That would have been 1940, so he had covered mares at the beginning of that year when French racing had gone on quite happily. After he was stolen – because French racing continued in a rather better way than the English – his stock turned out to be brilliant. There was a major scandal and row after the War because Monsieur Marcel Boussac, who he belonged to and who was the most important figure in French racing, said that no horse got by Pharis in Germany could be entered – so the next five crops of Pharis just disappeared. They had continued racing in Germany and the Germans in fact took great pride in claiming that they had more racing than in England. It was a Nazi boast.
>
> They also stole English horses because Lord Derby had a stud in France. They just pinched the lot.
>
> A large number of horses were shot right at the beginning of the War because getting food was extremely difficult and you could only get a tiny quantity. So the number was decimated. Most the race racecourses were turned into military establishments – the big grandstands were jolly useful as troop bases of one sort or another. Even the Rowley Mile at Newmarket was given up.
>
> The attitude of Germany is shown by the theft of the French horses. The Germans were an inferior racing power and obviously that wouldn't have pleased Hitler. There were all sorts of major German races and the whole of German racing was Nazified. It was a source of botheration to Hitler and the senior Nazis who did go to the races, and continued to during the War.
>
> I think they would have treated English racing quite seriously but taken what they wanted in the way they did everywhere with the aim of turning Germany into a superior racing country and no doubt we would have been allowed to continue

in the way the French were allowed to continue. There was a break of about a year at Longchamp and in fact there was quite a debate in France about how keen they were to start again. And the Germans insisted that Longchamp was reopened – I think in '43 – as a way of demonstrating there lack of fear of invasion. It continued while the Allies were advancing from Normandy to try and demonstrate normality.

Since 1945, the world of sport has expanded in the most extraordinary way to the point where, almost every day of every year, major events take place. Tennis, as we have seen, reflects that very exactly. The soccer World Cup, which was such a stunted child even in 1950, embraced some 200 countries playing in six continental zones in 2010. In 2008 the Beijing Olympics embraced 11,028 athletes from 204 National Olympic Committees, contesting 302 events in 28 sports. In 1936 it had been 4,066 competitors.

The expansion has spawned so much – in equipment, in administration, in sponsorship, in media, in press relations, in television coverage and most of all in money – that it has an *industrial* feel to it. Posing the question 'If Hitler had won …?' is a game anyone can play and you can find your own answers. What you can say with certainty is that global sport, and European sport in particular, would have had an overt political feel to it and the expansion would simply not have happened on the scale and the nature it has, if it happened at all.

The world in which the expansion has happened would not have existed.

Notes

1   Hilton, *Hitler's Olympics.*
2   The Sino-Japanese 'incident' was in fact war between the two countries, involving the occupation of part of China. The war lasted until 1945 and may have had as many as 20 million deaths.
3   This chapter is unashamedly speculative, perhaps outrageously so, full of surmises and guesses, and not to be taken too seriously. If you are a serious sports lover, it is not intended to make you reach for your blood pressure tablets. Is it?
4   Bonde, Hans, *Football with the Foe* (University Press of Southern Denmark, 2008).
5   However, a match in Denmark involving Admira (Vienna) proved anything but peaceful. The crowd jeered when the visitors gave the Nazi salute and reportedly attacked uniformed German soldiers in the crowd. The Nazis were so angry they forced the dismissal of the Danish Minister of Justice. Interestingly, when the war was over the Danes then used soccer to, as one source (Amazon) put it, 'demonstrate Denmark's emotional integration in the Allied club, culminating in a sold-out game at Idraetsparken on 10 July 1945 between a professional English and a select Danish team in the presence of the British chief commanding officer in Denmark, General Dewing'.

6   Helmut Schön (1915–96) had a long playing career, from the 1930s, and subsequently became a highly successful coach to the West German team from 1966 to 1978.

7   en.wikipedia.org/wiki/Gauliga_Baden.

8   forix.autosport.com/8w/deutschlandring.html.

9   Ibid.

10 www.independent.co.uk>sport1994.

BIBLIOGRAPHY

Bachrach, Susan D., *The Nazi Olympics* (Little, Brown and Company, 2000).
Baker, William J., *Jesse Owens: An American Life* (New York: The Free Press, 1986).
Bullock, Alan, *Hitler* (Pelican Books, 1962).

Caracciola, Rudolf, *A Racing Driver's World* (Motorraces Book Club/Cassell, 1963).
Cholmondeley-Tapper, T.P., *Amateur Racing Driver* (London: Motorraces Book Club, 1966).
Cleather, Norah Gordon, *Wimbledon Story* (Sporting Handbooks Ltd, 1947).

Daniels, Stephanie; Tedder, Anity, *A Proper Spectacle* (ZeNaNa Press, 2000).
Downing, David, *The Best of Enemies: England v. Germany* (Bloomsbury Publishing PLC, 2001).

Fern, Dave, *Donington Grands Prix* (Donington International Collection, 1993).
Fisher, Marshall Jon, *A Terrible Splendor* (New York: Crown Publishers, 2009).

Glanville, Brian, *The Story of the World Cup* (Faber and Faber, 1993).
Glickman, Marty, *The Fastest Kid on the Block* (Syracuse University Press, 1996).
Greenberg, Stan, *Olympic Fact Book* (Guinness Publishing, 1991).

Hart-David, Duff, *Hitler's Games* (Century Hutchinson Ltd, 1986).
Henderson, Jon, *The Life of Fred Perry* (Yellow Jersey Press, 2009).
Hilton, Christopher, *Hitler's Grands Prix in England* (Haynes, 1999).
———, *Hitler's Olympics* (Sutton, 2006).
———, *Murray Walker: The Last Word* (Haynes, 2001).
Hodges, David, *The Monaco Grand Prix* (Temple Press Books, 1964).
———, *The French Grand Prix* (Temple Press Books, 1967).

Jeffrey, Gordon, *European International Football* (Nicholas Kaye, 1963).

Lambert, Margaret Bergmann, *By Leaps and Bounds* (United States Holocaust Memorial Museum, 2005).
Lang, Hermann, *Grand Prix Driver* (G.T. Foulis & Co. Ltd, 1954).

Mandel, Richard D., *The Nazi Olympics* (Souvenir Press, 1971).
Mercer, Derrik (editor-in-chief), *Chronicle of the 20th Century* (London: Chronicle Communications, 1988).
Mogulof, Milly, *Foiled* (Oakland, California: DR Books, 2002).
Myler, Patrick, *Ring of Hate* (Mainstream Publishing, 2006).

Nixon, Chris, *Racing The Silver Arrows* (Osprey, 1986).
———, *Shooting Star* (Transport Bookman Publications, 2000).
———, *Rosemeyer!* (Transport Bookman Publications, 1989).

Owen, David, *Alfa Romeo* (Patrick Stephens Ltd, 1993).

Posthumus, Cyril, *The German Grand Prix* (Temple Press Books, 1966).

Reuss, Eberhard, *Hitler's Motor Racing Battles* (Haynes, 2006).

Schapp, Jeremy, *Cinderella Man: James J. Braddock, Max Baer, and the Greatest Upset in Boxing History* (Mariner Books, 2006).
Shirer, William, *Berlin Diary* (Hamish Hamilton, 1941).
———, *The Rise and Fall of the Third Reich* (Pan Books, 1971).
Small, Steve, *The Grand Prix Who's Who* (Guinness Publishing, 1996).
Speer, Albert, *Inside the Third Reich* (Sphere, 1979).
Stevenson, Peter, *Driving Forces* (Cambridge, 2000).

Unnamed, *1938 in Germany* (Memphis, Tennessee: Books LLC).

Vassiltchikov, Marie 'Missie', *The Berlin Diaries* (Mandarin, 1990).

Wallechinsky, David, *The Complete Book of the Winter Olympics* (Aurum Press, 1994).
Willis, Roger, *The Nazi TT* (Isle of Man: Motobusiness, 2009).

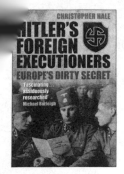

Hitler's Foreign Executioners: Europe's Dirty Secret
CHRISTOPHER HALE   £25.00

Heinrich Himmler had a secret master plan to create an SS empire that would have no place for either the Nazi Party or Adolf Hitler. Researched in archives all over Europe and using first-hand testimony, this book exposes Europe's dirty secret: nearly half a million Europeans and more than a million Soviet citizens enlisted in the armed forces of the Third Reich to fight a deadly crusade against a mythic foe, Jewish-Bolshevism.

978-0-7524-5974-5

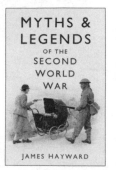

Myths & Legends of the Second World War
JAMES HAYWARD   £9.99

The Second World War gave rise to a rich crop of legends: the escape of an un-dead Hitler to South America, the Allied aircraft buzzed by UFOs, German parachutists dressed as nuns, a failed German invasion of Suffolk in 1940, and many more. This book offers a refreshing and intriguing perspective on the myths, legends and folk memories of the Second World War.

978-0-7524-5237-1

World War II: Book of Lists
CHRIS MARTIN   £12.99

Everything you ever wanted to know about the Second World War, from the highest-rated fighter aces to the most inventive escape equipment used to break out of Colditz; from army pay by rank to the largest battleships; from the strangest regimental mottoes to the plays most performed by ENSA; and from the dates each country joined the war to the most unlikely spies.

978-0-7524-6163-2

Nazi Princess: Hitler, Lord Rothermere and Princess Stephanie von Hohenlohe
JIM WILSON   £17.99

Princess Stephanie von Hohenlohe was a close confidante of Hitler, Göring, Himmler (who declared her an 'honorary Aryan') and von Ribbentrop, and was described in a memo to President Roosevelt as a spy 'more dangerous than ten thousand men'. In this new biography, Jim Wilson uses recently declassified MI5 files and FBI memos to examine what motivated both Stephanie and Rothermere, shedding light on the murky goings-on behind the scenes in Britain, Germany and the USA before and during the Second World War.

978-0-7524-6114-4

Visit our website and discover thousands of other History Press books.

www.thehistorypress.co.uk